Published in 2013 by Myrdle Court Press, London, UK
in association with This Is Not A Gateway

ISBN 978-0-9563539-4-8

Myrdle Court Press is an independent
publishing company that advances critical ideas
about 21st century cities

Unit 24 Myrdle Court, Myrdle Street, London E1 1HP
www.myrdlecourtpress.net

Designed by Karolin Schnoor
www.karolinschnoor.co.uk

Printed and bound by Imprint Digital, Exeter, UK

The Queen vs Trenton Oldfield: A Prison Diary

by
Trenton Oldfield

For Margareta and Marcus Kern
whose instinct was to come
close and to share.

For our daughter and her
generation for whom all of
this is for.

"As inequalities increase in Britain and across much of the world, so does the criminalisation of protest; my solidarity is with everyone everywhere working towards more equitable societies."

Statement made to the press by Trenton Oldfield on 29 September 2012 outside Isleworth Crown Court, London, United Kingdom – after receiving a guilty verdict for the crime of 'Public Nuisance'.

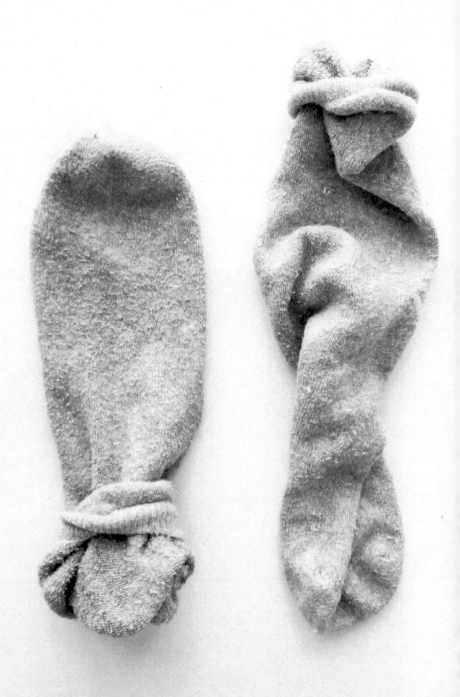

TEAR HERE

1001107/F

THE BENEFITS

Viva Semi-skimmed milk
pasteurised at high temperature
fresh for longer. It's perfect for e
use and its long-life makes it id
all occasions.

This quality dairy product mu
unopened and unrefrigerated fo
months. Once opened, the milk s
refrigerated and used within
See top of carton for Best Bef

FOR CODES ENDING I

IE
1065
EC

UK
N607M
EC

Made in EU

ViVA

LAKELAND
DAIRIES

SEMI-SKIMMED

MILK

WITH LONGER LIFE

UHT 200ml e

table of contents

Articles
& Documents

Appendix

Preface

Preface

Trenton Oldfield

This diary documents my experience in a category B prison in London, United Kingdom, in the last months of 2012. When I write of 'prison', even in the most abstract ways, I speak only of and through my own experience. Every prison and every prisoner is different.

I am publishing my prison diary for three reasons. Firstly, I wish to set about assisting in the process of demystifying prison in order to contribute to demystifying 'prisoners' – people who our culture inflicts endless unwarranted discrimination against. People who 'do their time' but whose lives 'outside' are significantly undermined by having been hot iron branded with the inequitable mark of a criminal record. Secondly despite human 'progress' the prison population in England and Wales is increasing at an alarming rate. Indeed, no country in Western Europe imprisons more people than the UK.[1] This is in part due to: devastating 'austerity cuts' that have increased crimes of survival; iniquitous 'terrorism' laws that have allowed for people to be imprisoned without charge for years on end[2]; 'pre-emptive' arrests of people suspected of potentially protesting[3]; increase in the criminalisation of communities[4]; resurgence of the archaic joint enterprise law used to imprison innocent people based on loose association with supposed criminals[5]; and, inflated charges aimed at jailing those who dissent[6]. It crossed my mind that more and more people might wish to familiarise themselves, get accustomed to the everyday practices of one prison in England at the start of the 21st century. Thirdly, I hope this book may contribute in whatever small way to provoking a closer look at the politicians, police, legal fraternity and judiciary clearly involved with the dramatic increase of prisoners in recent decades. I suggest it is these institutions that might need reforming and improvement. I also question if the parameters in which most charities couch their work isn't reinforcing populist media stereotypes of 'prisoners'. I wonder why so very few charities are working on the abolition of prisons. In addition, and fourthly, not only was I given a prison sentence but I was unusually also given court costs to pay. The diary is being sold in order to raise the monies needed to pay off these costs.

This book includes all the paperwork I was able to collect. It also contains a visual archive of my time in prison – photographs of my prison uniform, dishes and cutlery, the daily breakfast bag and other everyday items such as cigarette packets, nail clippers, disposable razors, milk cartons, drawings of my cell and so on.

At the back of the book are articles and interviews that were published in the press just before and after my sentencing; transcripts of my testimony at the trial; and an index of various prison resources and guides.

How I ended up in prison

I arrived in HMP Wormwood Scrubs on the afternoon of Friday 19th October 2012. I was transported from Isleworth Crown Court where earlier in the day I had been sentenced to six months' jail for a direct action protest I undertook on the 7th April 2012.[7] My action was an act of resistance, an intervention, a protest against the astounding and entirely unnecessary levels of inequality that have been exacerbated by a generation of politically motivated 'cuts' and deliberate dissolving of civil liberties. One of my aims was to draw attention to how the concept of 'elitism' – a construct where one group (almost always a minority) are perceived to be superior to others – has and continues to shape British culture, society, laws and foreign policy. Elitism is shorthand for the idea of some people thinking they are better, more deserving than others. It was an idea the British–ruthless–class tested out on its own peoples here and in Ireland before brutally implementing it on others right across the planet. It is a concept that enabled slavery and the European colonial project, which saw the genocide of vast populations and ancient cultures, and the exploitation of resources and land (that belonged to others), for their own profit. Despite its falsehood it is an idea that continues to permeate most social relations. If not resisted, if given free reign, it always ends in tyranny; it has to.

In the three days preceding my direct action the unelected 'government' received royal assent for its bill to asset strip the publicly funded National Health Service, it introduced the Communications Data Bill to legalise surveillance of all digital communications of UK subjects, and it called on people to 'shop' their neighbours if they suspected they might protest at the then forthcoming summer Olympic Games. My protest was aimed at drawing attention to these injustices. After a lifetime of seeing the devastation caused here and around the world as a result of the very apparent democratic deficit and elitist policies, I felt I had no choice but to do something outside of 'polite society' expectations but wholly consistent with everything I have and continue to work on.[8] My motivations are revealed further in the court transcripts included towards the end of the book.

Tactics and resistance

If there is a deficit of democracy what other choice is there but to use your body? If parliament is continuingly ignoring 'polite' protest and dissent and is working against the wellbeing of the most disadvantaged, if poverty and inequality have massively increased, if civil and human rights are being pulled and if what is left of publicly funded services are being asset stripped and the government that is supposed to represent you suggests reporting your neighbours and is planning to introduce secret courts, what choice is there but to use your body to intervene and disrupt? I had no choice but to swim into the Thames on the 7th April 2012. Everything tells me we are being pulled back into a period of extreme poverty, indentured labour and war. If we don't resist now I feel it will likely take 100–150 years to break free.

Many people have asked why I did the protest alone. Firstly I was aware of the re-introduction of the brutal Joint Enterprise common law, which has been convicting and jailing people with little to no link to a crime. I didn't want anyone else to suffer the vindictiveness of the 'criminal justice system' unnecessarily. Secondly, I was aware resistance groups have been heavily infiltrated by government agents and undercover cops. I wanted to make sure the action was achieved, that I wasn't arrested changing into my wetsuit in the loos of a cafe in Barnes, for example. Thirdly, I wanted to provoke a discussion on individual resistance tactics, drawing on the knowledge and practices of those that have actually successfully defeated the British elite[9]; be it the work slow tactics of slaves or guerrilla tactics of revolutionaries. I wanted to suggest that if polite marches of 2 million people on the streets on London (against a hugely expensive taxpayer-funded illegal war perpetrated by Westminster Palace with devastating cost of civilian lives) can be ignored ... then maybe we might want to think of other methods, other tactics, or value the everyday resistances a little more. If we really wish to depose the elitism that permeates throughout this country, I feel we have a great deal to learn from those that have overcome/defeated the British elite.

Trenton Oldfield

The research I have done on prison and prison reform since leaving HM Wormwood Scrubs has brought me no closer to understanding the purpose of prisons today. Many of the groups that work with and for prisoners insist that one is 'reformed' before engaging with them. As nobody has yet been able to confirm, let alone sketch out, what the function of prison is, it's hard to know if could consider myself a 'reformed prisoner'. There is advice to 'stay out of trouble, keep my head down' (though hasn't that always been the case?) but whilst I have no wish whatsoever to return to any prison, the potential or 'threat' of it won't deter me for a single moment from continuing to work towards a culture that values the pursuit of equality and stands up without hesitation to any form of elitism: imperialism, colonisation, sexism, racism, classism, homophobia, discrimination and capitalism.

1. See for example http://www.guardian.co.uk/society/2012/jan/27/rise-prisoners-budget-cuts and http://www.justice.gov.uk/downloads/statistics/mojstats/story-prison-population.pdf.
2. See for example http://freetalha.org/ and http://www.freebabarahmad.com/.
3. See for example http://www.guardian.co.uk/uk/2012/jun/02/olympic-games-2012-police-arrests.
4. See for example http://www.campacc.org.uk/.
5. See for example http://www.jointenterprise.co/.
6. See for example http://www.defendtherighttoprotest.org/campaign-statement/.
7. The aim of my protest was to focus attention on the long standing and entirely unjust inequalities in British society that are being severely exacerbated by government cuts and a culture of elitism. I chose the Oxford and Cambridge Boat Race because it is a symbol of class, privilege and elitism in Britain. I was initially charged with Section 5 of the 'public order act'. Hansard reports reveal that government ministers asked the police commissioner to increase the charge so that a custodial sentence could be achieved. On the morning of my first court appearance (23 April 2012) my charge was significantly increased via the ancient common law charge of 'public nuisance' under which conviction can result in life in prison. On the 26 September 2012 I was found guilty of causing 'public nuisance'. On 19 October 2012 I was sentenced to 6 months in prison.
8. I have spent a decade+ in London working on various projects to address this city's unnecessary poverty and inequalities.
9. See for example Britain's Empire: Resistance, Repression and Revolt, Richard Gott (London: Verso, 2011).

Statement

Statement after Trenton's sentencing
19 October 2012

Deepa Naik

Most nation states work very hard at creating and maintaining untrue myths about themselves. Great Britain has convinced many it is the home of democracy and the gauge for 'civilisation'. Anyone living here today knows Britain is a brutal, deeply divided, class–ridden place. London is today the most unequal city in the western world. This poverty and the inequality are entirely unnecessary and are being severely exacerbated by government cuts and reductions in civil liberties.

Right now as we speak there are many thousands of people working to address this injustice; either to limit the damage or to overthrow it – completely once and for all. I know Trenton at this moment would want to send a message of solidarity to every single one of them where ever in the world they might be.

Trenton has spent his adult life working on these issues and his direct action protest on the 7 April 2012 was a natural extension of his everyday work. Trenton's protest was a reaction to an increasingly brutal business, media and political elite. In the three actual days preceding the protest: (1) the coalition government introduced the Communications Data Bill to legalise surveillance of all digital communications of all UK citizens; (2) the Queen signed off the bill to privatise the NHS; (3) a cabinet member called on the public to go to the police if they had suspicions their neighbour or family member might protest at the summer games.

Trenton was initially charged with Section 5 of the 'public order act'. Hansard reports reveal that a government minister asked the police commissioner to increase the charge so that a custodial sentence could be achieved.

The criminalisation of protest and of protesters is a reflection of the hyper anxiety of the bosses and the ruling classes. Everyone alive today has seen with their own eyes that revolution and overthrow is possible. Putting Trenton in jail just shows how anxious, hesitant and 'on the ropes' members of the establishment are at this very moment. Trenton and I would continue to suggest people protest ... as the well–known proverb says 'when injustice becomes law, resistance becomes a duty'.

Prison diary

Prison Diary

Trenton Oldfield

Wormwood Scrubs

19 October 2012

My fellow prisoners are great – real comradeship! Lots of humour, banter and sharing!

Just made my bed. First night in prison. In a room with five single beds, two tables – one seems to be for the small TV which is already on it. There seems to be only two chairs. Looks like you spend most of your time here on your bed? It's a large room with low ceilings, feels more 1970s than 1850s. We might be on the top floor, I remember walking up lots of stairs. Sheesh, it is in very poor condition! Hope the rest of the prison isn't going to be like this. Hope this isn't it? Man! Someone said something about us being moved tomorrow. It can't be this bad elsewhere, people surely would riot!!

Long day. Want to chat with my fellow prisoners more than write here but will get some points down so I can step back inside here once I am out!

- Everyone I've interacted with so far has been very supportive – interested, wanting to talk about action, trial, sentence – all think it's 'madness'.

- Words from prison guards checking me in about my sentence: 'travesty', 'fucking joke', 'crazy'. Have the feeling I'm not the only one being pushed in here with such madness at our backs.

- Lots of solidarity and warmth from everyone – fellow prisoners and also the guards – even on the transport here – in what I've learnt is called a 'sweat box' – must be hot in the summer! Atmosphere is good – light hearted and supportive somehow.

- My fellow prisoners at 'reception' are great! They invited me to join them, to work on reception with them. It's all day but they seem wonderful people. They gave me extra clothes, socks and underwear! Would like to work with them but it's all day – not sure how much reading I would get done.

- Had my medical done. Young guy in the NHS section. Seemed quite up tight and very 'English–distant'. I don't know how they can live so far from feeling anything? I bet he speaks to his family and close friends like he does colleagues. Said he chose this job for the pension scheme. Seems like he is living for a time that may never come. Hope it works out for him, hope he lives to 100 and can retire at 60. Hope they don't change the retirement age nor the pension funds collapse. My heart would break for him. Made my first mistake – on the advice of a new friend I tried to suggest to 'the screws' that I was 'mad' so I could have my own cell. They all thought it was hilarious and said I would be in the cell with everyone else. My new friend told me I should have told them I was racist. If you are racist you automatically get your own cell. I have some memory of a white supremacist killing his 'black' cellmate. This must be why it would automatically happen. Everything about this is horrific.

This mattress must be 20 years old? Not sure what it's made out of – some ancient plastic foam? Chunks are missing from it. I'm not sure how my fellow prisoners will fit on these beds – they are very short and exceptionally thin. Must be beds from another time for a different group of people than those that live in London today? The beds themselves might be as old as the prison? The sheets are an aqua green though my sheet has many holes and doesn't fit the bed. The blanket is bright orange. It has holes all through it also – it's more like a shawl than a blanket? It's hot in here in any case, thankfully. Though with all the smoking the window needs to be open?
My fellow prisoners tonight include:

- Young man, maybe 26, was caught shoplifting. Has to serve 14 days as he couldn't afford to pay the fine. Has been nicking luxury goods for as long as he can remember. Was up for a chat. Was arrested at Heathrow at international departures. Seemed like he might have a drug problem, seems a bit distracted. Leaving now for another room – packing his stuff – screw tells me he is going to the drug rehab wing. Must be hard to go cold turkey in here but a good place for it, I mean you can't go out looking for stuff can you? But what do I know? Hope he manages okay.

- Across the cell under the window is what might be the fittest man alive? I mean this guy is fit! Seems silly to use an animal metaphor but he seems he could be a cheetah. He is svelte, anyways! He has two purple and black eyes and some long cuts on his cheeks. Someone asks him if he is a fighter. He smiles and says yes. He is waiting for his day in court. He has been in the same clothes since he was taken to the police station four days ago. He is in the same tracksuit he stepped out in before he got into a fight with people trying to steal his car. (He was still in the same clothes two months later when I left). He has a wife and child elsewhere in Europe.

• Been chatting to a lovely young man, again with a child and wife, though they are in London – in walking distance from here. Tough position to be in – so close but so far! He is a builder. He has such a lovely smile! Moved here a few years ago. He works near where we live in Aldgate East! I know the building site, I can see it from the kitchen window. Small world. Smokes a lot of ciggies! Loves a chat. He was jailed today for 16 weeks for pushing someone out of the way in a pub fight. His lawyer said he would just get a fine, so his wife and child were at home and he just took the morning off work. He is really angry at his lawyer. He is worried for his child, his wife and how they will live as he won't have an income. Just before we were put in here was the first chance he has had to call his wife since being taken from the court this morning – all of two minutes before it cut out! He really wants to talk. Understandable! Hope his wife is okay and not freaking out too much – at least Deepa had months to get used to the idea of me going inside. He is in the grey prison tracksuit like me – a convict. His clothes don't fit as he is too tall!

• Under the other window is another young man. He also is up for a chat. He is being held on remand for rape and harassment. He feels like he has been trapped by the woman because he could no longer afford to share his income with her due to losing one of his jobs. He keeps saying "she is meant to be my fiancée, how could she do this to me?" He says he would plead guilty to harassment but not to rape as he hasn't had sex with her for a long time. He seems shocked to be here, genuinely shocked. Was arrested at his work place and hasn't been home since – prison cell for two days, court and now in jail on remand. Talks of 'revenge'. This makes it even harder for me. He admits to harassment; though denies rape and talks of revenge – how does one navigate this? Violence against women is entirely unacceptable to me but he is currently innocent. I'm finding it very very difficult to navigate this situation. What will I do if I have a cell with someone that is convicted or on remand because of his violence against my sisters? Oh man, this is going to be tough!

On the way here I had the chance to talk to the young woman working for Serco. I assume she was a guard. I don't know what they call her now everything has been privatised. She must have been in her mid to late 20s. She rode alone in the 'sweat box' with us. She locked us in. As we left the court, she told me there were lots of photographers outside and that if I didn't want to be photographed I should keep my head down. I chose not to hide so instead I held up Foucault's *Discipline and Punish*. I don't think the mainstream media will have published that image. My fellow prisoners chose to pull down their pants and give the hunter–photographers moons LOL! So much laughter!

In a way it was a relief to be in the van as court and police cells are hugely uncomfortable in their ultra sparseness. Found it difficult to read and hard to sleep. Wrote a little bit mostly to Deepa for my barrister to pass on to her. Used the books I had with me as pillows, sang a little as the sound is quite good. In my brief conversations with this young lady she said she had been sent to Feltham Magistrates Court in April as they thought I would be taken to prison that day. She seemed a very kind person. It was interesting to hear her talk with the fellow prisoners as we were being transported to Wormwood Scrubs. They asked about her life, her interests. She found radio stations for them to listen to. Unfortunately the signal wasn't very good. She explained to everyone she rarely saw her partner as they were expected to work 72 hours each week. If they didn't they would be replaced by other people seeking work who were prepared/desperate to do it. They would go all over the country, anywhere, anyday, anytime. I could see her from my box – she was trying to catch some sleep on her desk even with the music turned up. All of us prisoners somehow. The person with the keys is even refused most of her dignity and freedom.

For some unexplainable reason a cascade of popular culture clichés of 'prison' started to flood my mind on that road trip here. Maybe it was because the heavily tinted windows already started to meddle with real and unreal? Maybe it was the music? Maybe it was that Deepa was likely to already be at home and I was only just making my way to Wormwood Scrubs now, already splintering time and place? Maybe it was the everydayness of slowly stopping at traffic lights when everything about being in here is wrong? Something happened. It was ridiculous however I couldn't stop it. Everything I know has told me 'prison' is not and cannot be what TV and films wish to show it to be. If you don't fear prison then there is little to fear from 'the authorities'. Prisoners must be dangerous people and prison itself brutal; long live the idea of the 'vicious poor' which authority can 'make good/reform' ... if we prisoners just repent and relent?

Nonetheless images from mostly American films didn't help me when I was ejected from the sweatbox into what was nothing more than a small ancient low ceiling cell just like you see in films. In this cell I counted 44 other men. Half had seats, half had to stand. I managed to find a seat on one of the few benches along the edge of the wall. Almost everything I have watched in popular culture suggested something brutal would happen here; a fight would start, people would try to rob each other and so on and so forth. There were, I have to say, many wide eyes. It wasn't long before a few characters started entertaining us with some kind of dramatic performance about time and prison. Can't remember what it was for the life of me but it really broke the ice between us all and passed the time while we all waited to be processed. Very grateful to them from that moment, the TV and film screen was cracked, finished. It took so long to be processed we ended up eating together in the holding cell, people taking turns to stand up so others with food trays could sit down. All the trays and dishes were organised in one area and stacked neatly. On Fridays it is fish and chips or pizza.

It also wasn't long before I was recognised (was on the TV all day today apparently, which in and of itself is ridiculous!) and much of the cell joined in with their thoughts. Apart from the absurdity of any charge, let alone jail, I was told in no uncertain terms that you should never wear a suit or take a bag on sentencing day – it's bad luck. Deepa and I knew it would be jail, luck or no luck. You only need to study a little of the history of this country to know this would be the case. I'm surprised my barrister seems to have been taken by surprise! When he came down to see me in the court's cells he said, "You are right, you have been stitched up." It is quite easy to read the institutions in this country; they are quite undemanding to predict if you put on a critical lens – even if they are out of focus.

After being processed by two kind men who were furious at my conviction and sentencing, I went to another holding cell, which this time included that ever patronising and at the same time insulting art of open rural landscapes.

Of course this time the artwork was done by prisoners, who I bet are strongly encouraged to paint places they miss or are suggested they might miss. I've also changed out of my suit and into my prison clothes, which were given to me by the prisoners who work on reception. These were some of the most handsome and kind men I have ever come across – extremely tall, entirely covered in tattoos and extremely athletic looking. I thought for a moment I might have been in the USA. These guys gave me extras of everything, which I've read, rightly or wrongly, as small acts of solidarity. They also said I should sign up to work on reception with them – they would try and fast track my application. I have a feeling it would be a lot of fun and I would learn a lot from these guys. I will apply as soon as I can. They were very welcoming and said my time here will be fine, not to worry.

In this holding cell with eight or so others is a young man who is also very tall and extremely athletic but he has a long beard without the moustache. Not long after he joins us fellow prisoners are asking him about Islam, people are drawn to him. He takes on their challenges very calmly, it's not like he is defending or converting ... he's just letting them know stuff. His main argument is the other guys are reading last year's newspapers. Islam is up to date, hot of the press. He asks them why they are not up to date, why they bother with used chip wrapping. More of the prisoners are drawn to him and wander over. He is quite compelling – very at ease. I ask one of the people beside me what he has done, as they seem to know each other. He said probably something to do with firearms as it sounds like he is facing an eight–year sentence.

Another tall young man in the cell with us has convinced someone in the medical team to give him some methadone. He didn't swallow it and spent some time working on a way to cover it, so he could transport it and sell it when he got to his wing. He ended up sliding it into his spare pair of shoes. I wondered what the going price for it might be and who might buy it. A little bit did spill when we were walking up the stairs to the next check–in.

Somewhere along the way we were given an HM Prison Service bag which contained two bread rolls, a small bag of muesli, a small box of long life milk, sachets of sugar, tea bags, shampoo sachets, a toothbrush and a reasonable sized tube of toothpaste. I think we were given a plastic bowl, plate and cup, along with a plastic knife, fork and spoon in the induction room – up here? One of the problems with institutions like schools, hospitals, prisons, is the rooms start to blend into each other ... become hard to differentiate?

The induction was run by three prisoners all wearing orange shirts; one older man and two younger men. The organisation or job (not sure which it is) is called Insiders. They also started to crack jokes about rivers, swimming, boats. Everyone, absolutely everyone knows! If it wasn't me there would be another person but it's great to have something to break the ice in each room we are brought together in! It's a great way to meet people also; instant new friends LOL! In this session we learnt about the telephone system – we have to register numbers on a form and we get two minutes free credit to start with. Also we got a bag with rolling tobacco. While I don't smoke, I ticked the box, so I could get some – I read somewhere, I think from the info Rachel gave me, that 'smoke' is the main currency in prison.

Other money can be added on Wednesday via 'Canteen' but will take another week to come on line. Two minutes on the telephone is amazing when you may have two days ago been at work or walking home and now you are in prison. If you didn't have any cash on you when you came in it might be weeks before you can arrange for someone to send any in and as long before it gets allocated to you? No idea what you do if you have never memorised the phone numbers of loved ones? I guess you write a letter and hope for one back? Hopefully you have been in town long enough to remember your address to send a letter ... I don't get the feeling they would pay for international post, I might be wrong. Hmmmm. With a misunderstanding/misuse of data protection laws, which means nobody is allowed to know where you are, you could end up lost/hidden in prison? And if you didn't speak English and your embassy has few staff, you could end up living here?

Back in the cell (door left open), each of the three induction guys pops in for a chat. Such nice people. I asked them for a bit of advice. They said just keep your head down and stay out of trouble. I asked what this meant and they all separately said don't get involved with other people's issues, particularly if it involves other people you don't know. Don't borrow anything if you can help it. Just like life outside really they said. All three reckoned I would be out in two months. I'm not so sure but I like their confidence. As I'm busy writing on my bed they all ask if I'm writing a book, all ask not to be forgotten, to be mentioned. Warm people! Lots of solidarity with my action! The older chap with the massive tat on his arm said he did it to help pass the time and that it's nice to help other prisoners – he can remember what it was like when he first came in.

Trenton Oldfield

Wow, just back from the 'bathroom' which is attached to this cell. It has a shower and toilet but my goodness I think you would be dirtier as a result of being in there! It can't be like this ... people would riot surely? Everything was broken, working but broken. Can't imagine the last time this place was cleaned, maybe it has never been cleaned? Most tiles are missing, basins have been removed, showerheads removed and the shower curtain is covered in mould and lying mostly on the floor due to the broken rail. This doesn't make sense at all. Why would we be so badly treated and why would our health be put at risk like this? Makes no sense, none. We rearrange the tables so we can eat together. We place one of the tables in between two beds, using the beds for seats. People that had never met before that could be old friends, advising and supporting each other.

People I want to remember:

'Screw' – massive guy with goatee beard, bald head and huge tattoos on either side of his neck – you might think he was a biker? Came to the cell to check–in on me, was up for a chat. We spoke about working at Cat A prisons (three main ones on the Isle of Wight) where the real heavies are, gang members and so on. Said Cat B was a better place to be but does miss the intensity. Think he said he changed prisons so he could be closer to his family who live near by.
'Screw' – beautiful beautiful woman who wore a bright purple weave. She was kind, helpful and seemed gentle. Someone somewhere has a very cool Auntie!

Saturday evening

Moved to B Wing this morning. Much of the day has been spent in holding cells, waiting to be moved to another holding cell. Some of these cells seem to also get used as shower rooms or were previously shower rooms? Everything is lockable and the shower rooms are no different it seems. Here we sit for hours, or it feels like hours. Luckily I have reading material with me. Us new guys sit quietly until one the characters in here takes over and starts to entertain, joke and almost dance in the cell. Keep having the pleasure of being in rooms with extremely funny and critically minded people.

So I'm in Cell B3.46. B Wing is another induction wing. Apparently we stay one to two weeks here before being moved wings or prisons. I would have liked to have shared this cell with T who works near me in the East End. I feel we would get on well. He was already teaching me Polish too, which is awesome. But I'm alone in this cell, which is also great in a way as nobody is smoking and I might have a chance for my throat and ears to repair. Always been very sensitive to smoke. I think someone was so desperate for a smoke last night they ended up smoking the tea from the tea bags. If you had an addiction to the chemicalised tobacco it would be insane to have to wait weeks for the next pack? My sympathy is with them!

Food seems better on this wing. Maybe I'm dreaming but seems better. Fingers crossed for the months ahead LOL. Nice guys in the kitchen – gave me extra servings and extra breakfast stuffs. Quite a few 'well done brother – fuck the system' call outs from them and people in the line, not sure what to do!

Have just had a visit from one of 'the screws', said he wanted to check on me, knew it was my first time inside. (Everyone, everyone knows who I am!) He asked if I was a bit of an eccentric LOL! I seem to have had so much solidarity from 'the screws', I asked him if there was something going on with the prison, with the prison staff? He said his colleagues probably had sympathy for me as they are also going through extreme funding cuts as well as piece by piece removal of their agreements – such as pension plans and alike. He also felt prisons were in the process of being privatised. He said the new people coming in have nothing, nobody wants to hear about prisons and absolutely nobody wants to hear from prison guards. Prisons don't even exist on maps – they are blanked out – just a blotch of one colour.

He seemed generally furious at Margaret Thatcher saying she messed everything up, not just prisons. Charities had done great work putting pressure on the structure to make it better in here. Cells now have toilets so prisoners no longer have to crap in a bucket and empty it once a day. He also said it's 'much more intellectual now'. Paying inmates to attend classes meant everyone was better ... it was a calmer place to be as a result. Everyone communicates better with each other. He said before it was just one big brawl. He had been working in the system for 30+ years. Tall, grey hair, softly spoken, seems gentle – though with a huge frame, you wouldn't have much chance if you tried to take him on!

He has just come back to see if I wanted to go to church tomorrow. I said "yes please". I asked to attend the RC service. I imagine the Roman Catholic service would be the most interesting. Sun knows the C of E services are by definition as dull and predictable as an English professor LOL! Will never forget the midnight Christmas service at St Paul's Cathedral Deepa and I went to, what a tragically sombre group of people! And this is the service for the day their 'saviour' was born, can you imagine!! And the RC service will likely include Romani and travellers also. I would like to meet up with them. He said he was confident I would be allocated as Cat D – which is the lowest category. He said it was a shame all the Cat D prisons were outside London. Means lots of travel for family members. Said it was a big mistake.

If I stand on my chair, I can look out the window. Trellick Tower is in full view. What a different day most on Golbourne Road will have experienced today. Will try to draw it tomorrow. Helpful in trying to orientate myself. Funny how I used to work and also live around here. Saw these walls from the other side so many times about a decade ago. Will be sure to go to Golbourne Road on the day I leave – have many fond memories of and around that street!

Day two

Woke in Cell 3.46. Was freezing overnight. No heating. Funding cuts or part of the punishment? No cover over windows. Oh man. Been in the same clothes now for a few days, they seem to be smelling? No night clothes. Same set for day and night forever?

The people I feel most for in here are those that are on remand – many seem to have been taken unexpectedly at work or at the airport or alike; they seem to be in a haze and understandably so. It seems like it would be incredibly difficult, if not near impossible, to fight a case from prison. When I think of the time I spent researching my own case, let alone the numerous meetings with both Ben and Mike (my lawyers) together and separately. Not surprised these men feel adrift and can't sleep. People on remand must be without a doubt at a disadvantage when trying to defend themselves.

In a single cell somehow my mood has dropped. I'm not sure if it's because I have watched some television for the first time in over a decade or more? It is terrible and AMAZINGLY MISOGYNIST. And why is the music shown so commercial and pointless. I am sure music had politics? Now the message is 'go dance'? How can we be living in this hyper–political time and the music/ lyrics be so aloof, so unrelated? How can television made and programmed by humans be so out of touch? If you watched television you would disappear into a world where everything is 'okay'. Adorno would be shocked at the colonisation of an entire medium. Heart breaking. Feeling quite down. Wasn't able to attend the RC service this morning, something about it being full, I think. My name was shifted to the Church of England service. There were many of us – I think people from both A and B Wings – maybe 150 people? I wonder how many went to the RC service? Or perhaps the chapel is smaller, if they have a chapel at all? The C of E church was huge so it felt mostly empty. I think it is located at the front of prison – near the gateway out? The scale is impressive. No doubt many prisoners suffered building it and the money used to build it from stolen lands far from this island. I learned in the service that the church is named/dedicated to Francis of Assisi – the chap that spawned the Franciscan monks and nuns (which I thought were RC?). The service this week was run by a Franciscan nun. She had a man with her who had an electric guitar and they seemed to be singing hymns from a 'modern' hymn book – pop culture version, 70s style. Both had lovely voices. I didn't sing but let me tell you some did! The service was very diverse. One man I couldn't take my eyes off looked like Malcolm X – ironically. And did he love to sing!

Service was mostly a history lesson on Francis of Assisi which was very interesting in that he was the son of a rich merchant who declined his father's comfortable life. He didn't devote his life to workers but the worship of 'god' and spreading god's word. He stole money from this father to rebuild a church. (Even then there were derelict churches – even then people didn't care much for churches nor Jesus Christ – churches have always been empty – they are built to mark land and are built oversized in order to suggest a large congregation!) I'm not sure if Francis just didn't swap one establishment position for another? We all know people like this – mostly those who have swapped running their parents' businesses for having their parents pay for a life in academia. If he was interested in defeating the class war on the poor by exposing the exploitation of his father's businesses then I might have been interested – enjoyed the sermon.

The church was 'policed' by a total of three 'screws'. Well over 100 prisoners and just three 'screws'. These prisoners have a lot of respect! Anyway it was great to see so many enjoy it – the nun was pretty cool and apart from a few dodgy hymns, there wasn't that much judgement, denigration or moralising – okay there was – but how could there not be? Have heard next week is the Pentecostal church – as the minister said – lots of hand clapping, so I might try and attend that as well! Maybe I won't make it to the RC service until week three?

Sunday evening

Just had dinner – I had chicken, I wasn't vegetarian tonight! Was great. The food on this wing is okay – must let the guys know. Had a quick chat with both the young 'screw' and also the guys on the food service. There is a solidarity with my action, especially when they know it was against the Tories. Happy to have a few extra breakfast bags from the guy that gives those out. Lovely guy, been on remand for six months, trial in another four months.

Monday morning

Didn't see the 'Prison's Minister' today. I guess that's why we were locked in all morning? I would have spoken to him. Everyone seems very cynical of him – of politicians and of parliament. Everyone talks politics here. Everything is politics in here.

Been told today I am probably 'the most famous prisoner in Britain today'. Been told by another prisoner everyone will want to become my friend but I should lay low, 'stay out of the limelight'. In contrast to this advice, much of me wants to broadcast that I am looking for people's stories to get out – so I can be the conduit for their stories. Feels like a good use of time in here. I don't really want to write about my six months in here when I can get their stories out. I wonder how I can lay low and also do this work? What could 'the screws' possibly do if they found me collecting witness to people's injustices? Would they care? Would it make me exposed as everyone is suggesting I shouldn't be? How long will I be on this wing, how long will I be in this prison? Does it matter? What happens when you stick your head above the parapet here? Out there it ends up with you being in here. What happens when you do it here? I will ask the guys on reception – they seem to know everything and have the most fun I've seen so far. I'm sure they will know what to do.

'Keeping quiet and keeping a low profile' is an interesting idea in and of itself. Is this not what has happened to the English person or the person that ends up living in England? Somehow people from around the world end up also learning this or at least their children born here do. Is this a nation of people with Stockholm Syndrome? A nation with this condition? Is this not a nation of people that will wave flags for those that oppress them? How did 50 million + end up sympathetic to their captors? Is it generations of abuse or just the repetition of sayings like 'keep quiet and keep a low profile'?

Started re-reading Fanon's *The Wretched of the Earth*, the introduction from Sartre is interesting, invigorating.

Swept the cell today – might try to establish a daily pattern. I guess sweep at the end of the day, so new day starts fresh?

TV advert analysis – seems the aim is the infantilisation of women. The commercial makers seem to treat women as children or suggest women should be like children. The greatest culprit of this so far seems to be this insane Littlewoods advert where women, fully grown women, are doing children's activities and their dresses spontaneously/magically change. Now they are children wearing 'cocktail dresses'? Phucked up, seriously phucked up.

TIRED – need to turn this TV off!

Monday 22nd – Wormwood Scrubs

Writing about Monday on Tuesday afternoon – yesterday seemed to steamroll quickly by.

Woken early and told to attend an education induction meeting. Was crammed into a room on the 2nd floor with 16, maybe 20, other fellow prisoners. Three men stood at one end, said they were from an outside agency to help prisoners. They said they couldn't help with anything to do with prison though, so don't ask them. After about five minutes I was called out of the room for a visit. Wasn't able to fill in the forms they gave us but will do it today in the cell and find a way of getting them to them.

Think I was in a bit of a state of shock at how abrupt and unexpected the unlocking was – wasn't prepared at all. Hadn't eaten, shaved, done my hair or somehow pressed my prison clothes, a little bit. Little bit annoyed with all the paperwork and sitting in rooms – would have liked to have stayed in my cell and read. Crazy I know but it's what I desire the most. This is my problem though, as from my conversations in 'association' many people thought they would benefit from the English lessons and alike – they seemed to be quite appreciative of the classes. I am the only one that came in with books though, maybe that's the difference?

Trenton Oldfield

The young man, the 'screw', who escorted me to the visitors block, while somewhat sympathetic to my actions started to share some very racist ideas including that non-white British people shouldn't be counted as British even if they were born here. This would mean most of my friends here in London don't count? That Deepa doesn't matter? If Deepa and I had children would they be considered British? Bearing in mind I'm Australian – but I guess this is a white thing? He said certain people behave differently: Jamaicans are in here for drug dealing, Sri Lankans for beating their wives, Polish for drink driving. I said "white people for paedophilia"? He chose not to hear that I think or I didn't say it loud enough! I suggest there might be some legacy from colonialism, particularly in relation to drug dealing and the way the role of women was undermined by British occupiers. He was sure: "It's cultural, it's what they have been doing for hundreds, probably thousands of years". Holy shit, he's an expert on so many cultures, across so many continents and across time too!

It seems this prison works via the methodology of 'holding pens' where the logic of keeping people apart with little to no association collapses and everyone from everywhere is brought together while they wait to go to x or y. It's both momentarily nerve-wracking as you pop into the room and everyone checks you out and then wonderful as the foremost characters start to shine and share their story and experiences – it's brilliant.

Yesterday the memorable people from the holding pen when we were waiting to see our visitors included:

- Tough though entirely charismatic North Londoner from Kentish Town, in a tracksuit – spoke about how prison was before – no toilets, just a bucket – no electricity much of the time; raw and brutal. Thought he was in his late 30s but he probably was in his 50s if he was talking about prison 'before'.

- Young guy – beard, jeans, coloured shirt with stripes – spoke beautifully, powerfully about David Cameron visiting the prison and how it's insane for him not to understand how if the British went around the world sticking flags everywhere that people wouldn't want their lands, lives and possessions back. People discussed the TV talk from Cameron et al suggesting they would take the TVs from prisoners. Same young man cracked the whole room up when one older man (overweight, brilliant grey beard) said Cameron etc could never take their TVs in here and so on – he asked "what planet you living on brother – if he could he would!" It was very funny and powerful. Whole room of 50 or more people were listening to him.

- Young hip guy with beautiful afro and a real side walk. Has worn a singlet rather than a t-shirt – despite the chill. Seems familiar to me, maybe from when I used to work in North Kensington? I'm too shy to ask. Hopefully he is on my wing and I can ask him another day.

- Youngish North London guy: talked about how annoying it is with all the cookery shows and the soft porn on TV. He said he races over and changes the channel as soon as any of it comes on. Told story of the time his cellmate had pissed 'the screws' off and they were going to separate them as he was to be put on 'basic'. He said he pulled the TV out of the wall himself and handed it to them. He was happier to stay in bed and read for two weeks than be separated from his friend. "They think TVs are more important to you than people"! He laughed about the pornos the prison used to show in the past, on Thursday evenings I think he asked, "what are you meant to do, have a wank with your friend in the room?"

People don't group together by race and so on as suggested in TV, films etc – maybe it's the randomness of when you get pushed into a 'holding pen' but there are no clicks, cliques, or gangs that I can see. Think that might be one of the myths propagated about this place. There is some attraction to others who speak the same language/s – which makes sense as everyone is trying to give or receive advice/support. Everyone seems to chat with each other regardless however. Maybe it's only 'the screws' that hold racist and classist views we see on the screen? I guess 'the screws' are as close to prison as those Oxbridge scriptwriters will allow themselves? Maybe they just want to believe we are animals in here, ripping each other apart like they like to do and have done to the people here and around the rest of the world. These are the sorts of people that think 'empire' was a good thing!

Everyone is very polite and helpful to each other though – letting people go first and helping each other with x or y form and suggesting ideas for their trial and so on. There is a tension whenever people are clumped together, people do size each other up – however this doesn't last long before good humour and hilarity takes over. There are some wonderful people in here, and of course some real characters.

It was both difficult and wonderful to see my love, my partner! Brilliant that Rehan could come – driving Deepa here and coming to check in on me also. Seems Deepa was on her way here yesterday and only a few streets away but took a few wrong turns and ended up at Wandsworth Prison! Oh man! Of course it's great to know he is here for us; a good friend, loyal and always so quick to do stuff, whatever it is. I feel fortunate. I'm not sure it was such a good idea to see them – I wasn't prepared at all; half–asleep, unshaven, un–showered, in smelly clothes and I've got some kind of tobacco smoke inflicted sore throat and runny nose. Of course Deepa was worried about this but I couldn't really talk much. I also didn't enjoy the process of being so alienated and disempowered by the process.

Speaking with my loves was surreal. I was allocated the red seat in a group of four seats all bolted to the floor. I was told not to stand up at any time and to limit touch to the beginning and end of the visit. None of us were allowed to take any material with us – notes, letters etc – just talk. As a prisoner I had to wear a yellow bib over my grey tracksuit, which is pretty alienating and humiliating. The aim of wearing a bib is to identify 'the prisoner' from 'the public' but I think it's more than that; it's emasculating and disempowering us in front of our family and friends.

There were a lot of screws in this room. They were much less friendly and supportive than the others inside the prison. A gaggle of them called me over to have chat with them. A number of them suggested to me that they believe in the death sentence. I guess they don't get too concerned about preventing deaths in custody then!? I'm not sure why they were volunteering this to me but we prisoners should also apparently 'pay our debt to society' – by cleaning spray–paint/graffiti, collecting rubbish, building roads and so on. We should be shamed in public and at the same time we should do hard labour. "It should be public, it must be public." Did they read Foucault this morning?

They did acknowledge they had no idea how to do this – how it could be organised. One lady screw did want to make it clear she didn't think they should be chained together though FFS! Though I have a feeling most of them wouldn't have minded this. They were pretty keen to keep talking – thankfully one of the screws noticed my hesitation in continuing the debate with them and told me to go through to the other side. It's always extra concerning when these views are held by someone from a 'minority' background and a sister that holds these views shocks me to the core – Stockholm Syndrome rules large over this island!

So David Cameron visited at the same time I was in my visit. The screws left their posts to come over to the window – like he was some sort of celebrity. I wish he had been passing in the yard when we were escorted across. He should be the one in here doing time for his crimes. Out of the corner of my eye I could see all his security staff fanning out across the yard. How pathetic. In here nobody would want to 'hurt' him – we would just ignore or laugh at him. He is seen as a joke, as a joker. Not many conversations have come up about him or the prison minister but the ones that have, people share how deeply cynical they are about him and the political system. People in here know the extent of how rotten the system is; these are the professors; this, friends, is where a deep knowledge is!

Before heading across to the visitors building (which I think is run by volunteers!) a fellow prisoner came up and said "brilliant fucking protest – phuck the system!" and shook my hand. If anything is apparent to me it's that 'Westminster Palace Democracy' days are numbered – there is no doubt about this! It's corrupt. It's too distant from us. It was never in our interests. There is too great a deficit now. Even if you watch a politics show on TV (whose aim is to project a normality, continuality and most importantly 'urgency' to a specific topic whatever it is this week) it is clear it can't continue. It can't last more than a few years. I'm sure they think they have decades. It could all collapse with a sizable controversy (aren't there enough already?) or even a half–arsed challenge from 'the public'. It's a mirage, a miracle at the moment. Even the screws don't vote.

I've written to Deepa about how I felt in our 'visit' so it's difficult to repeat it again here – but I do wish I was somewhat prepared – as I fear she may have felt somewhat distressed to see me so 'confused', 'distant' and quiet – as I was then. If it was today it would have been entirely different – my stomach drops at her thinking I'm still the same today as I was yesterday. I do hope I can call her today before she meets friends at our apartment for dinner. I'm worried I'm still locked in the cell and while it sounds like its 'association' time – though the afternoon does seem to drag longer than the rest of the day and I have no clock, no way to tell the time except from the TV and the TV rarely tells you the time! Feel ill thinking about Deepa – I just wasn't as upbeat as I had hoped to be – too internal and unclean! In the 'visit' Deepa told me of all the positive articles and support she had received – but somehow I'm not that interested. What can I do, I am in here now. I don't remember names or alike but I do know she sounded good about things.

Finally worked out when one can shower: 11am or 4pm – so showered as long as I was able – water temp was okay – far from hot but far from cold. With no bins people leave their shampoo on the floor – it's much like a gym – again like school – no separation and people showering in their underpants – not sure how to get clean with some clothes still on – time will tell, I am sure I will learn the methodologies! Being clean is very important to me!

Yesterday ended with more joy – post was delivered! Emails from friends and from many strangers sharing their solidarity and confirming I shouldn't ever lose sense of myself, that there is huge support and at the same time a profound disbelief at a six months jail sentence for an act of protest, of civil disobedience. Most painful and important was the message from my love sent at 3pm Sunday. In this message I hear words of love, solidarity and strength! She sounds strong and focussed.

I think I need to read it again as news of a forthcoming 'Immigration/Border Agency' visit has floored me. Somehow taken the energy/wind out of my sails – man, it's a rollercoaster! Well maybe the laws have changed and they will deport me despite being married, working here and of 'previously' very good character. Such is this life! There is a side of me that thinks the police, on encouragement from 'the Camerons', will make this life difficult now – I expect things to get complicated when I think I'm about to be released – not that I can think of things that will be of concern – so imagine they will be made up. Six months 'inside' isn't enough for them, that I'm sure about! It's not over with my prison sentence. That is why I'm reading as much as possible, learning as much as possible from these guys; these amazing authors or from these amazing lives discussed by other authors; reading Guevara's *Guerrilla Warfare*, Verso's *Book of Dissent* and Fanon's *The Wretched of the Earth*.

Dinner last night was very tasty and I imagine the meals will be perfect once my order for chilli sauce arrives – £1.09. The strangest aspect so far, the most worrying thing for me, is how unhygienic it seems to wash plates etc with no cleaning equipment and in the same sink as the loo – and the bin situation is pretty crazy also. Nonetheless it's okay. I have just bought detergent and scrubbers – so again sure it will be okay. Thankfully with the kettle, I can burn everything off in the meantime. Lucky I came in with some cash so I can order things from the canteen sheet. Though it's odd you have to wait so long for an order. And it's odd there isn't actually a canteen.

Keep having this feeling I'm going to be calling Deepa from Australia, "loves, guess what... I'm in Australia."

Dinner time is always great, there is some great solidarity between prisoners – and heaven knows I'm getting support and handshakes! Whatever this means I'm getting huge support; open support from 'black' brothers or I'm noticing it the most. It was like my experience in the talk at the 'Defend The Right To Protest' event – it was the sisters that were mostly nodding their heads with what I was saying. It was their response I cared about, was going to evaluate my ideas against. If they were disinterested or challenged my ideas then I would know I had done the wrong thing with my action. Maybe there is a shared experience or knowledge? And 'to be honest' (as they say in the UK) it's the ones whose understanding and ideas I'm most interested in. Maybe it's the colonial difference. The first hand experience of The Empire even though I'm white? I mean do most Brits know this place exists only because it dared to exploit other peoples and their lands? Do they know everything here is from the slavery it funded and organised? Do they know the empire used the idea of civilised and uncivilised to say lands were un-inhabited – the people living there were categorised as animals?

Tuesday 23rd / written 24th (morning)

Slept amazingly well – but woken by 'the screws' who said we needed to go to education – it was an uncomfortable moment – reality happens, here I am in prison being woken by a prison guard! 'Free flow' is one hour at the beginning and end of each weekday – where people move across the prison to courses, workshops, libraries etc. There is no doubt it's an amazing feat of 'People Management' and all seems to operate via a clip board with our names and cell numbers, all very old school. There is nothing digital about it. They did 'lose' someone yesterday, which was pretty entertaining for everyone particularly the longer-term prisoners. Not sure if they found him, I guess that they did. Before moving or throughout 'free flow', there is a lot of waiting, again in 'holding pens', yesterday it was in the stairwell – maybe 100 men from all different wings together in a stairwell. Lots of these people had manila folders – quite full, seems there is some serious study going on. Would like to learn more about the study opportunities in here. Lots of laughter and jokes whilst we waited and waited. Even if I was in here for years I don't think I would be quick and sharp enough to make people laugh like these guys do.

Our class and I say class cause it felt like being back in primary school – even the tables felt lower than normal. There were those positive and cute sayings on the walls – on every possible surface – I'm sure it was well intentioned but my goodness it felt disempowering and paternalistic. More disempowering was the evaluation tests we had to do – with two degrees, distinction for my thesis, four books and everyday working with words, it was very confusing and the most disempowering moment so far. No wonder most people just gave up in the middle of the test. If English wasn't my first language, as many in here, it would have been extremely difficult. Anyway there are five levels; I have been allocated to the second level. Our teacher said one or two people had made level three but there were in fact five levels and she wasn't aware of anyone anywhere that had got level four or five. What an insane methodology! Instinct tells me this must be run by one of those New Labour/Tory 'community interest companies'. I'm not sure there was anyone that left that room feeling good about themselves or their 'learning opportunities'. Completely phucked up! Also I have little to no idea about what actual courses and learning was available to me!

There was one amazing young man – our 'third floor education rep' – maybe 19–23, tall, skinny, clean cut – waiting sentencing for breaking into a car and stealing. He was profoundly lucid about many aspects of prison, talked amazingly fast and nailed the relationship that can exist between the prisoner and the screw. He is one of the most brilliant people I have heard speak and he both dominated and captivated the room. He also inspired me to clean my cell everyday – or at least develop a system – a pattern, a routine. Hopefully will get to speak with him later – I think he has court on Friday. Here's hoping he doesn't come back, that the judge is good to him. This guy should be advising, no making, policy – certainly a commentator on prison and the 'justice system'.

Have held back my education and work forms – not sure it was the right thing to do or not – but I'm not sure what I want to do yet – but it's difficult to know if I will be penalised for this? Might try for the education rep if that brilliant young man doesn't come back on Friday? It's hard to know if doing a job will keep me here in the Scrubs or show I'm involved and therefore able to be moved? The trouble is I'm quite happy in my cell – books and writing – I'm worried I will spend most of my time waiting in 'holding pens' than actually reading and writing. If the job needed doing and it would feel satisfying I would do it – hands down! Though I just have this feeling it will mostly result in me just waiting around... which would be annoying as the first masters course I did LOL – it would be terrible to spend hours waiting and waiting, been there, done that!

Last night I heard someone 'kicking off' for the first time – no doubt it is a worrying sound – someone slamming/banging on the door and sometimes wailing. What pain, terror and anger this person is going through! Heart goes out to him! It would be very unsettling and concerning to be in the same cell or in cell beside it. I think we were locked down today (Wednesday) because this person(s) was again 'kicking off'. There was an alarm set off as well – I assume to call the other prison staff?

Spent yesterday evening reading a new delivery of emails and letters/ postcards. Can only reply via snail mail post unfortunately. Replying to the thoughtful people that have sent messages, sent in notes and notebooks – wonderful people! Spoke to my love, it's at the same time very difficult and also exhilarating to speak with her, I know it's extremely difficult to place so much on her – the festival, home, bills, books, communication, waking up early and not being there to hold in the morning – it's awful feeling being in the apartment alone – so many memories and thoughts that spring up when there alone. Luckily we have sort of 'match fitness' of being apart and working alone. Thank goodness it's only 6 to 12 weeks apart this time! And great we didn't have to cancel the festival – even if I'm in prison until 19 January, the festival is a week later! Though it's a huge amount of work for Deepa to do alone! We have to make the festival smaller this year – which I think might be a good thing. We have no choice. We have always wanted to do less – now are being forced to do less – easier somehow?

Strange thing about being inside is somehow everything crazy going on outside seems distant. And everything here is aiming to get you 'outside' again – 'outside' is 'good', 'inside' is 'bad'. The TV makes it all seem like everything is a–okay – even good out there. Totally peculiar, when it's plainly untrue ... I mean the crimes we committed were done on the 'outside'. Jimmy Savile lived and roamed on the 'outside'. What people are not picking up on is the Jimmy Savile situation is this represents just another example or way into the deep corruption of our institutions. Can you imagine if a bent organisation can be an 'entertainment organisation' (BBC), imagine the depth and horror of corruption in other 'institutions'. Imagine what happens in organisations that take care of children or by organisations/people that are seen to be responsible/caring/better/experts, or where abuse (military for example) is expected. Phucking heartbreaking!! This is what happens when some people think somehow they're different, better or above other people. This is the tyranny I protested about. Sexual abuse can't happen without a deeper corruption existing – it's one of the outcomes of a culture that is fraudulent, dishonest, duplicitous. It is the 'canary in the coal mine'.

Wednesday (written on Thursday evening)

Wednesday was it seems the first full day without any organisational matters – spent most, if not almost all of it, in my cell. At this stage I still have the cell to myself, which I have to say is a huge relief. I'm not sure it would be possible to read and write with another in such a small space – there must be a methodology but I can't quite picture it yet. Just myself and one other chap have a cell to ourselves now.... every other cell now has two people. These spaces ... eating, shitting, washing, sleeping are too small for two people, there is no doubt about it! The cells further up at least have a separate toilet. Here the loo is just behind a sheet hanging from the roof.

Not sure but I think the hype around me being in prison has died down now... just part of the landscape now... one of the many. That is comforting in many ways... blending in, but it does make it everydayish now – which is unsettling also!

Spoke through the door to 'immigration' (Border Agency), a young lady, just gave the usual information; address, name, conviction and so on. Before she left I asked her if she thought my conviction could affect my immigration status ... perhaps too quickly she said she didn't think it would. That anxiety, the only anxiety I've had in here, just dropped away – for now. No doubt it will return again and again in the months ahead – hopefully Sun, it all works out – while internally it feels like it will – my major feeling yesterday was 'the bosses' 'the establishment' haven't finished with me yet – they haven't gotten their 'pound of flesh' yet!

My shock at actually being in here, along with my determination to establish a rhythm seems to be transforming into a rage and disgust like it was before I came in – like it was on 'the outside'. It's entirely phucked up a judge thought 'the wrongs' I did were illegal and I should spend six months in prison! As a judge she seems as bright as a fish... though she did manage to set the jury question up very well, to get the conviction, I have to give that to her! I'm not sure why I expected a judge to be bright LOL! Why would they be?

Spending a full day in this small room isn't too difficult! I guess I'm practised at it? Writing books, articles and doing white–collar desk jobs for so long now? I am content and have clarity of mind. Despite the difficulties with my love at the time of my protest it is if course her I miss the most and feel greatest urgency for. While I read and write, I leave her with many burdens – festival, apartment, books, interviews, TINAG, MCP and apparently #freetrentonoldfield too. I know all of this I've done will make sense in the future! May she hold tight for these two or three months! I'm sure what I did will start to make more and more sense as time goes on. Well I hope it does!

Boarding school

Prison is every bit like my boarding school experience but it's 'easier'. The boarding school is faux prison, which makes it worse than the real thing. It can't be any other way. Boarding school is 'worse' as it's the fake version – prefects, housemasters, forms galore, punishment etc. They try to be like a Victorian prison but clearly can't be so have no choice but to 'over egg it'. What also makes it worse at school is this fear they force feed of what might happen to your future and worse than everything – what will happen to your 'reputation' ... it's all about the threat of going down the social ladder. None of that here, people have been convicted or are on remand – reputations are different, it's not about fitting in but quite the opposite. All I can say is faux prison (boarding school) makes the experience of prison easier, much easier – well, this is my experience so far – let's see what happens when I get moved to a different wing or different jail. Sounds like Wormwood Scrubs is a much 'better' prison than Wandsworth or Brixton – which I could have been in if they took me to the Barnes side of the river rather than the Chiswick side. But other people say the opposite, so who knows! I am here, so it is what it is!

Trenton Oldfield

Writer

Many characters or personalities would do well in here – first I think the stereotypical 'couch potato' would – it is possible to lie on your bed all day and night, watching TV, only needing to move a few steps to the toilet or a few more to collect your food. Also a writer could do well in here as they have some experience of spending vast amounts of time alone in their own thoughts and not moving very far. What's brilliant is having the food prepared for you. It's also awesome having very few distractions or interruptions if you have your own cell!

A week in prison

In contrast to what the 'the public' and some of 'the screws' might think everyone in here wants to do a job or get training! Except me! It's only me that wants to sit still. I think many people will be shocked to hear this, but it's overwhelmingly the case – most sought after jobs are education assistant, reception, 'hot plate' and alike – these young men want to work. Let me be clear they don't want to work for corporations making cell phones etc but want to work on jobs that make it a better environment for their fellow prisoners and to also pick up some skills and alike. They call working for corporations 'slave labour'! Much of the conversation, when we come together in holding pens or in association time, is around jobs ... what job, where, who with, what's its mobility level and so on and so forth. So it is just me who is happy in my cell, alone, writing, watching some music videos and reading. There is a real resistance to the introduction to 'corporate slave labour' as a number have called what's happening in other prisons ... they said there would be strikes for sure if they tried to introduce this here.

Slavery and prison work

If you wanted to take examples from the past to help with taking an 'educated guess' at what will be the focus for the 'next wave' of slavery or indentured workers, it would have to be either the colonisation of other planets or the mining of these so called asteroids. Be it the building of spaceships or the labour of people who will be used to 'take' space. Sounds crazy? Heard nothing about it? I wonder if in the 16th or 17th century the 'general public' were aware of explorers setting out in search of other lands to colonise? Would you advertise it or would you keep it as quiet as possible? I wonder if prisoners in Millbank ever imagined they would end up working in chains without payment, to take the land of 'Australia' from the indigenous peoples for the very Crown that imprisoned them? If Richard Branson ever gets involved in private prisons or work for prisons/people on benefits, I will be sure to take a closer look LOL!

Private prisons

While in the holding pen for my visit with my love, the brilliant character from North London, very energetic, was relaying to the group his friend's experience of a private prison. Said his friend spoke about it in very positive terms – computers, electronic systems, was new, nice screws, something like a positive environment. It seems to me it is a methodology to get people to want these prisons over the existing prisons. Private = good. Public = bad. There is not a doubt in my mind these are Trojan horse projects. A few exemplary prisons will be built. These will be classic 'show villages' that will first engender support and generate complimentary and supportive statistics. These will be the prisons politicians and some crocked organisations/charities will visit. Reports by these 'independent' organisations will show them to be much better for prisoners – probably something along the lines of their obsession with re–offending rates and the quality of education resources. Politicians who have had little to no concern for prisoners – ever – will talk of how 'you judge a culture by how it treats its prisoners' and so on! Endless articles will be written by prisoner 'charities' and ex–cons saying something along these lines and before you know it everyone everywhere will want prisons to be in the hands of corporations as people care about prisoners all of a sudden!

Most prisons and most prisoners will be nothing like the small handful of exemplars! Most of us will be out of sight and out mind and in terrible conditions – mark my words. 'Charities' funded by the corporate prison owners via their Corporate Social Responsibility LOL, will report: 'things could be better but the results from the prisoners' surveys suggest services are being delivered to a high standard'. Most prisons will be brutal brutal places run by already damaged ex–military people or even worse men with small man's syndrome. Work for little to no pay will be compulsory – there might even be signs saying 'Work Sets You Free' in the sweatshops?

I'm sure some 'professor of business efficiency' has written a book or someone's MBA has been on how to employ the methodology of 'show villages' and how to use Trojan horses – in business. Business is always somehow separate from life, from living – "it's business".

Telephone call

Just off the phone from speaking with my love. Always a dream to speak, however this evening at the end of conversations about work, life, love, Deepa suggested we might be having a child. My love suggests we might be having a child! 'Outside' I might feel different, however with only moments to speak! Not 100% but highly likely! My goodness this is wonderful and terrifying! It's difficult being here and not being there with my love at such a time. There is no doubt she has been putting on some weight. This, my friends, might be it! How do I sleep tonight? Hope my love sleeps okay. Well my court trial back in September was good for something, truly wonderful LOL! Whatever happens I shall be 'out' in time!

News Channel 4

I'm revolted at UCL and sickened to the core by 'UCL Urban Lab' for their role (be it active such as their press releases or in their silence and inactivity now), in assisting the process of granting planning permission for a UCL campus that will demolish Carpenters Estate – destroying HOMES and hyper-gentrifying this area!! Entirely appalling people and the worst betrayal by something that calls itself an 'Urban Lab'. Why don't these people have any integrity? Or even compassion? They would betray anyone! They should have all resigned or gone on hunger strike rather than beg like desperate lickspittles for work doing UCL's 'consultation' on the demolition of people's homes! This shall be their albatross, there is no doubt. These 'company men' with their pathetic narcissistic low self-esteem might want to be senior university administrators/gatekeepers but it won't be possible now ... an uprising will clear these people out overnight. They should be arguing for these HOMES to be refurbished, full employment, free education and the end of the criminalisation of poverty.

Struggle around communicating 'prison'

Struggling a little at the moment to work out how I might communicate 'prison' to people when I'm released. I feel confident at demystifying it, doing lists about it, denuding it of its 'middle class hell' status, but at the same time I don't want to cause problems for my fellow prisoners that might be in here longer than I will be this time. There is no doubt I'm over egging my influence but it would be an awful outcome to demystify the situation of being 'inside' and that being used as an excuse to 'tighten' the conditions, bring back divide and rule tactics and alike. Unintended consequences kinda thing!

Also my experience so far is very limited – so maybe it's not so easy to say things about being in here and I could only speak of my experience not of others' experiences. There surely is no way one could generalise about prison. I'm sure it's different for everyone, and probably every prison is different. But if it is for political protesters like me, maybe I can speak about it with some confidence? I'm working my way through this idea – hopefully talking to more prisoners I can get a better sense of it. What they want me to communicate to people when I'm out. From some of the conversations so far – it's about the stigmatisation of being a prisoner and then an ex–con; of having been to jail. The older guys keep telling me that I should know my life is going to be different now – "it's harder with a criminal record". It seems less about the conditions in here and more to do with the everyday life once outside, once you are branded as a convict.

Reflection

It's seven days since I've seen my reflection! There is not a single mirror here – anywhere! Not in the bathrooms, not in the hallways, not anywhere! Aren't we meant to be reflecting in here? Isn't this easiest when looking into one's own eyes? And how am I to shave? And my hair? Does it not matter what I look like now? Which surface on the 'outside' isn't reflective? 'Outside' everything is about appearance.

Trenton Oldfield

No longer alone

I'm no longer alone in this cell. I guess nobody has to tell you you're about to get a 'flatmate' in here. Wasn't prepared for it, had my stuff all over his cabinets etc. Books, papers, all my extra breakfast stuffs. Well at least it wasn't the Border Agency coming to deport me! It didn't take long at all to move the stuff, such a small space LOL! Guess what? He's not a crack–smoking, arm–breaking gangster who is going to rape me for my milk, but a young man with two master's degrees! Maybe it's good to have a cellmate? Less time in my own head or in these books? Just hope he hasn't done any crimes against women or children, that's going to be tough! He has just said he is in here for 16 weeks for stealing £2000 from his employer.

Window

So there is no heating and it's freezing – tomorrow I understand it's meant to be below zero. Today my neighbour took his newspaper and my toothpaste and covered the open bits of the window. Everyone sets about helping each other in here. He pops his head in most associations and we have a chat about France, racism, Britain and the ideas behind fraud. Had a nice visit from M, hopefully his cellmate doesn't come back this evening – let's hope he gets bail!

Remand

Remand is one of the most brutal, unfair systems – someone I met today has been in here for three months already and his trial isn't until February – six months in jail waiting for his trial! He suggested to me there is no compensation if you are found not guilty. This is unthinkable; imagine! This is something that must be compensated if they get it wrong! It's barbaric, brutal and unforgivable. This situation combined with trigger–happy judges means not only are prisons rammed full but people, innocent people, are having their lives wrecked. And there is apparently no compensation for this!?! This struck home to me meeting Terry's lovely friend on the morning of my sentencing – he was on remand, miles from his family, for an entire year – truly heartbreaking – received no compensation! Imagine what this does to a family, to a person. What a barbaric idea. I can see it makes sense for some violent crime like murder and rape but for an alleged pub brawl, for alleged theft, for alleged fraud?

Saturday sunshine

So today will be the first real test for me I feel, as there is not a cloud in the sky – it is also the weekend we would normally have held our festival. Otherwise I would likely be searching for a spot in the sun this morning with my loves and for a coffee in the sun. I have heard there is access to the yard so let me see if I can find this. So far I haven't been outside for a week accept for the short walks to the church and then when my love visited. Does seem odd to not have any access to the yard. Today it seems important – maybe the buildings won't block the sunrays?

Work

There is such a great deal of work to do with our books, the festival and so on, it was great to start yesterday – even just to send my love the outline for the newsletter for the 8th November. It is frustrating we can't speak for longer than a few minutes on the phone once a day and that we can't exchange specific information. Sun knows I hope the post arrives otherwise it's a terrible waste of energy, time and to have Deepa waiting for the post – breaks my heart! It is probably my fault as I didn't put my prisoner number on the letters. If we are pregnant it's critical we get the messages to each other. I'm not sure why my post isn't getting there?! Hugely frustrating I must say.

TV

It's been interesting talking to one of the older screws who had previously said prisons are much calmer than they used to be. In his words "more intellectual, it was brute force before". Having watched quite a bit of TV in this past week, I'm wondering if the TV itself, which is such a pacifier for the population at large, isn't a main calming effect for prisoners, for 'calmer' prisons? Watching TV you can't help but think everything is okay! Not only is it a valium but it's this amazing reinforcing force. If you watched TV only, you would be quite surprised to step outside the door. It reminds me of those postcards prospective immigrants were given of how rich the USA was – money growing on trees, giant chickens and alike! I have been writing down the titles of the songs shown over and over on the music channel. They include: Turn Around, Diamond In The Sky, Standing In The Dark, Don't Worry Child, Sweet Nothing, Beauty & A Beat, Hottest Girl In The World, Troublemaker, Something New, I Found You, Whistle, Good Time, Girl On Fire, Locked Out Of Heaven, Let Me Love You, Wish You Were Here, Feel The Love, Love Is Easy, Beneath Your Beautiful – all in this revolutionary time. First it's tragedy, and then it's a farce! I'm starting to think everything is okay! Hahaha! I should just dance around the cell singing Diamond in the Sky!

Letters

For reasons unknown no post was delivered last night (Friday) but on Thursday evening I received the most wonderful mail – some 20+ letters and emails! It's wonderful, just energy giving! I'm very much looking forward to replying – such beautiful people out there – everywhere, inside here! It's just a small brutal group that cause such concern and make things difficult for many. These people have a condition; it's called narcissistic personality disorder which is a deadly and contagious virus. Little known is the fact that this disorder has created a new stronger strain, which is called capitalism – its carriers are called capitalists. It's an entirely treatable condition.

Dreams

First night dreaming – dreamt I was released today. True! Hahaha! Woken from my sleep and released! Hahaha!

Rehab

What is crazy, and needs to be overthrown as a matter of urgency, is people having a criminal record. While nobody has told me what prison is for (rehabilitation, punishment, retribution, vengeance?) what seems most damaging is having a 'criminal record'. What is the point of coming to prison? Are you meant to do your time? Shouldn't you be cleared of everything once you have done prison? So you do prison for x or y crime but then you have another punishment (possibly worse) which is a criminal record. This has to end. You should have one or the other, not both! When I was arrested during my protest, I was repeatedly asked over and over "do you have any previous convictions", "are you known to the police". It seemed an entirely irrelevant question to me then and certainly the least urgent question related to what I had just done. What difference would it make to this specific 'crime' or any 'crime' that may or not have been undertaken? It seems all crimes come together – there is no end. There is no rehabilitation, once you are a criminal you are always a criminal. Which means there really is no point going to prison as you have the criminal record. Or if you go to prison you shouldn't have a criminal record cause you just did your time. What I'm learning is there is no rehabilitation – people's misadventures somehow compound and compound and are never ruled out – even 10 or 20 years in the future. It makes no sense, and is brutally aimed at maintaining a 'criminal class', one that can be easily returned to prison. It also helps maintain those horrific ideas of 'a vicious poor'. Everyone loves to hate a criminal. 'Everyone we don't like should end up in jail! Jail is reserved for the worst people.' 'Prisoners' and 'prison' are the shorthand to most people's prejudices.

Symbols

The brilliant thing about prison is the lack of symbols. There is not a single British union jack or alike anywhere. People aren't concerned with creating any symbols of any kind – be they nationalist or otherwise. I know you can't have sports clothes etc with logos, sports teams etc, but nobody even seems concerned with even attempting to create symbols. Maybe they are 100% banned (is my beard a symbol?) but it's such a relief in comparison to 'outside' – particularly after this hyper propagandist year! It's like de–cluttering a room and turning a TV off that's always been left on in the background.

Socialist Worker

Received another '14 day rule notification slip'. This time "*Socialist Worker* from an unauthorised source" "Will be destroyed or handed out at next visit". For phucks sake why do they keep doing this with material people send in?

The argument that if Amazon sniffer dogs haven't sniffed the material they will be covered in LSD is pure madness!

Mail

Just received a huge pile of new mail; wonderful people from all around the world! Not sure if I will have the time to reply – I hope so, such wonderful people! News of Penguin and Random House combining doesn't surprise me at all; surely this is 'natural' for corporate capitalism? What seems odd to me is almost everyone seems to be discussing the political implications of this control of knowledge … only talking about how they had to do it to compete with Amazon? Along the lines of … 'If we didn't colonise India, someone else would have'!?

Amongst the mail from loves and friends are two pieces from the prison: first is an Application for Release on 4th December 2012. I would be realised with an electronic tag on home curfew. The other is a transfer note to Birmingham – and that I have been categorised as a level C prisoner – not level D as everyone expected. I didn't think our dear government and their lickspittles had given up yet – political protest with no previous record is now considered a Cat C offence and you will be jailed accordingly LOL! How can my love visit Birmingham to see me – this is insane!

Closed prison

Category C for political protest – this makes no sense to me or anyone else I have spoken to in here – will let it settle in before storming around. No doubt it's arranged by a computer somewhere else and little to nothing to do with the peeps here. Need to be calm. It's brought home to me that this isn't going to end soon – there will be no early release, there will be a pound of flesh yet still to be paid, a requirement of the nasty vindictive class. Wow, protest is now Cat C! It's starting to sink in now. My goodness. Insane. It's a long time to be inside for a protest, for anything really. And Cat C seems silly – like it's a game. I really have to think about this, what they are trying to do and how to react – not react. Cat C is a closed prison "for those who cannot be trusted in open conditions but who are unlikely to escape".

Middle-class hell

So I have been thinking about 'the stain' of prison and being a prisoner. I have been thinking about how the fear of this stain is surely one of the greatest control mechanisms, certainly a very powerful self-policing apparatus. Prison is an idea from another time. It was probably always a lazy and unimaginative way of dealing with difficult situations. My guess is prisons didn't exist in indigenous nations for example? If people didn't have this hyped fear of prison they would step up and do stuff that needs to be done, I'm sure of it. And prisons would collapse as they wouldn't be able to contain all the 'prisoners' ... the idea would be rendered useless. Imagine having to jail tens of thousands, hundreds of thousands of protesters. Imagine if people stood up to corrupt institutions without fear of some kind of stain on them.

Prison is some kind of middle-class hell, a middle-class family's worst nightmare. It's anti-aspirational and is seen as a slide to the bottom of the social and economic ladder they are so desperate to have a leg further up on. It is of course essential for the middle classes to have prisoners – so they can have a defenceless, silenced population to rail against, to demonise, to lift themselves above. However if anyone has 'match-fitness', the everyday practice suited for prison, it is the middle classes! Here are some reasons why I think the middle classes ought not to be afraid of prison or why prison should not be a deterrent to middle-class action, which is so phucking urgently needed:

- Britain's middle classes (BMC) are used to and somehow enjoy steamed vegetables and boiled potatoes.

- BMC are used to and enjoy being cold in their homes. They are used to never turning the heating on. They would no doubt be happy to put another pair of socks on, feel cold, be unable to write because hands are so cold but feel good about saving on the heating bill (which they would normally end up spending on beer so they can pass out in bed because it's so cold in the flat).

- Most BMC will have degrees, so at some point will have mastered or come close to mastering sitting alone for hours and hours with just books, pen and paper.

Trenton Oldfield

- Many of BMC will have been to a boarding school or better yet, a school so 'aspirational' it modelled itself on and pretends to be an austere boarding school/prison. Prison hierarchy, rules and regulations are super easy in comparison but they will know all the codes and how the hierarchy is structured.

- BMC are very used to irregular visits to their home from friends and family. Formal in nature with no long hugs, plenty of sitting, no touching, no arguments, always wondering if there is going to be food. Such visits parallel prison visits: one hour of formal, distant and polite chit-chat before the inevitable 'we must get on'. Surviving prison depends, one is told, on keeping a low profile, never rocking the boat, never putting your 'head above the parapet' – something BMC have perfected and pride themselves on, and teach as a good thing to their children.

- BMC will feel at home in the very simple 'sensible' austere furnishings of their cells. A few pieces of compressed timber furniture, the TV being the most important item in the room and magnolia coloured paint.

- BMC will feel at home in prison as every cell has a kettle. Drinking endless cups of tea as a distraction is a huge part of the daily routine 'inside' as well. And long life milk is 'normal' in here also.

- With so few provisions in here, there is little to no threat of having the possibility of being generous or to having to lend anyone anything. Certainly absolutely no threat of having to extend any hospitality.

- BMC are well practised at writing pithy cards or notes to family members rather than spending time with them. The canteen even has Hallmark-type cards for sale where the words are already written ... you can just write the name at the top and your own name at the bottom. Could add an 'x' if feeling sentimental.

- Well practised at insignificant and polite chit-chat even with people they have known their entire lives, the BMC could easily pass time in prison. I think they could do six years without any trouble of running out of chit-chat.

- It is well known the BMC are not concerned with cleanliness, in being clean. We all know they didn't have sewers until the late 1800s. There should be no problem with continuing this existence in here. There is no pressure from anyone to shower ... you don't even have to change your sheets or clothes if you don't want to.

Wednesday 31 October

It is one of those glorious days. First, woke up and read 80 or so pages of *Love and Capital, Jenny and Karl Marx*, then spoke with my love about the joy and the likelihood of us expecting a child, and then a good lunch – finally some spice in the dish!

Loved ones that suffer

Despite my neighbour telling me I'm wasting my time writing books and I should get a job, another avalanche of mail and goodness arrived. First I read a letter from my love – sent some days ago, which accompanied monies I can use in the 'canteen'. It is the first time I've had tears in my eyes since being here. I miss her and I can really now start to feel her pain and the sense of loss she is experiencing in her messages. This hurts like crazy and I feel responsible for this – terribly responsible. There are many burdens I have left her with, most burdensome is not being able to talk, to reassure her, to hold her close and explain, reassure her that while this sentence is insane it's a good thing. The trouble with prison is it punishes the loved ones more than the prisoners. We have been through much together in the last few years.

And where does the judge eat tonight?

It sounds from what people on the 'outside' have written to me there is clarity or increasing clarity resulting from my imprisonment – an Achilles' heel has been exposed, of the establishment's vindictive, brutal and aggressive core. While the judge was cunning in framing the jury's question, her sentencing statement was weak, childish, churlish and intellectually corrupt. I'm sure she is dining out with her other odd, aloof colleagues on her new-found media fame. She certainly succeeded in getting her name in the newspapers. You do have to worry when people do things for the motivation of getting press attention! I wonder if she knows almost everyone else that is aware of the case thinks she is intellectually weak, that most are laughing at her? It was incredibly, incredibly difficult not to laugh at her when she was reading her sentencing summary. I had hoped she would be a learned judge, a thoughtful judge, someone I could respect ... I was hoping for something meaty from her, something to contemplate while I was in prison. Her statement was frustratingly inept, pedestrian and inconsequential. Really quite frustrating! Never mind ... such is this life!

Newspapers

So in this bundle of mail was postcards from strangers: 'Vive La revolution Cubana', drawings from Chops, envelopes with stamps on them already, love emails from my love, books from professors I deeply admire, emails from lovers I'm forever fond of, ex-colleagues and new friends. Kind, warm, loving people!! My joy increased when a newspaper was delivered to me. Seems Marcus and Margareta have ordered the *Guardian* to be delivered to me each day! Their solidarity knows no bounds! Such wonderful, thoughtful and generous people! Think 2004 was the last time I sat down and read a newspaper cover to cover.

My goodness! If only I could hug my love right now. This afternoon I should receive my canteen orders. It is the chilli sauce and bounty chocolate bars I am most looking forward to. I didn't order much. I don't have a desire for much at all. These years living on very little income has prepared me well ... I have very few wants. Chilli sauce though, I have to say, will be very welcome! Will be good to go 'cold turkey' on those posh coffees I have spent years chasing around London. Hopefully I will lose the taste for them once and for all.

My spirits have remained high. For the last day or so with news that none of my mail was getting through I stopped writing to people and focussed on reading! I've mostly lived inside Marx's family apartments and wondered how our life with children will be. How to live a political life in this hyper-capitalist time? What world will they grow up in? Well I have more energy and reason to fight than ever before! I can't let them live without agency over their own lives, they will never be slaves.

The trouble is I feel terribly ill equipped and concerned our political agitation will harm them. It worries me terribly. But heaven knows I will love them madly, my goodness! What funny, awkward looking, skinny, hairy things they will be! Big teeth, big ears, but the sun knows full of love and that they will feel loved by me, by us! This is the most important aspect to me, that they feel loved and have books and warmth around them. Today that seems possible but I'm not sure how to do it on an everyday level. Well this year is something for us! Thanks sun for allowing Deepa and I to meet, to be together! I knew the moment I saw her – clear as clear it was – an equal partner, not a muse but my partner!

After a week of having no credit to make phone calls, it was wonderful to speak this morning, even if it is amazingly brief. I understand Deepa was interviewed for an article in the *Evening Standard* about my protest, the politically motivated charge and my sentencing. Seems the journalist 'got' most of what Deepa was saying. She said she was this morning on her way to Voice of Russia – she must be exhausted! My love!

Claiming asylum

My cellmate went to the Hindu prayer session today ... he has come back bursting with energy! He really didn't want to go but I'm pleased I strongly encouraged him. He seems to have had a good chat with the others there. I applied to go but I guess it was too confusing with my name? Maybe next week? I want to go to all the religious activities in here. Seems most in the session were 'Sri Lankans', who as H has explained to me have claimed asylum upon landing at Heathrow. They were either Tamils who were fleeing for their lives as a result of the genocide or they have come in with families based in the 'Middle East'. These families escape the heat by coming to London for the summer – they bring along all or most of their 'staff'. As they had been treated so badly by these families they destroy all their papers, passports and so on, on the plane. They can only do this when and if they have them – usually they don't have possession of their passports to avoid this situation. Without papers and claiming asylum, they are placed straight into prison until their applications can be worked out. H said most had been in prison for two years already, waiting for anything to happen. This tyranny seems very similar to everything Deepa and I experienced and learned when we were in Jeddah last year. Something happens when there is such a gap between the rich and poor. It's not something peculiar to one group or another – people we knew 'from Europe' who had their 'nanny' sleeping in the storeroom under the stairs. These men said to H, "At least we have two years of some kind of rest, we have been working since we were children, and we can learn English and we can eat. At least in here we live without the threat of violence as we had both in Sri Lanka and where ever we were with these families". We chatted into the night about how this tyranny could be overthrown. It seems to have really affected him, understandably so.

What is prison for?

After a week and a little in here, I've been turning my night's mind to trying to work out why I'm here and why we are here. The first chapter or so of Foucault's *Discipline and Punish* has also got me thinking about what on earth this is all about in the so-called 21st century. Mike and Ben's proposed appeal has me thinking as I've reread 'our honourable Judge's' statement on her six months sentence for me.

Of course I don't have a clue, but it's interesting to consider the accepted contemporary ideas for sending people to prison nonetheless. As I understand it up to today:

- Prison is the place where 'dangerous' people are put to protect the public ... not hospital

- To reform the individual

- To punish the individual

- To perform vengeance

- To undertake passive aggressive torture

- To try to force the individual to feel guilt, shame and embarrassment

• To 'work off' our crime

• To create a purgatory for loved ones – to enact
  a collective punishment

It might be worthwhile for the prisons' minister to explain, perhaps in an 'info pack' upon arrival here, what the point of prison is – does the government know exactly? Does 'the public' know? Does anyone know? I'm not sure anyone here knows! Certainly it's not been explained or even suggested why we are here. I kinda feel like we are just here 'cause this is what's happened for hundreds of years; a momentum that just keeps going? We have always had schools, hospitals, roads, cemeteries and prisons? It's difficult enough for those of us that were preparing for it but it's extremely difficult for people that were one minute on the street or at work and then two days later in jail to come to terms with this!

Immediate imprisonment

This is why I think in 'association' time so many people look 'dazed and confused' – staring into the distance. I cannot understand why people are not given six weeks' notice, even one week's notice to prepare for jail. Whole livelihoods disappear! Prison is an over–punishment, they lose their relationships, their homes, their jobs … they don't have any opportunity to address anything beforehand, to somehow prepare, communicate and so on. Imagine trying to arrange your life 'outside' with £2 credit and one or possibly two hours a day out of your cell – along with this brutally slow postal service? Imagine it? If they didn't have to keep up the bravado of prison being such a scary place there wouldn't be the flight risk (the reason they say they take you straight from the court). People would have the time to organise for the time they will be in prison. Why must M's child suffer like this? Why must his wife suffer like this? I don't think prisons should exist but while they do they should have a methodology that enables people to prepare … it is the families that suffer and it's without a doubt an over–punishment to lose sometimes everything! Perhaps, perhaps it makes sense for violent crime, but overwhelmingly the criminals in here are not violent and have just done one or two foolish mistakes – sometimes more but not often. Surely this needs to change or is this torture part of the punishment – the potential to lose everything? Always, always plead not guilty! At least if you plead not guilty you have some time, there has to be a case prepared. If you plead guilty, especially at a magistrates' court, the judge can sentence you straight away. And I get the sense these judges may have a few blinkers. What sort of person wants to judge other people day in day out?

Stacked juries

It was interesting, most interesting, to read in *Love and Capital* that the juries in the main trials in Germany were likely to be have been 'stacked' or have 'agent provocateurs' placed on them to encourage convictions or not. It was my feeling, my intuition about my own trial. It could only be possible, I could be found guilty of this charge as a result of some sort of bent or pressured jury. It was too fast, too furious, too universal. I'm sure in time we will find certain juries were stacked ... maybe not mine but it's a very real possibility! I mean what would be more perfect to corrupt than juries – you can't contact them and they are never allowed to speak about the trial. I have a hunch. Not one I will pursue for a while but in time, in time. I guess we will find out in 30 years time, like everything else corrupt in this country ... paedophiles, war crimes in colonial projects, murders done to look like the IRA, police deaths in custody, surveillance of 'radicals' and so on. Why people here are happy to wait 30 years for the truth about things I don't know! When does a 30-year rule of silence ever work in favour of the people? It always, always protects the interests (corruption) of the elite, those in power or those in desperate pursuit of holding onto the power they think should keep. Mark my words, we will find out a number of trials were corrupted by stacked juries or juries pressured by agent provocateurs. Maybe it didn't happen in my trial but if cops are okayed to have children with 'green activists' (FFS) why wouldn't you corrupt juries? The fact jurors are untraceable and so on means it's incredibly easy to 'get the desired results'.

Thursday

Almost two weeks. Things are speeding up now. This week certainly went quicker than last week; my goodness! Visited or had our induction to the gym today, this morning. I thought it would just be weights and running machines, but there is a gymnasium – for basketball, volleyball etc. There is, though I'm not sure where, also a fake grass football field outside. Once again it felt like primary school – with lots of waiting around too. Perhaps I'm projecting but all but one of the staff and prison volunteers were 'white' – which seems strange when the prison population is clearly very very 'mixed'. I'm curious how that could come about. Maybe everyone else prefers to work out, and not do jobs in here? Who knows? Again we were treated like children – even sitting on children's gym benches – all 55 of us. Maybe it's not possible to order benches or school desks for adults? Maybe adult sizes don't exist? Maybe it's a budget thing??

Younger

Starting to note an interesting difference between the younger prisoners – those in their early twenties and everyone else – there is gusto; a performance we older ones just don't do, or couldn't be bothered to do? Maybe they have to, maybe I did as well? Hell knows it's pretty bloody annoying! A real bluster about them! Reminds me of some of the messages scrawled around including in my cell like: 'SW6 Young Janis on a Adventure'. Hell knows I was happy to make it to 30 – all those years of mistakes and working out 'whom' and 'what' now largely put at ease. Have a feeling a juvenile centre/prison might be worse than prison? I picture them now as very hectic places where there is an over performance – of masculinity, of everything?

Words/labels

The strange thing is, and a chap said it to me today: all of us are 'criminals' in here but none of us think of ourselves as criminals. Well he actually said, "I look at everyone in here and they look like criminals, but I don't consider myself a criminal – I don't see myself as one of them." He thinks because he did fraud he is okay, different. His comments made me feel very uncomfortable. This statement has reminded me of the feeling that comes over me (and others from the look on their faces) in those first moments when we are herded into a 'holding pen'. It's a feeling of anxiety that makes no sense as we know the people beside us, these are the people we share a cell with, see every day in the line for food, the same people we see at our religious meetings and in the gym and so on. These aren't crazies – these are the same helpful, kind people. There is a suspicion of others, which disappears almost every single time you speak with them. Until then, somehow you feel apprehensive about everyone else. It's a strange thing which reflects that even we are suspicious of ourselves, because of how prisoners are perceived in our culture. We are prisoners and we are suspicious of other prisoners. This is madness.

Take

There is a window sill just close by the showers at this end that every few days displays items such as shoes, cups etc – items from the prison. Below the sill are two large metal boxes on wheels that contain the sheets and blankets we are given on arrival. If there is stuff here, either the person has been released or transferred. If the metal bins include these grey tracksuits, then the prison mate has been released, not transferred. It's a small but positive sign that people do get released! We don't stay here forever! It does finish! There is an end! Where we go after is an entirely different story but that is for another day. This window sill is where people also leave newspapers etc for other prisoners to take. I have just left my first newspaper there.

Gifts!

Marcus and Margareta have already been truly and amazingly loving and supportive with helping with my legals, but now I feel shocked and embarrassed they have also ordered a subscription to the daily *Guardian* newspaper and the *New Statesman*. Wow. Feel overwhelmed. They are truly wonderful, generous, thoughtful and loyal people. I'm touched. My letter to them unfortunately won't contain my thanks for this as it was sent some days ago... I will write another. Wow.

Cell

I'm choosing to spend time in the cell, rather than the gym, yard etc as I've so many people to write to. And at the moment, at this stage of my understanding, the 'association' time reminds me of 'play time' at school. Everyone feels like they should be doing something but there isn't really anything to do.

Yard

'The yard', walking in a circle round and round, is horrific. You can't help but feel disempowered by this action. Walking in the yard, to me anyways functions as shock – a reminder that I am here, I am in a prison. Somehow my training writing books, having desk jobs means if I stay with my books at this desk I can somehow function as I have done now for two decades? And there is so much to read! And so many letters I would like to write. And of course this diary to write! I keep meaning to ask if it is okay to run in the yard or is it walk only? It would be nice to sprint, maybe even with others – 'race', get the blood running around this body – to feel some speed. It's very 'pedestrian' in here. Everything is walking and very slow walking! Maybe the running machine will relieve me of this need for speed, to run, to sprint?

Media / Newspapers

Like the TV, the newspapers forge a feeling that everything is 'okay' or that the status quo is okay, everything is fine! The papers I have access to don't seem to reflect the urgency most people I know are feeling, nor the life of the London I lived in; rode through. Every moment in London life is charged, but like the TV, you wouldn't imagine it was like this if your knowledge was gained via the *Guardian* or the other papers I have read in here; *Sun*, *Mirror* etc. I get no sense of outrage, pressure or urgency that I would feel each morning waking up in the East End of London. It's very disconcerting and also of great interest to me – how can they manage to package it together so well? It really is a worry that historians often use newspapers as their main source. Hopefully future historians won't be so lazy and will have access to social media and so on? There is no doubt the newspapers are not reflecting what is really going on at the moment.

E1 Revolution

Every tag in here seems to be postcode related – so I've started tagging too LOL! 'E1 Revolution' or 'R(E1)VOLUTION' LOL!

Trenton Oldfield

Saturday 03 November

So I have just been moved from B Wing to A Wing. Spent the last hour cleaning the new cell, trying to think through where x or y could go. For some reason I'm in a single cell. For reasons I don't understand it's possibly 30 degrees in here – the complete opposite of B Wing – which had no heat. It's likely I will have to shave this beard as it's just too hot and my skin will just flake. Now need to work out how to undertake a full shave. I'm on the fourth floor looking out over a 'normal' street; a street on the 'outside'. I think I'm looking straight out at what might be a hospital – seems like lots of NHS signs on the ground floor of the building. It is, as everyone mentioned, much larger than B Wing and of course everyone seems older – which can't be the case, but funny how it seems like this.

No 'fame' for me this time – news has moved on, thanks sun! 'The screws' don't seem to recognise me. Just going to keep my head down – as everyone advises! Was a bit sad to leave behind the very nice people in B Wing; good people, nice people. Particularly the guys on the 'hot plate' team. I'm pleased I got to shake their hands when I was leaving. I wish them well! Would be nice to stay in touch though not sure how to do it? Well, will settle in here a day or two and then see what happens.

So hot in here, just took off my shirt – noticed a white hair in the middle of my chest! Should a man with a grey hair be having his first child! Haha! What can one do? Will be amazing!

The difficulty with a single room/cell is that the loo is always there staring at you, it's not hidden in anyway. This loo made me retch when I went to clean it. It's going to take serious cleaning to get this smell out of the room. Yeesh! The other difficulty is not having a chair to sit on – asked 'the screw' and they said there may not be any, as they are so often smashed up. So now I'm writing on my bed, which in the end isn't so bad, but if it's for months then I'm not sure about it. Just spotted that I'm also directly under a massive external light which shines light on the ground four stories below – this is going to be bright at night! Now I see why someone has tried to cover the window. Well, I'm sure I'll find a way to sleep – let's see – maybe it's more directed than it looks?

Only concern is post from my love and the newspapers. I guess it will take a few extra days to get here – back to reading and writing until then! Reading all that news from friends is very energising – took up half my day! Love it.

Will try and get a pattern together – gym, writing and reading. But phuck me, this loo needs cleaning – can hardly concentrate due to the smell! Feeling pretty pissed off today, the move and the fact that I have an apparent visit with my love but with no phone credit there is no way for me to contact her and let her know. So I should be hanging out with my love for an hour so but it's just not going to happen – I'm pissed at the paperwork, the delays between the paperwork and action, for example it will be two weeks before I'm able to get anything from the canteen, top-up my phone credit etc. They really need to digitise this stuff man – let us prisoners do some of this stuff for ourselves. If we had an ipad or alike with an internal net, we could do things for ourselves and maybe continue with learning materials etc? I'm also pissed with my 'legal team'. Since I was convicted they seem to have just abandoned me – I know they are busy but not to have just even written a personal note seems odd to me. I've heard so little from them after my conviction I'm starting to become suspicious, which isn't a good way to do, to exist, to feel! This is what happens when humans act as business people not people! I know it was a 'business relationship' but even people that do one off business transactions keep in touch. I mean, I'm in jail. They were my legal team, which I guess failed. Maybe they feel embarrassed they couldn't defeat an ancient law with all their modern knowledge and so on? Anyways! It is England after all! I shouldn't expect more than this culture is capable of? The heat in here makes one think it's summer outside – I do like that the window is lower here, maybe it's because it's the fourth floor? You can just stand up to look out. In my other cell I had to stand on my chair – which is always a hassle taking shoes on and off.

I'm a bit pissed at myself also for not drawing the last cell and for not noting down the graffiti. Should have made the time to this. I doubt I will forget it but as time goes I'm sure my experience here will just blend into a feeling rather than detailed observations. Should have drawn my view from the cell window also: Trellick Tower, part of The Scrubs and onto the prison gym. There were some big trees also – some of which still have their leaves. Hoping my cellmate is going to be fine – I think he's a few doors down – might have a chat with him in 'association' time – he seems a little alone, no family, girlfriend or alike here in the UK. Man, this loo stinks so bad I prefer the smell of my two-week-old socks! Mother phuckers!

Trenton Oldfield

Two things stand out in this room: (1) racist graffiti I have seen; "fuck all black monkeys" with an illustration of a monkey's face and a large penis; (2) someone has thrown jam on the wall. When I first came in I thought it was blood. It still looks very much like blood sitting here, but at least close-up it's clearly strawberry jam. Tried very hard but just couldn't clean it off with the soap and cloths I have.

I miss my love, I wish for her.

Loads of paperwork to do – but might read for a while re: calibrate. Am happiest when reading. I always wished for a job where all I do is read. Sure I will find my groove again – maybe in an hour or so. Need to write to my love.

Nuclear

Nuclear: the issue isn't accidents or terrorism threat but waste storage. How does this not get coverage? The waste is the issue!

Saturday evening

In fact I'm in D Wing. This Is Not A Wing! D Wing is single cells – the entire block – as it's intended for people who are dangerous, too dangerous to share a cell with others – these prisoners are thought likely to kill, beat, or rape (etc etc) someone else in their cell. Yep! Three of us from B Block, who should be on E Wing really but thought we were going to A Wing, ended up here. These are the mistakes one fears in any part of our life but the sort of mistakes that can really make a difference in here. It is quite different I gotta say. The line for the medicine is <u>long</u>. Plenty of line jumpers and the chap in the cell beside me speaks not a word of sense – though is very keen to try and communicate with H and I. I wonder what illness he has. It's worrying. Was good to find H again. He was only a cell away. Not only does he have no furniture but also has no kettle. Have made him a cuppa to take back to his cell.

Lost in prison

I feel a bit of a fool cause I knew we had turned the wrong way when we came out of B Wing. I knew we were meant to turn left rather than right but I didn't say anything. Feel a fool I knew where D Wing was and A Wing was but followed the screw when he took us all the way down to D Wing. Phuck me! Really disappointed in myself for following when I knew it didn't make sense. When we arrived there was a young man collapsed at the bottom of one of the stairwells – his torso and head on the floor, his legs lying up some stairs. There were ten or so screws standing over him. I asked what was up and they said he had a fit. I'm deeply suspicious this was the case. I should check on his condition tomorrow. It's quite worrying.

Saturday is 'kit change' day. In line for clothes etc, I ran into the chap I met when I first came in – from the very first holding pen, the person that told me how to get a single cell and so. Told me that the chap we were in the second holding cell with (and a friend of his) was released despite apparently "punching the shit out of a screw the day before he was to leave" – yep yep yep. Saw J too – he's happy here – own cell, can watch whatever he wants – mostly music. Doesn't have to deal with anyone else. Seems to be trying sell headache tablets? I think? Always after some tea bags too – which I have plenty of as people kept giving me extra stuff. Nice guy. He has spent 25 years in jail across his 50 odd years of life. Said booze is his problem. Started drinking after the priest raped him back in Ireland.

Despite being quite sure Deepa wouldn't be at the visit, I went anyway. Had a small hope she might be there. Visits mean you cross one of the courtyards – are in the open air; no roof. It was good to be in 'city air'. The air was fresh. All hope to see my love dashed. I think I've got the holding pen zen/meditation down now – zone out, it's quite enjoyable – maybe was just happy to be out of D Block for a while! Goodness what a day.

Private prisons

It was interesting to talk with one of the screws (also thinks voting is a joke) about the privatisation of prisons. He suggested private prisons in the UK would very quickly become similar to US prisons. He said day–to–day life would transfer quickly to prisoners who would be ruled "jungle style" (his words not mine!). He was suggesting it would be a dog–eat–dog world where the 'strongest' prisoner(s) would control the prison. He said incarceration rates go up even more. People wouldn't be doing education but factory–style work. He thought it would happen in the UK in the next five years; all signs pointing in that direction according to his indicators. He is making plans to leave as soon as possible. He does happen to be one of the more engaged screws I've met in here. I'm sure those private prisons are show villages and it's a Trojan horse methodology! Try getting an international corporation to care for people they make money out of when most people don't care about prisoners now. Hilarious to imagine 'charities' holding G4S, Serco, Blackwater or whomever to account ... asking them to change their 'behaviour'. Worse still would be 'charities' providing services to prisoners that adhere to their aims and objectives – repent, reform and so on! Imagine if judges and so on held shares in these companies? Or their pension companies invested in these companies? And even better would be if the police were privatised as well. Beautiful.

Fireworks non–stop outside; such an odd country this one; bread and circuses do so easily distract! No emails, newspapers, letters etc. If they get lost in the system this will be an awful shame!

Sunday 04 November 2012

Now I know why the loo stinks so badly – it doesn't flush! It's now making a sound along the lines of air caught and it's incredibly loud and thuds. Stops and starts. It's been going on now for 20 minutes. I feel sorry for my neighbours – must be driving them up the wall. Certainly annoying/frustrating me.

Just realised some of the graffiti is National Front stuff – there is even a swastika!! 'NFs' written all over the room I can now see. The guy that wrote this bullshit would certainly have been on his guard here for obvious statistical reasons alone! What a phuckin idiot! Left my own R(E1)VOLUTION tag over his where I could find it. Well 'god of small things' and all of that.

Something more than 'lickspittle'?

Need to coin a word for the people that are not 'in power' but enable, encourage and support those 'in' to gain and maintain their likely illegitimate 'power'. Not just 'lickspittles' but something more. They are people like Andrew Marr from the 'Andrew Marr Show' and other 'useful idiots'. His television shows on 'civilisation', 'empire' and alike are abhorrent and deeply problematic. How could he imagine this is okay? There are numerous examples of low self–esteem people across every aspect of our existence, not just television and politics. You can meet them at work, they can be family members – those weirdoes are people that lack such self esteem they let these people take advantage of them, in their pathetic hope of some of the stolen gold landing in their pocket? They flatter, support and help put forward the most abhorrent ideas and people. They are sycophants, lickspittles without a doubt but we need a new noun to describe them. One for the list of the festival lexicon event. They are not bureaucrats alone, nor just mandarins, not just sycophants, nor just Tories – nor just apologists. They knowingly assist the most abhorrent violent ideas and people. They gain some material wealth, but nothing in comparison to those they support. Some fame possibly? But it's not this for them, it's something about thinking by being close to power they are themselves powerful. It is the administrations of the empire that really fascinate me. It's the administrators of today's subtle tyranny that fascinate me. How different this Sunday morning is to most people I studied with at the LSE. Entirely different paths taken though with the same 'education'; fascinating!

Let's take one of the 'lecturers' from the programme I studied on. This chap once said to a room full of people "take an airport lounge as an example of a space whereby every person's experience is equal" (true as true!). He now runs an advice company for wealthy people and corporations etc to 'invest' in property in London. As well as 'teaching', he now runs a private company that collects data on the expensive properties over time (400 years) in London, in order to show ultra wealthy 'investors' where to put 'their millions'. Something along the lines of London prices always go up across time – he can provide a service for your millions while the economy is down without the risk of other investments. These are the people from Greece, Russia, Colombia, South Africa and so on that research has shown are taking money, often the people's money, out of their countries and investing it in property in London – because it consistently makes money. It's abhorrent and shows the level of intellectual corruption. Worse yet, I think I remember his website said his 'unique system 'benefits from experts from the LSE!

No doubt his company donates to a housing charity ... I bet his website says "London faces a housing crisis, everyone should have a roof over their head and we want to support ongoing efforts for housing sustainability in London" ... or some such bullshit. I can't tell you how intellectually compromised and corrupt 'urban studies' is. There may not be another discipline that promises the world's abused and exploited so much while directly increasing and contributing to their subjugation and oppression. I dedicate my life to two things: (1) the British to know all about their empire – particularly the ideas underpinning and excusing it; (2) the forever problematisation of 'urban studies', particularly by those that use 'critical' or 'urbanist' in their 'blurbs' when clearly they are gutless sycophantic lickspittles.

Need to understand

Why he made this decision we will never know. With his degree and his own personal experience in the family business he could have written about how these people are destroying London – making it impossible for people to live a decent life here, how they manage to get the money out of their countries, how the money is laundered and what it means for cities like London but also the suburbs in Sardinia and so on and so on. Instead he invites these very people into his office, using his academic logo to woo them in. Why he chose to support these barbaric people is what I am desperate to understand. How did he make the decision to support these brutal people rather than fight/ undermine them? It's even more confusing when he is amazingly comfortable already – he needs not a penny more. To me there is absolutely no choice, but for him the choice was stark and he had all the evidence – from 'both sides' – and he chose, in this time of all times, to be the provider, the assistant to their brutality. This, this is what we need to understand.

My love

I'm hesitant to write to my love in this wing as I fear my frustration of being here will come through. But I feel I need too. I miss her. Trouble is it takes a week or more to get to her – so she might worry about me when hopefully there will be no need to worry about me anymore. No mail has arrived for me on this wing. It's been a few days now. Might reread old mail and reply to those I haven't yet had the chance to? Have all these books too but want to work on the festival, but not in the mood despite the festival being such a good vehicle to address these issues. Though I shouldn't be surprise no one applied for the 'Urbanist Like Me' theme, I am kinda disappointed. Why don't these people have any self critique or worse yet any sense of humour?

What power now?

If you think Jimmy Savile was in a position of power, imagine what people involved with 'competition format shows' like X–Factor, Apprentice and so on get up to! Unlike Savile et al (and there will more, has to be!), these people have real power – they 'select' those that will become 'rich and famous', they 'train them', 'coach' them etc. Unlike Savile who was just an entertainer, these are 'gatekeepers'. Who is better placed to take advantage of their position than a gatekeeper – and a gatekeeper potentially to millions? Imagine the abuses of power that happen in a context like this? This is just the entertainment industry! What happens at reading and literacy classes run by bored posh charity volunteers in impoverished neighbourhoods? The trouble is it's not hard now to want to investigate those Oxbridge outposts like Toynbee Hall and Oxford House? Imagine the abuses of power that happen in a context like this? This abuse they now show on the news isn't a thing of the past, like everything in this country they try to suggest it was 30 years ago and so on, it is happening now (and probably to a worse extent) and will happen in the future if there isn't an uprising and an intellectual project that tackles head on 'those that dare to win'.

Sunday evening, 04 November 2012

Of course today wasn't as much a concern as yesterday ... its remarkable how quickly one can adjust ... even if 'the screw' said today "welcome to hell" when we arrived. Another screw said make sure you get moved from here on Monday morning – visit the 'people management' first thing in the morning (nothing happens on weekends). I have to admit to myself I do have a sense of fear on this wing – even if it's gone down significantly even in a day. I'm sure it's more to do with films and television shows than reality, but it is here with me, in me. Let's see what happens tomorrow, how I feel, I'm sure it's not as dramatic as it seems.

Monday afternoon

'A Wing'. What a difference, what a huge fucking difference. H and I are on the fourth floor. We are back together in the same cell. Cell this time has a separate 'bathroom', one desk and two chairs, and 'a view' over the rooftops of houses. Currently direct sunlight is coming into the room. The room is warm but with cool air also. It's entirely, entirely different. The wing is larger than B Wing but smaller than D Wing – or so it feels. As soon as I walked in I recognised many faces that were at some stage previously on B Wing – nice somehow. And guess what, the 'hot plate' guys recognised me – which is awesome; cause these are the guys with the food and somehow have such a nice character to them. Can feel my 'stress levels' reduce <u>measurably</u>. Arriving on a new wing my stress levels would normally be quite high – it's the same prison but new somehow at the same time. And of course somehow one's own niggling prejudices return – "who is on this wing" and so on and so forth. Feels like I will be very productive in here – hopefully; in'sh'allah, please sun! Feels like it. Once the mail and newspapers start arriving I'm sure I can be quite productive here; develop a good routine of work. Started writing a letter to Channel 4 about the Thames documentary idea so will finish it this afternoon – send it off tomorrow. Channel 4 probably don't commission documentaries now but hopefully they can point me in the direction of someone who would want to make a people's history of the Thames – to challenge the insidious propaganda of the 'Royal' river exhibition. Lots of good examples including preferred suicide venue for women, ports for colonial exploration and then processing of colonial loot and murdered children with satanic markings. A hugely productive day in Cell 4.21, on A Wing!

Little bit like the films

D Wing was a little bit like the films, let's be honest! I'm particularly interested in how the material conditions made it feel very different, how my behaviour started to change as a result. With no chair, no table, with the toilet always in eye view and the incredible heat mixed with the stench from the un-flushable loo, it was like a mini torture chamber! I could feel myself changing, that the situation was starting to change me. I could feel myself adjust to it … preparing myself for what it might mean to have a long stay here. The 'association' times were more intense, you could feel it. It makes sense, cause if it was intense for me in that cell it was also likely intense for others too. I was becoming less interested in my own health (shaving, washing, cleaning plates), the condition of the cell, and more interested in projecting a sense of power, disinterest and solitude. I cleaned less, cared less and spent more time watching TV. It was so hot I could only wear my underpants. I would have been naked if it wasn't for the random door and cell window openings. Wrote no letters (but one to Deepa this morning) – felt like a few days 'lost' in another place.

More not less

I wish these prisoners were given better conditions – separate loo area, undamaged sheets, a desk, a chair, painted cells (no racist graffiti!), more room and better food. It is in my mind these fellow prisoners ought to have more not less. If anyone needed more support and comfort it is likely to be these prisoners, I feel. It would be crazy, for example, to take away rights every citizen has. While most prisoners are likely to think voting for Westminster Palace democracy is currently a joke, it makes no sense whatsoever to remove voting or any other 'rights'. You are a citizen until you are dead. Denying rights to x or y people means you, the denier, are the one with the issue, as you can't deal with the fact that they are citizens, that as citizens they did some of these acts that have resulted with them ending up in prison. Reducing material or any other culture makes no sense whatsoever. There is no doubt these people are the same as every other person alive. Most are likely to have had very little comfort in their lives: emotional, physical, monetary and so on. It makes no sense to me to reduce it even further; to strip their dignity even further. Now with them in prison, without the slips and slides of 'outside' everyday life, is this not some chance for comfort and full human rights? Why would you miss this?

The door policy

Having said all of this about how calm A Wing is, there are more doors being banged right now than anytime in D Wing – it's very intense indeed. Wonder what's going on! Crazy man. Crazy days. Will watch the sunset – looking out directly west. Time will tell. Look forward to finding out what this demonstration is all about. Settling in for a night of silent TV; it's US presidential election day!

Trenton Oldfield

Wednesday 07 November 2012

Have woken to the news Barak Obama seems to have won the US presidential election; his second term. Unsure of the actual stats but it seems clear cut. As H is sleeping I've still got the sound off; I am making assumptions based on my interpretation of the body language of the people they interview. Doesn't look like it has been confirmed but seems like he has won. Apparently each candidate has spent one billion USD each on their campaign ... $2 BILLION USD! Who has that sort of money? Who could possibly have such money? Elections are great, especially ones that seep into every part of your life (which $2 billion will ensure!), as they create a wonderful novelty of something important happening; the feeling that the profound mechanisms of democracy are in action. The scale of the operation, its theatrical and dramatic nature and its ever-presence is very good at suggesting everything is working as it should be; everything is okay! It seems like it gets another shot in the arm, or is being shocked back into life with one of those defibrillator machines. Well, fingers crossed this all works out okay for the people of the world – for the workers of the world.

James Bond

Not sure if I've written about this before – but I've been thinking this for a while – the James Bond thing is without a doubt as problematic as the Oxbridge boat race – it also needs taking apart piece by piece. To me 'James Bond' boils down so many of the deeply problematic aspects of 'British Culture'; royalty, 'who dares wins tactics', meddling in other people's lands, extra-judicial murders, subterfuge and institutional misogyny, juvenile snobbery and so on. Somehow 'James Bond' has made its way into the elitists' cultural calendar; the launching of a film may soon be as regular as, or even start to meld with, the annual armistice events. It seems to have endless support from establishment institutions such as the BBC. You would imagine it was funded by the government it has such support. Because of their sheer longevity and advancement of elitist culture certain events seem to capture the cultural industry. It's not hard to see how a nation afflicted with Stockholm Syndrome would also support it. It is now, in my mind, among Ascot, the Oxbridge boat race, MBE awards events, the poppy appeal, Remembrance Day and so on. These are sacred/holy cows that ought not to be challenged! If you do, be warned, you will face jail LOL! Someone really needs to challenge the ideas underpinning 'James Bond' head on – as a matter of urgency.

Prison

One of the great things about prison is the walls are so thick that there is very little sound that comes through from other cells! Last night when the football was on the banging on doors went nuts when they scored a goal – quite powerful and also fun. The banging on the doors on Monday was due to prisoners not being let out, having spent all day in their cells – I think missing classes not just association time. Apparently a fellow prisoner had barricaded himself in his cell. I wonder what barricading consists of and how they do it – must take lots of brute force and ingenuity to block the door – I mean we have so little furniture to do it with. Barricading yourself 'in' is an interesting idea as it plays on the idea that people want to get out of here and must confuse the hell out of everyone that works here as everything 'outside' is always better – everything is geared towards the idea we want to be 'outside' – outside our cells, outside prison. I really hope the chap is okay.

It's another beautiful day outside – stunning sunshine over the rooftops of Acton(?) – I do of course feel like sitting in the sun! Never mind, at least I have lots and lots of training of sitting, writing and reading when the sun is shining! It could be worse.

My love

With credit finally on the phone I was able to call my love. Very difficult to hear my love has been proper sick – in bed with flu, sore throat and alike. It's very difficult to hear. I wasn't there to get shopping, bring her tea, make lemon, ginger and honey tea and hold her! I feel awful knowing I haven't been there for her. Feel silly I'm in here and my loves is there in bed ill – very silly. Hopefully she will be better today, but I'm sure it will take at least a week to recover properly. My guess is she needs a break – it's been an intense few years and very intense last year and my goodness the last few months. My wish is she could take a holiday – spend some time in the sunshine somewhere or go to Zagreb and drink and debate with our friends there. There seems no point being here in London waiting for me – a week in the sunshine away from everything would be very important I think. I do wish my loves would do this, consider this. She will probably suggest the "3 days in bed was enough of a break"! Oh man!

I have just been given a document from a friend listing prohibited materials in this prison: KKK, BNP, NF and Black Panthers – all 100% available outside. Black Panthers and the BNP are political parties. Very curious to know what the arguments are for banning this material – particularly the Black Panthers. I guess they didn't pick up on my Huey P Newton biography when I came in! What might the punishment be? Should I hide it? Would that be worse if they raid your cell?

Britain

How is it possible to communicate 'Britain' for what it really is? How is it possible it manages to maintain any sense/veneer of 'civilisation' when if you just take a moment to look at almost any aspect it's a brutal brutal culture ... though somehow it manages to disguise, seduce and conquer? Thing is, most of the world knows, it's just those living here that don't seem to know their own history. It's odd.

Hunger

I am so hungry on this wing I'm drinking as much tea as possible to stop my tummy rumbling waking H!

Post Thursday

Holy moly, I have more mail, glorious mail, than I think it will be possible to reply to. I will be up late tonight reading! Overwhelmed such wonderful people in my life and strangers too!! Feel alive!

Sunday 11 November 2012

First argument with Deepa – think I am in shock! Awful. Think my temper is rising having been in here now for a little while and knowing my love is ill, that I can't assist in any way. She isn't well, nor is she taking steps to rest properly. It's hugely frustrating. Her stubbornness on issues of rest drives me a little mad! Rather than taking a week or more to recover – if she just switched off for two days she would be well again. I suggested she take two days' rest somewhere else – as a change is as good as a holiday – and she exclaimed with force "we can't even make rent!" which is entirely untrue. This has always been such a point of tension between us – her refusal to take any rest and respite. It makes no sense to me. If she went somewhere, anywhere, for a few days, she would get perspective and recuperate. It's been a source of our rare but heated disagreements from the beginning – our two holidays were almost forced upon her despite both those times being very important to her, for us. In six years we have had two weeks off! Two weeks in the sun! And major decisions were made in those two weeks. Why would she prefer to stew in the same troubles rather than breathe and recuperate? It's not admirable; it's silly, tiresome and unnecessary. I wonder ... will it change? I mean, even those Judeo–Christian–work–ethic–nutters say one should rest so one can reflect. Will this be our life?

I fear the clarity I get from stepping aside from our daily routine will never be understood or appreciated by Deepa. Somehow I have to find a way to change or live with this – I will perhaps have to find a way to take breaks without her and not feel guilt or concern about it. If my love wishes to stay with the view we will never be able to rest – walk in the hills, lie on the beach – then it is I who will have to do it with our children! We will have to agree it is her decision and that she can't make any of us feel guilty about it – it's her decision to be obtuse and difficult. To rest, to walk in the mountains is not a luxury, it is the point of living, and it doesn't cost what she thinks. My goodness I'm so frustrated by this – how can we ever reconcile this? Why does she not see that work 'doesn't set you free', that it's the greatest myth? Sheesh man, this going to drive us mad! In the weeks I've been 'inside' she has admitted she hasn't been able to work; because we work together on everything. It makes no difference, makes no sense, to be sat at home ill or staring at a screen – THE POINT IS TO LIVE. We have just one life; just one. This isn't a rehearsal, this is it, it's for living.

Monday 12 November

Wrote to my love last night, a letter of 10 pages or more (posted it this morning) trying to explain the situation as I see it – I've never had any debts, always had very good jobs, never been late with rent (but for one week), have had not inconsequential savings I had built up myself ... received a scholarship for my studies. I've always been able to secure good jobs and Deepa knows this. This Is Not A Gateway and Myrdle Court Press came entirely from us – I didn't work on someone else's project – was zero to hundred in just a few years! My philosophy has always been 'don't worry until you need to worry'. You can't worry about something that hasn't happened because it doesn't exist yet and probably won't happen/exist. Worry/anxiety is a disease afflicting too many! I have no evidence for this but I think it also limits one's ability to deal with issues when they do need addressing. If you are alive there is the possibility for good stuff to always happen. I've suggested to Deepa in the letter that I can't deal with the alarm and anxiety about money anymore so I've asked her to confirm exact figures that would stop or significantly reduce the stress, alarm and anxiety. How much savings and how much income per month would make her relaxed or at least without alarm and anxiety? I/we will get a job to secure this amount on the agreement anxiety and worry is finished – all we do then is live; love!

What became apparent to me yesterday afternoon was how happy I am when this stress doesn't come up, when Deepa's love is unconditional – if I can achieve this alarm–free environment it's worth it for me to return to daily commute public service jobs. I can't explain how deflating it is when we argue about these concerns; this concern. Everything crashes for me – it's like all the energy suddenly drains and I see everything from a negative point of view. It's distressing and just energy zapping. It's the one and only issue between us!

Monday 'job club'

I'm always up for courses, religious services etc in here, so this morning I was woken and told to go to 'job club' – in 'Workshop 6'. Submitted the form a while ago, hadn't heard anything, so it was a bit of a surprise this morning. Luckily in the five minutes I had to get ready and down to the gate, I remembered to take some reading material. I had a feeling it might be needed. Read three articles in the *New Statesman* and went to the loo before we were called into the room – eight of us. The guy that ran the session seemed really nice, up for a chat, bit of a storyteller and I'm sure very genuine about the possibilities of his job – his work and what he could do for us prisoners. The session included lots of talking about not so much – anecdotes, entirely unrelated stories and so on. Lots of half sentences – jotted a few of them down after I started to realise they were very much from a specific frame/lens on seeing/experiencing the world. Examples: "dog–eat–dog world", "London as city is a feed–me frenzy but this is where the money is", "set up by yourself and always make money", "you gotta fight for your life out there", "work for wealthy people", "I want you watching Alan Sugar, all those competition shows, definitely the Apprentice – love these shows, they teach you so much".

We had a nice chap come from Bounce Back – new social enterprise that trains painters and decorators – lots of questions from fellow prisoners about pay and conditions – I mean endless questions – all very suspicious about who benefits and who doesn't – good questions about who funds the organisation (a wealthy benefactor, government and European Union etc). I took their card. I have always wanted to be a skilled painter and decorator. Seems like one of those amazing jobs where you can see the work you have done. And those clean lines, better colours has always impressed me. Seems one must need great patience to achieve such. I can apply up to six months after release. It's very badly paid work from the social enterprise – £20/day for three months, then two NVQs which you get when you work for big property developers etc. Lots of encouragement to set up own businesses after working for a big company for a year. Our main trainer, who is a very enthusiastic capitalist, suggested if you ran your own business you could take a cut of £4 from co-workers to pay yourself when you charge the client £10. The worker gets £6, the boss £4. "You could even make £52,000 per year!"

The job club course is every morning and every afternoon for nine days. You get a CV and a certificate at the end of it. It was very manual–work focussed and again in a classroom type of setting.

When I explained or suggested I didn't think I would come back in the afternoon, he suggested it would be worthwhile because I could make enough money to keep me in tobacco for a week (you get paid £0.60 per session). If I didn't have so many letters to reply to and so many books to read and the festival to work on (I'm working from 8am to 8pm each day in here but for Sunday – my day of rest LOL), I would probably go along – no doubt learn much more about the values and aims of such services – but with so little time in the day – even in here – it's critical I don't sit for such long periods waiting for x or y to start. It's just too difficult for me to be in the holding cells or even

Trenton Oldfield

hanging around the gate – time just evaporates – huge amounts of time.

Teaching/facilitating has always seemed like something fruitful to be involved with. Decades of being taught and my recent experience in here have certainly helped me clarify the way I would teach. I don't think I would teach … I think I would facilitate. I would find out what the students' interests are, what they want to know more about in a particular subject and then design the course around this – hopefully with them. Some will say it would be too much work and so on but I'm sure it would be the same or less. I'm sure this will take some practice and forethought but I'm clear it's the method for me. I mean don't I get to keep learning this way also? Apart from capitalism demanding factory schools/universities, I can't think why people don't employ this method.

I did learn from one of the quizzes he got us to do that I don't like 'being taught' but like learning visually and in an organised/well-communicated manner. Funnily enough neither occurred in the first session and may be the reason why I chose not to go back this afternoon!

Asked the landing staff if there was any penalty for not attending, he said "no just tell the 'people management'. Went and told them at the gate where we are checked off each time we go in and out) and they said I will be given a disciplinary if I don't attend. Went back to landing staff who said "Don't worry; I will make sure you don't". The trouble is if I go my 'outside' employment prospects will dramatically reduce as I won't be sending off documentary ideas, working on the festival, reading these really important books and so on. Bit of a Catch 22. Hope it doesn't penalise me. It's curious to me why all the training available is 'blue collar'? If you want to do a degree you have to make special applications and also pay for it – normal fees – £9,000pa. Painting courses you get paid for but you struggle to get onto a degree course and have to pay for it. Why wouldn't prisoners be able to study? Why isn't this available to everyone in here for free? Why would you get paid to do low paid jobs and but have to pay full fees to study? Is there some kind of class or race assumption here?

Notices and services

The following notices were up on random notice boards across the four levels of A Wing. Most are advertising services available to prisoners:

New Deal
Phoenix Futures
Substance Misuse Services
Alcohol Intervention Services
SOVA London
Job Club
Pre-employment skills
English as a Second Language Courses
Prisons and Probation Ombudsman
Criminal Cases Review Commission
Introduction to Group and Team Work Communication Skills
Personal Development with Debs
Debating – Every Friday by the Honourable Society of Grays Inn
PRISONERS ARE NOT ALLOWED IN ASSOCIATION ROOM
(Staff only recreation room).

Service offices

Spread across the four levels of cells though mostly clustered around the 'landing office' – which is towards the northern end of the wing – are the offices of a range of services. It was almost impossible to access these services as most prisoners at Wormwood Scrubs are 'banged up' for 23+ hours of the day and while there may be an office it might only be visited once a week, as funding cuts mean one or a few people work across the entire prison. After a while you start to find out what days and what times certain staff are likely to be on your wing. H spends hours on a Tuesday standing on his tippy-toes looking out the gap at the top of the door and then quickly sliding from the gap at each side of the door in the hope that the staff member he needs to see would possibly be passing by and he might somehow catch their attention! Our cell is close to the northern stairwell so we can see whoever is passing. This part of the landing seems to be where the wardens like to gather as well. So far H hasn't had any success but I'm sure an 'artist in residence' choreographer would be motivated by his moves and no doubt try to reproduce them!

Of course many of the organisations are run and staffed by volunteers, which are as expected, imploding as a result of Blair's professionalisation and Cameron's Big Society. A small handful of these services are provided by us prisoners ourselves. Unfortunately the service I wanted to work for doesn't have any volunteers to train me up so I can then volunteer in here. Nobody knows when they might get volunteers again. The post I wanted to work in was to assist people who want a hand with all the countless forms there are to fill in. Seems like a nice way to meet new people in here? And the sun knows nothing happens in here, let alone out there, if forms are not filled in.

These organisations had offices (staffed or unstaffed) in Wormwood Scrubs at the end of 2012: St Mungos Housing Association, RAPT – Substance Misuse Services, Drug Strategy Team, Mandatory Drug Testing Unit, Alcohol Intervention Service, Citizens Advice Bureau, Home Office.

'Time to Connect – Building Better Relationships through Play'

After six months of 'good behaviour' prisoners can apply for a scheme with an outside charity which enables them to spend up to one hour each week with their young children in a 'supervised environment'. Like every single sanctioned/official programme in prison the assumption is we prisoners need reforming, that we are ill–equipped, incapable and that we certainly need guidance/teaching from a 'normal person' – usually from a government-funded charity or worse social enterprise, which is essentially a government department pretending to be independent and client focussed. Even if the activity is in and of itself not a paternalistic and patronising experience (though most of the ones I attend were) it seems the conceptualisation and communication of the activity must be couched in this way, regardless.

Coffee mood

I've been in a mood these past days, I'm not sure if it's the coffee I've started drinking, the lack of visiting the gym, the very indifferent screws, my disagreement with my love, the forever returning paperwork from the mysterious prison administrators with no positive news, the screws who don't deliver post (days now) or finishing *Love and Capital* or just plain frustration at being a political prisoner? Maybe it's my cellmate's wish to watch game shows that have no logic – just random like. I need to cool down somehow – not sure how. Maybe it's in the stars ... I just have to be patient.

Right now I'm pissed the volume is so high on the TV but it wouldn't have bothered me a week ago. I'm pissed we are only out of our cell for one hour a day – how can we do everything in one hour? Most of the time it's only 30–40 minutes – how can I shower, clean our cell, get and submit paperwork for the prison, ask to be on the list for the gym, call my love, check on washing, have a chat, take a walk – visit a friend? Really frustrated at the moment! Hopefully the gym tomorrow, so for a moment I won't be pedestrian! On the treadmill (ironically) I can have a sense of movement, of speed ... anything but this feeling that holds onto me that comes with pedestrian pedestrianism!

Jenny and Karl

I've written to Deepa about the book by Mary Gabriel, *Love and Capital: Karl and Jenny Marx, The Birth of a Revolution*. I've written about how I had expected the book would energise me and provoke me. I bought it for Deepa's last birthday, when we were in Vancouver. I remember she couldn't put it down and she would speak about it being a difficult read due to the tragedy that befalls their family, particularly the children's lives. Should I have read it before giving it to her at the time her father passed? It drew the first fountain of tears from me in here. I couldn't stop crying. The combination of all (but the 'hidden/ illegitimate' son) dying, including two suicides, Jenny and Marx's premature deaths and the abuse Engels experienced when accused of taking Marx's work. It floored me on Sunday – brought up many concerns already in our life and also early deaths by cancer and other illnesses. It was also very difficult to have many of the difficulties I have had with Marx and Engel's ideas confirmed.

Most pressing, of course, is our financial situation which is very similar to Marx's – in some ways better because we've significant experience of working (unlike Marx and Jenny) but worse in that we have no 'Engels' and no wealthy family members to fall back on as they seem to have had. We do have our health currently and our rented apartment to live in, which is in good condition, waterproof and full of books. We also currently can live in three countries because of our marriage – our passports. But it does hit home the impact of 'revolutionary' endeavours can have on one's life, one's family! But with a family I am sure to become more committed to working towards equality than without one! Oh no!

Trenton Oldfield

Post

Apart from three days of post missing I've just received five wonderful books in the post – all Verso titles, which makes me wonder if it was Verso that sent them to me? Whoever it is, is a wonderfully generous being/organisation. Unfortunately there was no note with it – must have been taken by the prison post people? Or maybe there was no note. I'm particularly over the moon about Richard Gott's *Britain's Empire: Resistance, Repression and Revolt*. This is the book I always wished existed in the world and thought I might have to write myself. Thank goodness he has done it because it's huge – unsurprisingly. I have only read the blurb on the back, which can be heartbreakingly unlike the material inside, but if it is what it says on the tin, then this book ought to be beside every Gideon Bible. I wonder if there are people that will pay for this to happen like they do for every hotel room to have a Gideon Bible to be there. It's another 600-page book – like *Love and Capital* – very, very excited! Thank you sun! Maybe it's a sign that this mood can lift. Also had a good chat with my love earlier.

Dinner and *Bhagavad Gita*

Another gift – the *Bhagavad Gita* I requested some weeks ago but it came this evening of all evenings – Diwali! What an evening – maybe the mood was because of the stars after all. For some reason I'm thinking about Bha – hope everything is okay for her, she is still with us!

Thursday 15 November 2012

Most of my energy and thoughts have been taken up with a new argument/ debate/misunderstanding between Deepa and I. It's been pretty all consuming. I'm not sure where it has come from but think it's a combination of work, family, finances, illness and the separation – the madness of this sentence and our separation. Just thinking about it sends a surge of nauseousness around my body – eyes close, throat fills, heart beat slows and have to drink water quickly or perhaps fall over – legs falling out from under me or blackout like what happens to me sometimes when I'm in hospitals. It's a tale of much heartburn and trouble in both our lives. How do we exist as one when we are two very strong people? I worry that for no reason other than being my love's partner I'm seen somehow as 'the enemy' at times. I'm often saying "it's okay, we are not invading Iran" but I'm wondering now if those moments we are on separate sides? If I am her enemy? I had always thought we were together but I'm starting to be concerned that actually we are on separate sides for these brief fallouts. I'm certainly not, nor do I have any desire to be the enemy – that would be the opposite of everything I've ever wanted or imagined. How could it happen that I could even think I could be her enemy? I am her partner. How could it be so far from what it is? I need to understand this situation – once and for all! I want to find the nub of this concern, so hopefully it can be addressed, finished. Cause it can't be possible can it?

After telling H about this feeling we have entered into a very difficult conversation – H seems to be a proper traditionalist and misogynist! It is clear he thinks women are 'the weaker sex' (funny seeing it is he who was 'trapped' by her and so came to be in here). He said that women had different muscles etc to men and thus needed to be protected by men. He continued with this argument despite my pointing out and his agreement that women do all the work in India – children on their backs, forging railroads, working in the fields and on building sites, in the home and so on. Kinda funny too as he took steroids.

The smell of misogyny

What I suggested to him was women can smell this misogyny a mile away and they will make your life hell as a result of your views and abuse of them. It's a reflex response. Everyone knows, inside them, that every human being is an equal, we are all different, all unique but we are all equal. Anybody that sets out to undermine this is any way, disempowering another, will not have a quiet life. They will be haunted in their everyday practices. Women, who for centuries have been in a lower position (according to men!), can almost immediately ascertain if you're sexist/misogynist from the very moment they meet you. One can smell misogyny.

I gave the example of racism/racists – suggesting to him he would have known from the moment he walked into the cell whether I was a racist or not. It's a 'sixth sense' people who are 'looked down upon' fine tune but something we all have. You learn to fine tune the smell of prejudice. You can sense it when it walks into the room, you can read it quickly in statements put out by institutions; it is preventative and self–preserving. He agreed. I suggested to him women have this too and they can 'spot', 'smell out' a sexist. I suggested the sooner he gets rid of this elitism – where he sees himself better than women – the greater the chance of happiness he will have. If he doesn't, any woman he's with will quite understandably seek to even out the power imbalance in whatever method is available to her – which will certainly cause him heartache, frustration and significant stress. Or jail, like now. I've said this to male friends with sexist tendencies from high school – it is in our interest that all people are equal, that women (our sisters, partners, children, aunties after all!) are not discriminated against. Our lives will be trouble if this isn't the case. Our lives are in trouble because of these prejudices. NO people thankfully accept being 'below' as he suggested the women he knows in India are happy with!

Unfortunately for H, 'power', I think, is one of the 'undiscovered elements' – it finds a way to create balance. Since I was a kid I wanted to understand how someone's mood could change and why it could change sometimes quite quickly ... and why people 'acted up' sometimes and not most of the time. I found it very odd to see people change. Not sure when exactly I noticed it but it became apparent to me that people who had something done to them, where their power was reduced almost immediately set out to gain that power from someone/thing else. Of course this means it keeps on happening ... the next person then sets out to gain the lost power from someone else, sometimes thinking they can do this through inflicting pain on animals, the forest or whatever. While I have no evidence whatsoever for these arguments, I feel there is x amount of power on earth and we need x power within us. I know I can feel when it's been taken and I think I see when it happens to others. Thing is you can't make more power. It doesn't diminish either – it's a fixed amount. Those that accumulate it, and it can be held, have too much. I wish I could say they suffer because of it but I'm not sure how yet. Maybe it rots them like too much alcohol does? But I know others suffer significantly from those it is taken from.

In shorthand – 'we' know when power is taken from us or we are deprived of it. It might have a mathematical number, it might not, but we know when it's missing and this is when we set out to replenish the x amount needed to feel good, centered. I wonder how we could find what this power is/measures up to be. It's no surprise to me that crimes against children – as on the front pages these days – are undertaken by those who were themselves abused. Sex crimes are not about sex but power – and the search for equalising out the power that was taken from them. Hurtful and horrific cycle, but one I'm sure could be broken with some focussed philosophical work and possibly some scientific work also. Seems clear, to me at least, that if we work towards equality in all aspects of our lives we might have the greatest chance of understanding this issue of 'power'. Perhaps it's something for our 'Centre for Post Capitalist Thought'?

H.

H. told me his employer didn't want to press charges but a girl he had been seeing, who he met on the marriage website Shaddi, had set him up and arranged for the police to arrest him. Earlier in the year the college where he was studying had lost its immigration licence. The college closed and the business running it folded. He lost over £5000 in student fees he had paid. He had 60 days to find a new college to enrol in or he would have to leave the country. £5000+ down he ended up taking £20 to £40 a day from his workplace and nipping next door to gamble, hoping he might be able to reclaim the £5000+ he had lost. As he was running out of time before the cut off point the amount of money he took to gamble increased. He thinks he took no more than £1000. His boss started to notice the money was missing but didn't fire him or call the police. He asked him to pay the money back. He didn't fire him as he made lots of money for his boss; he was very good at up selling products people didn't need.

His colleague who was also friends with the girl he was seeing ended up telling their mutual friend. She had also learnt that H. had been seeing lots of different girls on the website where she had met him. Apparently she had found out he had set up lots of different profiles, for different age groups. H. said he also had told lies about what his job was, saying he worked at x computer company one one page and for a consultancy company on another page and so on.

Apparently she set about establishing this, when H. said he didn't want to marry her and just wanted to be friends. This amazing woman then arranged for 10 of the women he had been stringing along also to confront him at one meeting. She broke into his Facebook page, Shaddi etc pages to get this information. He said he couldn't remember which lie he had told to any of them, especially when they were all asking questions. That would have been an extreme experience for everyone! Ouch!

What happened next flawed him. A few weeks later she got another girl he had been meeting (none he ever slept with or took any money from) to arrange to meet H. in a hotel for a drink. It was an ambush. She had arranged for the police to arrest him for the theft. Two plainclothes police arrested him as he walked into the hotel. He said he had a feeling it might happen as he saw someone looking out the window and then dashing inside. He said he was surprised he kept walking even though he had a sense something was up. I don't know enough, but I would have thought the police couldn't press charges without the agreement of the owner? Maybe they did anyway cause they knew they could get one extra deportation this way. It seems deportation is one of the main endeavours of the police? This prison seems to be holding many people for deportation? Do the police get bonuses for deportation numbers?

Afternoon

Back from the gym – thank goodness – it's been two weeks and I was starting to feel almost desperate to not be pedestrian, to move faster than a slow walk. Even contemplated running on the spot in my cell. I went straight on the running machines, of which there are many, but I'm all alone on them – everyone else is in the free weights room – working on their upper bodies! It is hard not to be impressed with most people's upper bodies in this prison! Wow! Someone made a joke that they should spend less time on their upper bodies and more time on their legs – suggesting it's the reason they keep getting caught – top heavy and chicken legs! I ran four separate miles on incline 2, all 8–minute miles. Took a break in between each dash to lift some weights in the same room – and went on the rowing machines – my goodness rowing machines are painful. Gone are the days when I could do 5,000 metres on them. I'm done, completely shattered, after 1,000 metres these days. Such a painful activity to do. Like swimming, it seems you use every part of the body – those rowers are quite some athletes! From memory I always found rowing machines worse than actually rowing. I remember this from school days – somehow I would beat everyone in the single skulls but never on the machines. A curious thing – sure there is an explanation.

The trouble with being here is the pedestrian nature of prison – there isn't any chance to run or ride – certainly no chance to ride! Movement is very slow. Not only with the holding pens but also people don't want to rush back to cells it seems? The yard with its anti–clockwise walk is more depressing than anything else. It is not large enough to run. I'm surprised the running machines aren't used more often. Must only be me with this affliction. But I do wish I had their upper bodies!

The gym is superbly kitted out – and might take up a good percentage of the overall building space; the prison's space. It's difficult to get on the list to go but it's a great joy to do so when it happens. The other great thing about the gym is the music – load music. I'm not one for 'missing things' on the outside but music is something I do miss. I miss the Funk and Soul Show and the Huey Show without a doubt!

Mail

For some reason since I've been in here I've never received emails on a Thursday or Friday – post yes, but never emails. Is it possible every other day I get 4–8 emails? Hard to know why this is the case – perhaps it's the person in charge on these days or just a blip in the system? Perhaps nobody writes on Wednesday or Thursday? I'm not sure, but Deepa recently wrote and said she had sent 22 messages – my count of her messages was just 14. Another frustration is the failure that many, so many, books and some newspapers are not getting through. I've a pile of forms here that give me the choice of either having them destroyed or paying for them to be sent back. It's very difficult indeed when people have taken such care and thought to send them to me. I'm sure other prisoners are in this situation also. I'm concerned for example that Professor Dorling wrote to me with his new book but they've destroyed it. My goodness, imagine!

Reflection

It's strange, and I am not sure it can be so, to know that no other prisoner receives the *Guardian* – the screw telling me that I'm the first ever in his six years of working here. I give him the copies after we read them in cell 4:21. I'm worried he is trying to flatter me. And I can't work out why he would even want to do that. The other day he said he couldn't treat me as a prisoner; he just didn't see me as a criminal. That was very difficult to hear and I'm not sure why exactly but made me feel strange when so many others in here aren't as well – why me? Cause I had press he knows of me and my ideas but what about the thousands of others who come in who are innocent or over criminalised? Cause I read the *Guardian*? I know he meant well but made me feel very uncomfortable. Why me when there are so many like me? He said his friends asked him all the time if there were innocent people in here. He said I would be the first one he could report to his friends. I'm just not comfortable with this. It worries me that he treats people differently ... somehow criminals should be treated differently than other people? The only difference between us and everyone else 'outside' is we got caught. They were waiting for most of us, ready and wanting to criminalise us. Most of us in here are brown or black. Most of us in here are poor. We know your crimes and you know your crimes ... stop pretending we are different.

Another screw told me I had his sympathies today – a conviction and sentence being a "travesty". I wonder what they say to other prisoners? Heaven knows I've been feeling like a criminal since I have been in here. As I am now watching TV it also speaks almost non–stop about criminals. Is every other show about criminals? Are we always the bad guys that must be stopped?

You can really start to doubt yourself in here – you start going over every discussion, every action. You start to see if x or y happened in a slightly different way you could be in jail. People say they start to get nervous around cops – feeling guilty for things they did years ago, small misdemeanours and so on; a type of paranoia sets in. Imagine what being in a prison does. Makes you go over every single moment in your life. You hear other people's experiences and you start to see how thin the line is. It's much, much thinner than you think when on 'the outside'. In here you can see that almost any situation in your life can go the 'wrong way' ... end up with you being criminalised. And once you're criminalised, that's it.

The trouble is there are police and so on waiting, just waiting for some groups to make mistakes, while nobody is even looking at other groups. I bet the Windsors, the House of Commons and without a doubt the House of Lords have done more crimes this week than everyone else together LOL! Those 'entrepreneurs' our 'culture' holds so dear to its heart ... would without a doubt be in real turmoil in here. Everything they do is about taking advantage and daring to win – if they looked back over their deals, what it has meant, how they went about accumulating that money, they would soon see they crossed lots of lines of legality and certainly decency. One mistake will mean a lifetime of confronting their decisions. There is without a doubt a special purgatory for those 'social entrepreneurs' and 'company–men–academics'. I wonder what thoughts they would start to have about themselves if they were in here? Most capitalists – all capitalists(?) – would be confronted with the way they have exploited people and our earth for their odd idea of accumulation/profit. They would be in purgatory in here without a doubt. They would be in a very difficult position first thing in the morning and just before they fall asleep. It won't take long for them to think of themselves as criminals – surely they wouldn't think they were innocent after a few weeks in here. No chance.

Mornings

A great struggle for me is the mornings – life 'outside' means I'm always awake at 6am or 7am – and the prison is silent – it's a torture that gets worse as the prison wakes up but there's no place to go – nothing but the cell and the prison screws – clanging doors, speaking over the intercom, birds outside, the railway and my cellmate turning over in his bunk above me. It's when I feel most alone, most frustrated. It's when I question myself the most. It's a torment. It's tormenting. I read for as long as possible so H can stay asleep. He sleeps to escape from his feelings about being in here. Reading sometimes helps, sometimes makes the feeling worse – particularly reading about 'failed' revolutions as I have been doing recently!

It's better when I'm up at this table writing letters, this diary, and reading. It soon pushes the morning thoughts away. Once I've eaten, had coffee, written to Deepa or a close friend I'm a–okay – then work begins on my book about land ownership or reading the latest book to arrive. Sometimes the door is opened and I make a dash for the phone – which I probably shouldn't – it's too early. The door is sometimes opened for me to attend workshops – the 'job clubs' I've not been going to. My day passes very quickly with writing replies to the generous and kind people that have written to me – will do a list of tasks for the two weeks as it seems I'm staying here – not moving to Birmingham, which means I can get more of a routine.

Trenton Oldfield

Home?

Hopefully the home detention tag thingy will go through soon – on Monday afternoon I can plan to leave here – head home and get back to working on the festival and our books and finding a job/doing a PhD? The question is do we stay in the UK or do we move elsewhere? Is one able to make a life in London? Can one live here? Is it a place for living? Would our child become 'English' by living here? With this barbarous government and these outlaw corporations in full action, maybe it's 'the' time for an overthrow? Is this the chance for revolution? Would it be 'the' very worst time to move elsewhere? How could we live with ourselves not being here, contributing to it? It was hard enough to be abroad when Occupy was underway. Can we be more productive elsewhere? Would we be able to contribute more to a revolt being elsewhere – having time to write more? Nothing will change anywhere if the UK doesn't change. Doesn't matter if there is a revolution elsewhere and not here – cause this culture, these war–hungry people will end up undermining anyone else. It has to happen here. The culture of 'who dares wins' needs to be addressed – head on. There needs to be reparations for crimes past. People here need to understand the mechanisms of empire and what these troops and companies are doing now, right now. If they try to throw me out of this country, it won't be me that is 'tired of London, tired of Life', it is the authorities that will think London can't handle me LOL! That would be too funny!

Films

With films etc being so 'anti–criminal', I wonder what 'criminals' feel when they watch these films? I suggest sometimes it's very difficult to watch. I wonder if anyone has done research on this? I wonder what emotionally this does to 'us'? I think it might be something that needs considering – I suggest it could be both emotionally draining and also possibly a methodology for therapy? Depending on what prison is actually for … does anyone know what prison is for??

Saturday 14 November 2012 / Screw conversation at kit change

While waiting in line for kit change I had a conversation with a screw. Said the British, no, the English, elite, would never stop as they have too much money – can just so easily buy people and institutions. He said, "I can't say this officially but good on you; what you did took a lot of guts." We spoke about their pensions and the privatisation of prisons. They all seem very concerned about this and that prisons will go back 50–100 years to much more brutal places. He said he gets lots of flack himself for not being 'English'. He said, "The average Englishman is totally fine, good people, most of them, it's the elites that look down on us – see us as less than them, just because they took our money. They think because we are nice and didn't kill them we are weak. I wish it could change, but how?"

Gym

In the gym again this morning, thank goodness! Lots of wise cracks about there being no swimming pool and rowing machines – "should get a photo of you on the rowing machines and send it to the papers". It's quite wonderful jovial fun – so odd that everyone, I mean everyone knows. Feels like a shared experience somehow – feels like they were part of it also somehow. Anything against this phucked up government is understood and appreciated. Let me know there will surely be more like me coming in, keep an ear open for them. I'm always asking what they would want me to say about prison when I get out and they always say or almost always say "let them know we aren't too bad, we've done our time, let us get on with it"; "Let us get on with our lives once we are out"; "Let them know we are alright innit". Ran only three miles today – short gym session; happiest running not walking!

More jokes were cracked again this lunch, more by the 'hot plate' crew. I'm fond of all these guys – their sharp wit, their warmth, and their own personal situations. Always come back up to the fourth floor smiling and sometimes still laughing. Like it how most people set out to help each other.

Visits

I'm not putting in the paperwork for visits. I feel it's crazy people coming out of their way to see me just for 40, maybe 50 minutes – going through all the hassle and checks and so on. And I'm not happy with how the prisoner is treated in that room either – wearing the yellow singlet sitting on the red seat, wearing a grey tracksuit. I'm not sure I want people to see me like this. Along with the holding pens, this is the experience that is very disempowering; humiliating. If I'm not out in December then I'm sure I will be missing people and wanting to see them face to face. But just two months – it seems too much to put people through as well! Maybe if I'm out in December we can have a 'Christmas party'? Everyone together – everyone in one room? Think we have one or two bottles of wine left over from the book launch? I would like that. I wonder if it's possible to arrange – cause so many people leave London at Christmas time?

End of trouble

Spoke to my love today and I think we are both passed the trouble of last week – can tell from the sounds in our voices. Trouble is yesterday I sent a slightly stroppy letter – about how we need to communicate as we are not enemies – by the time it will get there it will seem silly, bit 'naf' and probably a bit OTT; certainly out of date! Writing another note, hopefully will arrive on the same day cancelling out the other OTT letter? LOL. Fingers crossed. Should know the wind changes direction... six years together! Should know about this! Feels good – boost of energy. It's remarkable how much it affects me either way.

H

So yesterday H had a visit from his cousin and brother–in–law which has had a tremendous impact on how he will see women forever. The woman who took the law into her own hands has also apparently contacted all of his family members and told them everything he did. From what he told me he basically set–up a number of profiles on shaadi.com and was in constant contact with around eight women – some he met up with, some only online. He said he worked at Microsoft as a programmer when he in fact worked in a retail shop. Not ideal but no worse than a trustafarian setting up a pseudo company/ organisation in order to dress themselves up as 'successful' and actually doing something. Also he seems to have only done something most people in their 20s do – exaggerate their jobs and position in life. How many 20–somethings are focussed on job titles and extend what they are actually doing at work and school? It's a tough decade – away from home for most people and constantly making mistakes in order to find out more about who they are – what they think about, what they want to do, who they want to be with, spend their time with Heaven knows, meeting potential partners is a priority. It was for me!!

Now H feels entirely abused by this woman and keeps saying: "Never trust a woman." "Women are trouble, man, I'm done!" "Of course in India this information will have a big impact on my life – people will talk." "People will forever have an opinion of me regardless if it is true or not." He speaks of getting revenge on her or her parents in India. Try to talk him down and also point out what's wrong with his sentiments ... but we are not understanding each other – he is really angry and I'm pissed he could even imagine revenge is something suitable to think or do. We've not spoken more than a few words – he has been asleep most of today since he returned from his visit. Not sure how to help him.

I've been making lists of books I want to get hold of when I am 'out' – from reviews I have read in papers today: *Former people: The last days of the Russian aristocracy* by Douglas Smith, *The sound of things falling* by Juan Gabriel Vasquez, *Falling Sideways* by Thomas Kennedy – fiction, *Border veils: keeping migrants out of the rich world* by Jeremy Harding, *Derrida: A biography* by Benoit Peeters, *I Am Spain: The Spanish Civil War and the Men and Women Who Went to Fight Fascism* by David Boyd Haycock, *You aren't what you eat: Fed up with gastroculture* by Steve Poole, *Meme Wars: The Creative Destruction of Neo-classical Economics* by Kalle Lasne and Adbusters.

Wednesday 21 November 2012

So very much to write about, so very many people I should be writing to; causing one of those 'frozen in the headlights' moments – 'but where do I start' moments. Have put together a list, well three lists; now I not sure which list should I start with! The day goes so quickly in here, it's dinner time before you know it.

The good news is that it was H's birthday yesterday so we shared my pack of ginger snacks (everyone is given one small pack every Saturday evening). Ms Deepa Naik and I are communicating wonderfully again and there is a good chance I will be outta here in exactly two weeks time! The probation officer visited Flat 24 and gave a positive report for me being allowed home on curfew. Deepa mentioned on the phone that the probation officer was shocked by my sentence and all the probation officers she spoke with saw it as a "political sentence, hands down, clearly". Hard not to forget these words.

The officer mentioned that if they don't release me on the electric tag it again would be politically motivated and I can appeal it – the governor of the wing has to make the case for keeping me in prison formally. It could it seems only be political but it will be interesting to know what they will use as their excuse – if it happens it will be very interesting to see how they couch my continued incarceration. I'm not confident of being released on December 4th but I was the only one who thought I would end up in prison from my protest. I hope this time I'm wrong and I'm released on curfew and then license!

Some guys on the 'ones' were released this morning – over the moon for them. They were imprisoned for some robberies of some commercial offices while drunk and similar. I wish them every happiness! One of the laundry guys mentioned he wanted to write a book about being in here – must stay in touch with him – I would really like to read it! There are so many interesting stories in here. I really look forward to reading it!! I have a feeling there will be lots of prison books – as more and more of us are incarcerated for smaller and smaller 'crimes'.

A4E

Since Monday I've been attending 'Workshop 6' 2–4pm which is a Microsoft course for using Microsoft applications. I understand the course is part of something called a 'European Drivers License' – I'm doing stage one but I've learned a great deal already! It's great to have access to such courses. I particularly like it as it's done by oneself – no group projects etc. I understand I can continue it 'outside' as well – will be very helpful for our work, any work I will do in the future.

It was of some significant concern to notice it is run by 'A4E Justice'. How ironic even the name is! I love it when these businesses are just brazen and open with their bollocks. How can one make money from this? How can our interests as prisoners even be close to the interests of a business with international shareholders. I had hoped the workers were employed by the prison, by us. But they have been outsourced, no wonder all we hear is pro-capitalist rhetoric from them. In regards to the course, it's been quite funny to go through the sections, particularly the sections on 'computer security'... us prisoners; us criminals get a special reference LOL! They use these amazingly clichéd images and constructions of crime! It's all crime, crime, crime! Fraud, thieves etc! Wonder what the others are thinking as they see these images and constructs of them? Brilliant!

Everyday practices of prison

It has become apparent from letters from friends and supporters that it might be worthwhile taking my time to do a bit of anthropology of the prison. There seems to be a real interest in the everyday practices of such a place. As a result I've started recording daily activities. There is a real interest to understand what a day in prison feel like, looks like. It's true, prison is an unknown to so many and it seems there is a real interest in trying to empathise with the prisoner's life. (The day before sentencing I looked up Wormwood Scrubs on Google Maps to get a sense of the layout and it was rendered as 'a blob, 'a gap' and an 'unknown' in this city – just one large orange shade!) I'm sure there is also some fetishisation too. There will be some middle-class people that feel frustrated that they don't know something about a part of our cities that others do! These are the people who are used to 'access all areas', not used to being limited. Reminds me a little of one academic I know, lives in the UK but was born in Israel, who once complained to Deepa and I that they were annoyed with Israeli tyranny on Palestinian peoples because it prevented them from visiting places, limiting their experiences – as an Israeli can't travel in most if not all of the 'Middle East'. They argued that they were missing out on things, parts of the world because of things that had nothing to do with them. Yep!

I want to share the everyday practices of prison, or at least my experience of one prison for two main reasons: 1) to stand in solidarity with my fellow prisoners who have shown me and my fellow prisoners kindness, humour, warmth and provided support, and 2) to demystify prison so the middle classes who currently who fear prison and the stain of prison more than anything will no longer fear it and feel more emboldened and confident to undertake resistance against those who set out to enslave us – that they shouldn't fear prison. That if they all took action, it would be impossible for the concept of prison to exist, it would collapse.

Trenton Oldfield

An average day

Until fairly recently ex–military men had a monopoly on the prison guard job market. This prison would be a very dangerous place I imagine if the prison guards were soldiers that chose to fight in Afghanistan, Iraq, former–Yugoslavia and so on! In typical brutalist neo–liberal methodologies, when the Blairites gave into what sounds like a sustained campaign from fellow prisoners to end the military's de facto control of prisons, they took with the other hand, creating a new precarious workforce who are underpaid and overworked. This morning I had a brief chat with one of the new prison guards (started three weeks ago!), a chap from Scotland who has six children. We talked about the architecture of Wormwood Scrubs. We shared a knowing laugh at the passive aggression of 'the Victorian's' designing a 'humane prison' whilst forcing the prisoners to build it themselves in unsafe and brutal conditions!

He explained how the wings were designed to achieve the maximum amount of sunlight, which means, depending what side of the wing you are on, you either have direct sunrise or direct sunset. Here on A Wing I get woken by the sunrise. There are no curtains so I wake anytime between 5am and 7am. Some of my fellow prisoners cover their windows with either a black plastic bag (which is readily available from the landing office) or with newspaper. Both require using lots toothpaste (glue) and wanting to live in a very small cave. Happily H doesn't seem to want to cover the windows and can sleep through most things including sunlight.

As most of the prison is set a long way back from most roads (apart from D wing) and has a large park on one side it's an incredibly quiet place, quite unlike my experience of the rest of London. Unlike the apartment we rent in Aldgate East, very little sound can be heard from the neighbours – these walls and floors have been made well LOL! Mostly I am woken by bird song, something else I am not sure I can ever remember happening in my ten years living in Aldgate East. Some nights I sleep facing the window, some nights I sleep facing the cell door. It makes no difference whatsoever unfortunately to the moment when I reach around looking for Deepa. Is she awake yet? What will her day bring? Is she feeling okay? Oh shit man, I'm in a prison!

In the middle distance 'the tube' (now overground in this part of London) makes those gentle industrial noises where speed, electricity and steel come together. While my liberty has been unduly taken from me, I wouldn't want to be on that Central Line destined to sit in front of a computer screen of make–believe numbers at Bank or Liverpool Street. My heart goes out to these aspirational dream/storm chasers. Mostly my heart aches for their children if I am entirely honest.

As my cell is on the 'outside world' side of A Wing, a window that opens is replaced with a perforated screen. This must be to stop the world's strongest and most accurate thrower being able to regularly and purposefully throw something into the correct open cell window? While 'the ones' (ground floor) is the best place to be as it means you have an important job (server etc) being on 'the fours' is brilliant as you are up above the perimeter walls. On this side I have a horizon and a view of trees and rooftops. Somehow the giant netting has come apart right in front this window so it's possible, looking out, to have few reminders of jail, of being jailed. Under me is the prison's perimeter road. It starts to get a little busy after 8am with the 'sweatboxes' (Serco prisoner transport) coming to collect prisoners for their day in court from the prisoners' reception at the back of the prison. It seems some staff need to walk to this reception as well – which might be quite a distance from the main entrance, maybe a ten minute walk? Normally the sound of heels or wooden soles frustrates me as it seems such an unnecessary and repetitive sound made by an inconsiderate person who is likely oblivious to it. However for now I am enjoying the occasional 'civvie' letting everyone know they are on their way down the road.

From around 7.30am a handful of cell doors begin to be opened. Specific cells only ... people with special jobs, maybe people who work on reception, people off to court, gym orderlies and people who will be released today. You know it's happening, not because of the sounds of doors opening but the sounds of the screws' radio auto–bleeping and them swinging their key chain up into their hands to open the cell door. Around this time the first broadcast over the internal intercom system occurs. Like most of the communications, it is almost impossible to understand. It is likely this message is announcing the first 'free flow' of the day. It's the first of many.

By 8am it's impossible for me to be asleep. It's loud in here! Being on 'the fours' I'm tempted to describe it as a 'volcano' of sound! While most of us are still locked in our cells (and will be for most of the day) the wing cleaners, whilst working, are busy yelling out to each other and having a chat. The loudest sounds come from fellow prisoners now waiting at the gate. Despite the time of day you can hear loads of laughter. It's loud like a school playground at lunchtime or the interval at a play or concert. It reminds me of the crescendo of noise that happened on the change of classes at school. It rises gently, becomes amazingly loud and ends suddenly. It's hard to pretend you are not in an institution.

Even though H seems to sleep through the most amazing noise and bright light I stay in bed reading so I don't create the possibility of waking him. On the floor beside my bed is a collection of books, newspapers and writing materials. It's hard to know what I might want to read or write about in the morning ... best to have almost everything in easy reach. Read and write in bed until it's impossible to stay away from the water closet or my tummy starts to rumble.

'Out of bed' day starts with press-ups, sit-ups, ablutions, the loo, making of my bed, shifting books and papers from beside my bed to the small table by the window. Check on the weather by looking directly out the window. So many sunny days! Autumn is such a wonderful time of year in London ... beautiful. Every meal is eaten in the cell. Breakfast comes out of a small plastic bag given to us by a fellow prisoner when we collected our dinner the previous night. It is either oats or something like coca-pops, something like rice bubbles or something like special-k. Collecting dinner is a bit of a balancing act as you also collect four pieces of bread (more if you're friends with the chaps), a box of milk (hard to get extra milk as a screw stands in the kitchen watching) and a bowl full of dessert (pudding with custard). On Sunday night the week's butter is also dished out. It is a particularly pedestrian walk back to the fours. Breakfast milk comes out a longlife box. I leave my boxes by the window so they chill a little. Happy I've had to go 'cold turkey' on my posh coffee addiction. Now my canteen order has come, breakfast also includes a large mug of instant coffee. I only have one coffee these days, as with so little physical activity I don't wish to be awake again all night. All walls are tough to steer at three in the morning but the three walls and door of a prison cell are something else altogether LOL!

If you are lucky your cell door can be mistakenly opened – due to confusion with another prisoner (maybe previously in this cell?) or if a cellmate has an appointment or alike. Sometimes screws do it out of kindness. Down goes the breakfast bowl, across the top of the coffee mug goes the book I'm reading, on go the shoes and straight to the phones. That's where most of us go. You might have ten minutes before cells are locked down again. Most people waiting to use one of the three phones check in with each other – see how they are. Everyone is just waking up. It's sometimes so loud in the prison that it's difficult to hear what Deepa is saying on the other end of the phone.

Unfortunately "End of free flow, all prisoners to return to their cells", repeated, is quite easy to make out over the intercom system. Over a period of around five minutes the decibels drop with each bang of a fellow prisoner's cell door. Soon the wing falls silent again, strangely quiet. H settles in for his next period of sleep. I try to work out what I can do without making too much noise, though I am quietly happy when he does continue to sleep as I find it hard not to watch the 'real life' TV shows he watches; Judge Judy etc. I have found a way to write when the adverts are on though – when combined they can be as long as the show itself. As only the screws have keys to the cell doors, other prison workers can sometimes be heard yelling through the gaps of the door trying to speak to prisoners. The busiest people seem to be the staff of the UK Border Agency unfortunately. Sometimes you can hear someone from Working Links getting a few details, probably from a new prisoner. Otherwise it's amazingly quiet. For me this is wonderful for writing and reading, though I wonder if it is difficult for the younger ones, and those used to being outdoors. I've spent much of my life with books, pens and paper ... and being deskbound for most of the day.

This silence after the noise is the second time in the day that it hits me that I am in prison. With morning tasks checked off, and either the bed or the chair to work from, I am once again confronted with the fact that I am in prison! I can't help but laugh out loud at how absurd and vulnerable the wantabe ruling class are. They keep proving my arguments for me LOL. It's this laughter that gives me the exact energy for the hours ahead. My greatest worry is that I won't have the time to reply to everyone who has written. I am also determined to map out some chapters for this darn book of mine that has been around my neck for over ten years now. I think I am making good headway on the issue of how land came to be understood as property but mostly how monotheistic religion was used to rip apart the idea and practices that held those ideas together. Most problematic of all perhaps, how such disentanglement allowed the creation of hierarchy, with someone (god) always on the top. Progress.

My body aches for music. H isn't a fan of the one music channel we get in here and I entirely understand why but I do wish to pump it up loud on the TV just to have something to push through me. My mistake was bringing a radio that has a detachable power cable ... something the check–in prison staff suggested could be used to charge mobile phones. It was not allowed. I put in a General Application every week asking for it. Yet to receive even a reply. If I could listen to the Huey Show etc, I think I would be okay in here.

'Association' or 'Domestic' happens either in the morning or in the afternoon. Sometimes, sometimes, it happens in both the morning and the afternoon. It alternates with each day; morning today, afternoon tomorrow ... sort of. I think there is meant to be a pattern like this but it doesn't seem to be so predictable ... seems to depend on staff resources? The fours and the seconds are 'let out' at the same time and the ones and threes are 'let out' at the same time. Never is the entire wing out at the same time.

Association/Domestic never lasts more than one hour and it is regularly much much shorter. You never know how long it will be, so you have to be quick to shower, send post, drop in General Applications, find the fellow prisoner who is responsible for clothes washing, check boards for visitors, make phone calls, see a screw about x or y, go for a walk in the yard, add your name to the list for the gym, find a broom and mop to clean your cell or just have a chat with a neighbour. Mostly it's just great to stand in different air to the cell. Sometimes the cell can be so hot it is a joy to stand in the cavernous halls. Some prisoners play pool. The other day I noticed a ping pong table that I hadn't seen before, might be new? There is no place to sit, not a single chair or bench anywhere. It's difficult to meet fellow prisoners unfortunately.

Some days there is a gym session ... if you managed to get your name on the list the day before, if the screw remembers to let you out of your cell and you make it down to the gateway before they lock the gate. Sessions average around 30–60 minutes. As a regular prisoner you could get the gym three times a week – which would be around three hours of physical activity out of a possible 168. It takes as long to get there and come back and the schedule includes the 'movement' time as well, unfortunately, so actual running and lifting time is quite short.

Most of the time is taken up in the holding cells at either end. I've taken to taking the *New Statesman* with me. As it is so rare an experience to actually get in the gym I can take old editions with me to give to the one of the gym orderlies – a chap who said MI5 tricked him when was working with the Indian secret service. He's been in jail for four years waiting trial and going through re-trials. I've left editions with other gym orderlies to give to him and they ask me every time if I've left him coded messages in the magazine LOL. I said if I were planning a break out it would be for everyone not just for two people.

Lunch happens before you know it ... anytime between 10.45am and 12.45. You would have thought prison would have be regimented, predictable, organised. Wormwood Scrubs certainly is not. It's very unpredictable. You could be washing your breakfast dishes and already your door is opened for lunch. Most of the time you have to pop your head out the door and see what other prisoners, let out just earlier, have in their hands to work out what is going on. Many a day H went from sleeping to eating lunch.

Lunch, like breakfast and dinner, is eaten in your cell. It's carefully executed by the guards. Being on the fours we are usually the last to be 'unlocked'. Each and every door needs unlocking, there is no central system ... but this suits as only a handful of people at a time can make it down the stairs to the 'hot plate' area where the food is served. The guards hold and then 'release' a number of us each time one makes it down to the next landing. At meal times the stairs have a one way system – down the stairs at one end and up the stairs at the other end. The 'hot plate team' are fellow prisoners who serve food that has been prepared elsewhere in the building. The food comes in large metal dishes – maybe 50 x 30cm. When one dish is finished they pull another one up from the warming system below.

On A Wing we have a menu which we submit the week before. You get to choose from around five options. There is always a vegan, vegetarian, Halal and Kosher meal to select. Halal seems to run out pretty quickly. You take the menu sheet with you when you go to collect your food. The meal you circled earlier in the week gets marked off by one of our fellow prisoners. Naturally I forget my menu sheet all the time, perhaps 80% of the time. Often H sees it resting by the TV and brings it with him! Kind! It's always great to see the 'hot plate' guys – they are always up for a laugh and a bit of banter – always some cracks about swimming. After most of the day without speaking, it's great to have a bit of a chat and some laughter. They start to seem like family somehow? Maybe it's cause I see them so often and they are related to food? There is a familiarity LOL. You can click your kettle and be back in your cell before it has finished boiling. Either the small kettle takes a long time or the entire process is quite quick? The screws are waiting to close the door behind you. All very efficient and helpful cause you don't have any spare hands!

Not sure we have eaten a meal without the TV on. It needs to be up around 10 extra notches to compensate for the noise that now echoes once again through this institutional building. Now it's a combination of chatter but mostly the noise of doors slamming, keys turning and screws yelling out that x or y floor is finished. In about 20 minutes the wing will fall silent again. Sometimes after lunch I wonder if everyone just suddenly fell asleep. It goes amazingly quiet again. Could be a monastery? I would be curious to know what most people get up to between lunch and the next 'free flow'. Do most sleep? Do most read? The screws will know ... as they come along opening and then closing the window, checking on us. If H has received bad news the previous evening or not been able to see the staff he needs to see, he tends to sleep after eating and washing his dishes. I regret and feel for H's troubles and totally understand that sleeping can be just wonderful at blocking almost everything out. Dishes are washed in the small sink in the toilet area. One of the first things I bought through the canteen was dish soap and scrubbing brushes. Nobody, I mean nobody, comes to collect their food with dirty plates. Everyone's plates are spotless. Cleanliness is paramount to prisoners it seems. Cleanliness is one of the reasons why it is imperative association/domestic happens – we need access to brooms, mops, rubbish bags and so on. Some cells are spotless, most are very clean. Lots of effort goes into cleaning them.

The second and final free flow of the day happens at 2pm. This is usually for education sessions and workshops and sometimes the gym. Hundreds of prisoners from all five wings make their way to different sites across the prison. There is one long straight corridor that runs like a spine connecting all the wings. Think the shape of an E, a spine with wings coming out of it. The spine must be 500 metres long? The same corridor is stacked above itself, connecting each floor also. The prisoners only ever use the ground floor corridor – but for the laundry transfer and alike. The other corridors don't seem to be used that often, though some staff seem to have keys. These corridors probably operate if and when the prisoners barricade the main entrance – like back doors where the riot squads can come in, probably unexpectedly in most cases? Those 'humane' Victorians thought of everything?

In the afternoon again I sit at the small desk with books, letters, newspapers and pens and write and write and write. Sometimes I read in bed but have a fear of falling asleep and not making full use of this time. There is also too much to do and how can I sleep with all these brilliant books and magazines to read? How could I not write to these beautiful people who have written to me? My ears are now peeled for the sounds of a guard's keys and radio bleeping – hoping for either post and/or newspapers. These hours hold the greatest expectation for me. The sound of keys turning means there is too much mail to be pushed through the gap between the door and the wall.

The silence is pulled apart around 4pm when many prisoners return from their courses, legal visits, work, personal visits and so on. Hundreds of prisoners make their way back along the connecting hall being checked off back into their wing. Surprisingly though reassuringly the method is rather old school in Wormwood Scrubs; when you leave the wing your name is highlighted. When you return to the wing a line is drawn across the length of your name. Somehow I imagined everything would have been digital ... maybe with a chip being placed in your arm or alike that we would scan or would be automatically scanned when we passed key sites in the prison. Apart from the highlighter pen, I imagine the same methodology has been used here for well over 100 years. Hope it doesn't change. Hope we aren't chipped! Though I do think we should be given something like a tablet computer when we 'check in'. The tablet could have pre-loaded videos discussing the idea of prison (which would be unlikely as they are intellectually untenable propositions in the 21st century!), videos in different languages explaining the routine of each wing, how to apply for jobs and so on and so forth. They could be connected to an internal internet where we could download books, educational resources and alike. If we are not 'allowed' access to the World Wide Web itself we could have access at least to an email system which the prison staff could monitor like they monitor our regular mail? We could submit General Applications on the system which could be tracked for progress? Money could be transferred electronically to an account we control and monitor? Our canteen could be ordered electronically? Someone must have suggested it to the powers that be – wonder if it is being considered? I'm sure this would make a huge difference to our everyday life in here and have a major impact on our access to educational materials. But no micro–chipping or alike!

Not long after the returning prisoners are locked in their cells, if there is enough staff available the ones and threes or the twos and fours will be let out for their domestic/association. Some days it doesn't happen at all. While it is unusual, a prisoner did barricade himself in his cell on the day I came here and it's happened again today. This means no association/domestic as the screws try to work out what to do with him, how to get him out of his cell – ironically. The other day there was no association and we were escorted to the 'hot plate' because two prisoners had taken one of the guards into their cell and he was so badly beaten he ended up being hospitalised. He hasn't come back to work but the other prison guards seem quite relaxed about it ... "part of the job really". The two prisoners have vanished; assume they are now in high security and in 'solitary' at the moment ... certainly on 'basic'.

Around this time the sun comes directly into the cell. I've taken to standing and resting my book or this notepad on the window sill. Here I can feel the sunlight directly on my face, on my body. It is a true pleasure. I've even stayed put and watched the sun set behind the horizon a few times, something I haven't done for many years. There were leaves on the trees when I came in. They are all gone now, all of them. I've seen them fall. I'm getting in touch with our natural world in here LOL! This is when I write most of my letters.

Dinner happens anytime between 4.45pm and 7pm. It's the same drill as lunch, however this time you need to remember your bowl, for dessert. I pop some letters in the letterbox, have a bit of a chat with the 'hot plate' guys, slow walk to the other end of the wing, up the stairs and I'm back in this cell in no time. Thud goes the door and clunk turns the lock. Down goes the noise level of the wing with each door closing. Something sad about it in a way and I picture this happening all over the country, all over the world, people retreating to their rooms, stepping back from the public realm, turning on the TV. No doubt it's happening more than ever. We always watch the TV when eating. It's usually when I get the chance to read my mail. There is intensity, warmth and clarity in these messages that is just awesome. I worry that once I am out life will take over and it won't be like this. It's beautiful.

As H sits closest to the TV on the makeshift table we made, he seems to have control of the channels. He is a big fan of these reality TV shows of which there seem to be many. I convince myself, like I have always done, that there is lots to learn from these shows, purposefully ignoring how very much it is edited for dramatic effect. In our old cell I was closer than he was to the TV so popped the news on ... which I guess is 'same same but different' to these reality shows. There is one game show in which there is no competition between 'contestants' called 'Deal or No Deal'. Everyone eventually has a shot at being the player and the level of money you win is entirely random; there is no skill, training or strategy you could employ. It's really a show about 'how much is enough' and 'isn't life random'? As a result there is only warmth and support from fellow constants and the host of the show.

Nobody, as far as I am aware, now leaves their cell after being locked in having collected dinner. On weekends this can be amazingly early, even before sundown in winter. The wing falls silent again. If you turned the TV off you could picture yourself anywhere: monastery, retreat, forest. Our social welfare 'contract' ought to include once every seven years a choice of retreat ... the chance to be 'away', in our thoughts and outside of the practice of everyday life. I suggest up to three months every seven years. I imagine some monies would need to be allocated for children to stay with relatives or perhaps there is a way to do it with children? The quiet is only interrupted if there is an international football match on or if someone 'hasn't taken their medicine' and is kicking off. The only way to make noise others will hear is by kicking and banging on the cell door. H and I seem to have come to an understanding – he gets to watch reality and game shows and films if we don't watch any football matches whatsoever. One evening recently England was playing another country. We assumed England was winning or doing well as all the doors kept being kicked. However the next day when we checked the paper to see the score, it was clear the vast majority of the prisoners were going for the team playing against England.

In the evenings the TV seems to come into its own – its role as pacifier is at its best. Most evenings, and they are long, the relative silence seems evidence of the TV's success. This is the toughest stretch of the day, for me at least. The day has sped to this point, with lunch at 11am and dinner at 5pm. Even if I have done 200 press–ups and 200 sit–ups across the day, I still have loads of energy and after a day or reading and writing my mind is wired. I want to do stuff. This is when H is in full control of the TV and, while I struggle against it, I almost always give in and end up watching it also. He likes to watch films, even films he has previously seen. Having watched a bunch of them with him now, they seem to have a very similar plot and it's very easy to predict what is going to happen next. It probably annoys him hugely when I say what is going to happen next. I cannot get over how many people are killed in these films!!! I'm so very curious to know how these films affect my fellow prisoners ...

You know it's 9pm as someone comes along and opens and closes the cell door window. It's amazingly quick. I assume it's to check two people are in the cell, that nobody has escaped or hung themselves? Those on suicide watch are checked every hour. By this time I can no longer pretend to myself I will continue writing at my desk and I usually end up lying on my bed looking at the screen when the guards come past. I continue to hold a book in my hand. I do read and make notes in the adverts, but I think I hold it for the 9pm prison cell window door opening: "I'm not lying down, I'm reading and making notes!" I feel guilty the guards are working so late in the evening away from their families and I am lying down watching television! Oddly somehow I think reading a book or ripping articles out of a newspaper is better.

The second most difficult part of the day for me is the period in–between switching of the television and falling asleep. Mostly I feel awful for watching the same film every evening and having not taken the time to write to people. H is the bed directly above me. Sometimes we speak in the dark. These are interesting conversations, about the future, about what might happen to both of us, what that film was about, and what does this all mean, being here. Most nights we just say something along the lines of 'another day down ... they might have the keys but can't stop the clock, sleep well, we will both be out soon!' I always find it difficult to fall asleep. I think I could read until morning but have no light to do so. So many unfinished thoughts and points I want to make sure I correspond with friends mean I end up writing in darkness on my notepad. Most words I can't make out the next day LOL. I wonder if Deepa is asleep yet. I wonder about her day. I hope my letters arrive. I feel joyful about our future together and very very energised about our work together.

Key days

Here is a shorthand version of my observation of key days in HMP Wormwood Scrubs; Tuesday (Hindu temple), Wednesday (canteen), Friday (mosque), Saturday (lock down, kit change, gym), Sunday (church). Some important paperwork; canteen sheet, food sheet, post, phone etc.

Saturday

Saturday is a busy day. Doors are opened around 7:45am when you have the chance to run down to be admitted to the gym. I've now started to arrange my gym stuff on Friday night – as being on the 4th floor makes it less likely to be down in time before the gate is locked. You must take your gym card with you to be admitted too! The gym is around three minutes walk away – down the core corridor past B Wing and up 100 or so stairs. Of course it can take much longer to get there if you're held in a holding cell or on the stairs – though Saturdays seem pretty quick. At the gym you are given shorts and a tank top – you have to wear them regardless. My religious brothers wear the shorts over their long trousers and the tank top over their prison grey tracksuit top, so as not to expose their body. Which is pretty impressive, disciplined, and kinda nuts at the same time.

When we first arrive at the gym it's a little bit of a rush as people are keen to get to certain equipment before others – this seems the case of the free weights in particular as there are limited benches – but it seems everyone ends up sharing in the end so it's odd, the small rush. The free weights room is the only room in the prison I have come across that has mirrors. I pop in before showering to get a reminder of what I look like – look for dry skin, acne and so on.

I'm very curious about my religious brothers in here – it must be very hard for these prisoners to deal with a criminal conviction. It must also very difficult for their families who might also hold religious convictions. I've been reading the *Bhagavad Gita* and it very clearly points out the prohibited activities for which many of them are in here or, at least the police and judges thought they did. How do they reconcile their actions with their very strong religious convictions? This is from the *Gita*, "Total renunciation of prohibited acts – non-performance in anyway whatsoever, through the mind, speech and the body, low arts prohibited by the scriptures, such as theft, adultery, falsehood, deception, fraud, oppression, violence, taking of interdicted food, wrong doing ... "

On return from the quite short Saturday morning gym session (30 minutes) it is 'kit change'. It's completely organised and administered by fellow prisoners. If you like to be clean, feel clean, this is an event you just don't want to miss! Kit change is the wonderful moment once a week when you can change your clothes, bed sheets, underwear and socks, and towel. If you've been to the gym you have about five minutes to strip your bed, collect old clothes and get in line for them to be exchanged. The laundry is done by the prisoners and fellow prisoners then hand out the new kit. The blanket, sheet, pillow case and towel have been rolled together. It does feel a bit military like – you could imagine this happening at army bases 100 years ago. I'm not surprised a word like 'kit' is used. Each wing is slightly different. First you drop your bundle and then you are handed a card with a dot beside each item you have returned. You then go over to a cell turned into a storage area where a screw and some prisoners hand out what is on the dot – most people have a single dot beside 'full kit'.

Power outage

Power just went out ... people banging on their doors. Only lasted a second or two – has happened a few times though.

Rain

Rain is pouring down from the roof of the prison all the way down to the ground floor. It's like there is no roof or sprinklers are on. It seems some of the dungeon cells are also wet – which I guess exposes their vulnerability to escape? If water can so easily get in, there are plenty of holes – must not be escape proof then?

Clothes

It was a shock at first but having only one set of clothes becomes okay. When I say one set, I mean that is one set for both day and night; there is no separation between day and night. Same clothes 24 hours for 7 days. If you are convicted and sentenced you get one pair of grey tracksuit pants – all large size – some extra large. They have an elastic band so they stay up okay. One light blue t–shirt – again all rather large – oversized certainly for me. One tracksuit top – grey – mixed cotton and synthetic. These are made at HMP Manchester. Something remarkable happens about one week in – you no longer find it odd that people are all wearing the same clothes. That odd feeling that everyone is wearing their pyjamas disappears. All I started to focus on are people's faces – mostly their eyes, the rest just blended away.

The sheet is green – a mint green. The blanket is bright orange. I feel confident to suggest the blanket is synthetic, doesn't feel like wool or cotton. The blanket is of crochet style. The sheet is a material cut very roughly, possibly with a semi blunt instrument. Sometimes they fit, sometimes they don't. The pillowcases are mint green also and cover a rubber pillow. Quite recently 'the screws' came in to the cell and did a 'kit inspection' where they were looking for extra blankets, clothes, towel etc as the prison was running low on all items. Unfortunately H had his second blanket taken. My second blanket was somewhat disguised by being under the other blanket.

Two pairs of boxer shorts (light blue – 'baby blue') are issued as well. Fortunately I brought seven pairs of socks and seven pairs of underpants with me. Outer clothes for a week in here is okay. But one maybe two pairs of underwear is just not okay! Someone is allocated the job of laundry. If the wing hasn't run out of soap and you can find him and if he's not busy, you can get clothes washed! The clothing situation is very difficult for those on remand. This I think is the most difficult for those on remand – many who have only the clothes they came in with – that they were wearing at the time of being 'arrested'. Quite intense! I'm not sure how they manage! It doesn't seem they are able to wear the prison clothes. So I don't think they can even have a change of clothes to swap into while they wash their other clothes.

I am quick to take advantage of the fresh towels and clothes – dashing to the shower; long shower and shave! Feels great! My goodness! My goodness, fresh clothes and a shave!

The weekend also means no 'menu' but lots of beans, vegetable sausages, hash browns. I'm not sure why there is no menu on weekends but there you go. All meals are early: 11am for lunch, 4 or 5pm for dinner.

Sunday

If you're Christian this means you have a bit of an early start on Sunday but also a walk in the outside air. If not you can sleep until 11am (lunch) without being woken – the prison is almost silent until 10am. Like Sundays on the 'outside' there is a real change of pace and energy, it feels different, time is different. I'm still up at 7am reading or writing. Though I have also spent more than one or two Sundays yelling at the BBC's 'politics' shows; Andrew Marr, Sunday Politics! How is it that people like Andrew Marr, with such low self-esteem seek out and are offered such jobs; offered shows named after them! There are no 'rush hours' like Monday to Friday (no 'free flows' on the weekends). It feels very different. I love it but H hates it.

On Saturday in A Wing two pieces of paper go up by the 'people management' or whatever it's called office. One sheet is to register for the Roman Catholic (RC) service. The other piece of paper is to register for the Church of England (C of E) service. It has come to my attention over the last few weeks that the RC church has double, sometimes triple, the amount of people that sign up for the C of E service. This week there were 25 for the C of E service and 63 for the RC service. Who knows if all the RC signatures attend or if all the C of E attend? Nonetheless it is an interesting statistic which raises the following questions for me; are there more Roman Catholics in prison? Do Roman Catholics identify with their faith more than C of E prisoners? Are RCs 'better' at attending services? Are prisoners drawn from RC communities more than C of E communities? Are the police and judiciary biased against certain groups that have the RC faith? I have noticed that most of the 'white' prisoners in here do seem to be travellers and young men. The other group that comes to mind is Romani. There seem to be many Romani here considering their population size in the UK.

Dinner is so early on Sundays and with daylight savings you can get confused and be in bed fast asleep by 7pm. There is of course no clock. You only know what time it is by the TV programme. Trouble is you are then wide awake from 9 or 10pm until 3 or 4am! Somehow you have to stay awake and not get hungry again. Most Sunday afternoons H falls asleep after dinner and then turns the TV on at around 10pm because he is wide awake.

Cash and canteen

One of the reasons to always carry £20 cash with you is if you end up in prison it will immediately get put on your canteen system. I had £17 cash with me by accident, which meant when I was 'checked in' they could take the cash straight away and I could then allocate it to the phone, buy/order nail clippers, ear buds, detergent. If you don't have any cash with you, it will take weeks to get cash onto your prison number. I have been told by some of my fellow prisoners to keep a very close eye on the amounts – apparently our money goes missing all the time. Sheesh, I can imagine it must be hard to try and get that back! Must take years!

The canteen form comes sometime on Tuesdays. It's pushed through the gap between the cell door and cell wall. It lists numerous items you can purchase – mostly it seems sugary items and materials like ear cleaners, nail clippers and alike, which one might have imagined would already be available without cost? It does seem to me 'black' goods are very expensive relative to other goods – skin care, hair care etc. You mark the number of the item you want next to it and then you tally up the total number of items and cost. It needs to be placed in the canteen box by end of lunch on Wednesday. Phone credit will then be updated for the forthcoming Monday afternoon. There is no other way to put credit on your phone allowance. It takes a full week for the ordered items to arrive. You need to be very clear what you think you might need/wish for in a week's time. One of the difficulties with HMP Wormwood Scrubs being a 'holding prison' is you don't know if you will be moved to another prison. So you may not even get the items you ordered as you might be in Birmingham? Whatever the case, I will never walk the streets of London without £20 cash, the phone numbers of those I love on a piece of paper and the phone number of a lawyer on a piece of paper. It must be on paper as your mobile phone will likely be confiscated – you certainly won't be able to bring it into the prison.

Interestingly the canteen order seems to be arranged, organised and administered by DHL. When they gave me the wrong batteries the lady that came to sort it out (but unfortunately didn't so still no music from this radio!) was wearing a DHL uniform. Canteen comes in a large plastic bag about 50 x 50cm, sealed and with the receipt in the top also sealed. You don't open the pack until you have checked all items are there. You sign for it and then someone from DHL also checks it. The meal sizes are so small in here I'm sure the larger and hungrier guys must supplement their meals via the canteen sheet, which must be amazingly expensive for them.

This week I received plastic sandals/flip flops, a bar of chocolate – 'euro shopper', two Bountys, two cards – one for Deepa and one for Laila's birthday, phone credit and a pack of Doritos. Apart from the chilli Doritos which I demolished in moments, I have no appetite for chocolate – doesn't interest me. I have also received my order of more hot chilli sauce and a BBQ sauce. I'm sure these two items will be very helpful at meal times LOL! Aside from the Huey Show, all I have desired is chilli and pepper! I doubt only desiring these two items will meet the needs of those prison charities that love and only publish poems from prisoners that yearn for everything life offers on the 'outside'. And why does it always have to be poems or fiction? You won't find any charity publishing work by a prisoner saying he is content in prison; that they have no desires for things on the 'outside'. They wouldn't know what to do with this LOL!

Saturday evening

Is great as you are given the week's supply of margarine and a packet of biscuits; one week it's ginger biscuits, the other week it's tea biscuits. The packet is around 10cm high and contains 20 separate biscuits. You can average three a day and make a full week a–okay. H prefers to eat his entire pack on Saturday evening.

What will it take?

It's funny watching that aristocratic David Cameron on TV enlisting the war against the Nazis in his artificial 'war on no–growth'. Everyone knows the first person to mention Hitler has lost the argument! And even funnier when it's clear the Nazis may have lost but Nazism won – as embodied in people like Tony Blair and David Cameron et al. I guess I'm flabbergasted the people in this room with him haven't taken off their shoes and thrown them at him! Rotten tomatoes, bad eggs, bad apples ... whatever!

I'm forever amazed at how the generations of abuse perpetrated on people that live on this island results in retreat rather than revolution. Perhaps there is a point where, after say 600 years of continual abuse, your instinct is not revolution but hiding and sympathy for your abusers? Maybe there is a time period where it's no longer possible? Does it become part of the culture to be indifferent, silent, easily led, resigned to the abuse? It fascinates me that the people on this island, particularly those that identify as English, lash out and are extremely violent to those that challenge this situation. I've wondered if it is out of embarrassment for themselves, for not doing something, anything? It seems to me the English psyche (currently) is one very used to being abused, cheated, lied to, used, scape-goated. Like abused children, they find ways to hide or not draw attention to themselves, seeking out a life in mythological worlds, unable to relate well to people due to the lack of trust, and pre-disposed to erratic, unexpected, often violent, behaviour themselves?

Again I'm wondering, really, sincerely, if it might also be possible to suggest a type of Stockholm Syndrome where the captive and oppressed start to sympathise with their captors and oppressors? Surely that's the only way to explain why people would turn out to wave flags for the marriage of the two people that through procreating are going to continue over 1,000 years of disempowerment of them? Or why, despite hundreds of years of fighting (and being killed) around the world for the elite's interests and then being thrown onto a fire like wrapping paper at a royal Christmas, they believe fighting for 'their country' is honourable. It certainly and without a doubt is brave!!

A very dear friend has sent me a review of a recently published book that illustrates there are only 22 nations on planet earth that the British haven't invaded without 'royal' and then later royal and parliamentary agreement. The book lists only the known formal invasions, not the ones taken without official status or those the author didn't feel had enough documentation to confirm. As the review of the book points out, no other nation comes close. The British, particularly the English, know how violent, brutal and ruthless the elite are – they've experienced it themselves and then taken part in this brutality.

It seems like the same pattern of the way those abused children end up becoming child abusers themselves. Lashing out, sometimes violently is a common behaviour of people that have been abused. I wonder if the comments left online by 'the English/Anglo-Saxons' are different to the comments left by other people? My guess is that they are. It's a perfect way for them to abuse but remain hidden? Someone must have done research on this? <u>The question for those on this island and those where British people live around the world or nations set up or influenced by 'British culture' is how can this cycle of abuse be broken, so it doesn't repeat'?</u> How deep is it though?

Darwin's 'survival of the fittest' and 'evolution of the species', and so on, no doubt suited those who set out to establish, as was so popular at the time, the concept of a hierarchy and elitism, of those at the top and those at the bottom. It may have challenged some aspects of 'god' but only reinforced ideas of evolved/civilised, un–evolved/uncivilised and injected the brutal unfounded belief in competition as the root to all success/evolution. I always did wonder why such an idea took off so quickly, had such support. One must question if 'the myth of progress/evolution' suited the interests of the elite and their colonial ambitions? Should it be a surprise it was an 'upper–class' Oxbridge Englishman, already involved with colonialism aboard man–o–war HMS Beagle, that promoted the idea? It is no surprise to me it was an establishment Brit that promoted the theory – it is how they wanted to see themselves after all? How else would it be possible to suggest the millions of indigenous peoples could be seen as animals/uncivilised and thus no impediment to the brutal theft of their lands?

Is that a head sticking up above the parapet?

This culture has become peculiarly and worryingly anxious about those that 'stick their head above the parapet'. They rightly fear a collective punishment will ensue. Despite having very little to lose (limited comfort, limited peace, limited rights), most people on this island somehow think it's worth suffering and inflicting suffering on others to 'protect' their ever smaller and smaller material conditions and dignity. That small though vulnerable 'nest' that they choose to retreat into is likely to have been collected together as a result of participating in invasion, exploitation or cultural sycophancy, but it's still seen as worth protecting, even if they know it's evaporating in front of them.

'English' people are well aware of collective punishment, having experienced it over many centuries. The memory and knowledge of these experiences are, we know, passed down generation to generation through conversations, family behaviours, everyday practices. The desire to preserve the crumbs is understandable. In Britain the aim of life is to try to make it through a life of hoarding without drawing attention to one's self – like prison: "keep your head down". If you're the 'adventurous one' of the family you might migrate to Australia or Canada.

Like those that grew up in an abusive family one just wants to get as far away as possible, as soon as possible, and attempt to start one's own life independent from the abusive family – a chance to break the cycle. Those that stay behind join the culture and set out to preserve what little good they can see in it. It's understandable though desperately sad. Certain rituals then become important, those that celebrate the oppressor. Main themes tend to revolve around competition, rewards for sacrifice, valour, innovation and success. Competitive sport is becoming more and more important, of course.

Everyone but the British?

What is remarkable is it seems everyone except the British people themselves have defeated those that oppress them; the establishment, those that dare to rule them. Of the many nations that have been invaded by them, all have defeated them, thrown them out or set up their own nation. However despite having more people, a longer experience of the abuse and awareness of tactics, it hasn't been possible for the people of these islands to rid themselves of those that abuse them – everywhere but here? Little bit embarrassing? The rest of the world has chased the British establishment off their shores but here, today, most are happy to hide and it's ever so easy to find sycophants everywhere ... such as those currently in the NUS, who prefer to ruin the lives of millions, saddling them with huge debts, coming up with ludicrous slogans and forging divisions amongst those that could easily have been united on a very clear agenda and could have brought down a 'government'.

What has always been profoundly different here (and in Australia), to other places I have lived in and visited, is the noticeable absence of critical reflection and something of a fear of philosophy. There is a simple, resolute and unchallenged resignation to the nature, practices and rituals of their oppression. Visit the former Yugoslavia for example, where people have lived through great trauma, invading armies, civil war etc, and there is a philosophy, a way of looking at the life and moments in an attempt to understand, to question, to discuss. And with that also comes warmth, a generosity, a kindness to strangers, an awareness of complexities and an openness and willingness to debate. It's an openness along the lines of something that suggests "we've all been through a lot, what's your story, what do you make of x or y? What would you want to change? What are the things that are important to you? What makes a good life for you?" It's only, in my experience, England and some people in Australia, Canada and the USA that argue for 'polite conversation' and even more terrifying polite conversation where one doesn't speak of politics, religion and land. All the topics for much needed discussion! I'm sure some sycophant wrote a 'manners book' suggesting these 'social rules'. The only people to benefit from 'politeness', from a 'polite society', are those who don't want to be confronted with some hard facts. I can't tell you how much it frustrated me in court how polite everyone was to each other and how I was told not to upset the judge in anyway and so on. It was in fact my 'freedom' at stake. I'm charged with some phony law and I'm expected to be polite, well mannered, not to upset anyone. Of course I was going to end up in prison ... who was going to challenge anything?? Who benefits from politeness?

My hope is that 'the English' listen closely to those who have come to this island from the nations that defeated the barbarous invaders. They have much to share with the peoples of the UK. I wonder how it could be done? I wonder how the people of the UK could start to learn from those that have come here from elsewhere? I know they could share their knowledge of becoming free from these murderous, cunning elite. Rather than bemoan 'immigrants', these are the very people that can intellectually, emotionally, psychologically assist the English to finally remove these brutal elites once and for all. How can this happen?

William Windsor

Keep starting to write a letter to William Windsor. I'm curious to see if we could start a correspondence as we have things in common; he studied art and geography, he and I married at the same time, he will be having a child around the same time, we're both staying in a 'house' his grandmother claims is hers – both at the expense of the people! I wonder if over time I could convince him to contribute to abolishing this monarchy and paying reparations to the world's indigenous peoples from whom his wealth and power come. I make good headway on the letter and then I see him in a military uniform somewhere and throw the letter in the bin! Once he joined the military there was no chance – only a very rare specimen makes it out of there with any critical faculties!

The Gate

To leave the wing to attend a visit, class, medical centre, gym, church etc, you have one gate to go through which is centralised by 'people management'. You have to be ticked off a list to go anywhere or be accompanied by an officer. There is almost nothing digital or electronic about it – it's a printed sheet in which your name is highlighted when you leave and crossed through in black ink on your way back. You just provide your name, no prison card or otherwise. It probably hasn't changed for 100 years or more. When you get past the gate you can often be searched – I seem to get searched each time – they pad you down – front and back – check the elastic band – front and back – and check your papers with you. Your towel etc gets checked when going to the gym too. It's wonderfully old fashioned.

Showers

In A Wing there around 80 cells on each floor and there are four floors. Every alternate cell has been converted in a toilet room. Each floor has a shower room the size of a cell. In A Wing there are no doors in the shower room, just panels like a gym shower or school toilets. You can only see from the shoulders up if you are walking past. There are on average four showers – some floors have a few more. You ask around where the best showers are on your way in – people happily tell you. 'Best' means hottest and sometimes 'cleanest'. Ground floor showers are usually good as people on the ones often have the most 'privileges' – it's the floor where the hot plate servers are, the gym orderlies, gardeners etc. The showers don't have handles, they have a single press button, which can turn the shower on for a second or a few minutes. To keep the shower on you just keep pressing the button. Sometimes you have to press on another unused shower to bring the full force of the heat on. Surprisingly you can usually get a shower straight away. I've been showering every other day just cause there is so little time to get stuff done in 'association', but with the gym on the schedule it's a shower every day. My observation, be it correct or not, is that the cleanest fellow prisoners are the brothers of Muslim faith and black British prisoners. They shower and clean and clean – super clean folks! It is true to say very rarely have I seen an Englishman in the shower. There are many people that don't shower very often at all!

Unlike filmmakers want to imagine, there are no attacks in the shower etc. It just hasn't happened. If there is any 'agro' it's almost always between a prisoner and a screw. I saw no sign whatsoever of gangs in here. All I saw in the showers were good people chatting to each other, giving each other advice and support. No horror stories to report so people build sympathy for me on the 'outside'. No excuses yet for those who pull back from action for fear of going to prison. Most people shower in their underpants and with sandals on. Almost everyone is fit. There are very few unfit people in prison and they do tend to stand out.

There are no walls or barriers between the showers – two showerheads on the three facing walls – six in total. I've never seen six people in there. I've not been to many gyms (at swimming pools etc) at all but I imagine it's quite a similar set up? Soap and shampoo are available from the screws in the landing office – when it's open. Oils etc can be bought from the canteen list. Nothing can be brought in. Shavers can also be obtained from the landing office.

Ties

I noticed this evening a screw (nice chap) had his tie undone and that it was a clip tie. Mentioned it to him and he said if it wasn't, if it was a normal tie, the guards would be very vulnerable to being strangled.

Accounting

Had a nice chat with the chap that works for Working Links – the people that place us on computer courses etc. Mentioned that he used to be an accountant but left as he found it dishearteningly political and deeply corrupt. Said he had to stop working at a very well known architecture charity because of the political accounting that was going on – never looked back, but quite disappointed by the experience of it.

Cops in prison

Overheard my first conversation today that suggested there were many undercover police in prison. One chap in the showers was speaking to a guy about x and y, and then when he left he said to his friend, "They better get that guy outta here soon. Everyone knows he's a fucking cop." The guy did seem very uneasy. But with tattoos on his neck etc. He was either a con they have turned or a crazy mother phucker like the cops that have had kids with activists and so on ... prepared to tattoo their necks or have children with activists etc.

These people are nuts! Imagine being so fucked up, so ill with Stockholm Syndrome or so blackmailed, you would have think it's a–okay to have children with 'green activists' or get a tattoo on your neck and live in prison?

When the 'undercover cop' left, the guy and I then spoke about his last 16 years in and out of prison – he's 32 and wants to go straight, "live a quiet life". "Move to Bournemouth and never live in London again. It's too expensive, brother, too crowded, too hostile, too many problems here. Never coming back, brother, never want to see this place again." He was a religious convert and you could again see the power and strength that came with this and how other prisoners were drawn to him because of his composure and stature.

Drugs in prison

He spoke of what prisons were like when he first came in – nothing like today with a TV, toilet etc. He said the screws were brutal, ex–military, racist and the governor was always military like; "violent people, all they know is violence. Nothing like it is now – but you have to watch out for the drugs they inject you with, brother we seen so many go mad from whatever that stuff is."

Tense

The wing has felt tense over the last few days – the screws particularly so. Not sure what is going on but it's here, I can feel it. Hope nothing serious is about to kick off. Just seems tense – seems to happen every few weeks – the tension just steps up. The screws become very efficient on their communication; their eyes and pupils are a little smaller. The prisoners jostle a little more waiting in line for food, hassle the servers for more food etc. Maybe I'm over sensitive to these changes. But something is definitely up.

Saturday 25 November 2012

First dreams of a life with Deepa and the children; our little ones. Two of them. One in each arm. Was hot, we lived somewhere hot. It was joyful! Try not to think about it too much as things still don't always work out. Even though we are 'in the west', pregnancy and birth are still very dangerous periods for mother and baby. Well through trials comes joy LOL!

Trenton Oldfield

Sunday 26 November 2012

There was a terribly energetic wind storm last night! It was pulsing, sweeping through the prison. It must have been very dramatic on the outside as it was dramatic in here. Wind, let alone a wind storm, is such a rare occurrence in London that I tried to stay awake and feel it, listen to it. As the windows have grates on them the air just comes rushing in. It's wonderful having these pulses of cold air dropping through the windows and then feeling it come across one's body. As the rain came in through the roof the other day, so too does the wind, and it was pulsating through vast empty halls and pushing under the door making wonderful noises and providing the opportunity to feel the wind pushing and circulating across one's body. So rare are these extreme 'natural' moments in London, I've begun to cherish them and to pay as much attention to these moments as is possible at the time.

If anyone has asked me what I miss about living in Australia I always say without hesitation, I miss the breezes, the air. The way an ocean breeze drops into a room from outside and glides over one's body is life giving to me. It's very erotic/sensual, for me in any case. Those swooping ocean breezes are hard to ignore, hard not to pay attention to. They are not spirits but it's not hard to imagine that they could be! London is most of the time a city somehow just perfect for work – people only really pay attention to the weather if it's snowing or a cloudless hot day – both as we know are very rare – happen once or twice a year. It's a city that feels to me as if it has a dome over it – regulating the weather to cloud cover all year round. It's rare to feel anything emotional or be affected by the weather here. I know my moods are rarely affected by the weather, which is quite different to other places I've lived. Rarely are there wind storms, thunder storms, hot cloudless days or snow covered streets. Is there anything more arresting than an unexpected late afternoon thunder storm in the heat of summer? I have the fondest memories of watching storms develop over the ocean and roll in across the city; the smell of rain on the forest floor, on the tarmac roads; the cracks of thunder and the excitement of watching the lightning rods, watching the line of clouds shift day to night; the giant puddles which you could drown in; the feeling of being soaked but not worrying as you will dry off again in half an hour. It's an emotional rollercoaster that forces one to leave here and wonder about our natural world, our place in it. I miss everything about this.

In London you can rely on constant cloud cover – constant emotionless cloud cover. The last relatively decent summer was in 2006. For the past six years I have worn a coat every day through six summers. In fact there would be only a handful of days I've not worn my 'mackintosh' since I bought it on sale in 2003. It's perfect for 363 days of the year! This is a weather, a city, for work. It's brilliant if you're working or studying as very rarely is any day a 'down tools' and enjoy life type of day. You could live here all year and only three to four times a year be reminded that you're part of the natural world, feel part of our natural world. Work seems a very good option on another cloud covered, non-descript, emotionless day. It's addictive. The other aspect that makes it addictive for me is the fact that it only takes me 15 minutes to walk between capitalism's HQ, the Bank of England, and Amnesty International's HQ. This is both physical and metaphorical. How could there not be a clash of ideas in a city with this situation? How could that clash not become addictive? That said I am increasingly concerned with Amnesty International's 'leadership' these days and wonder if they are not just an arm of the UK government's Foreign Office. There is of course this great worry forever at the back of my mind that while London is forever and always busy with talks, conferences, activities and so on, it may not be that critical. It might just be busy treading water; the busyness a confusion to substance?

Nonetheless, today is one of those very rare days when the sky is without clouds; a wonderful day to be out and about! The sun is shining and the storm seems, from the trees I can see, to have brought down all but the strongest leaves; it's winter now, there is no disguising it! Today, the ground will most likely be covered with those beautiful leaves. And if it rained in the storm, it will have helped wash away some of the dirt so well known in London!

Thinking about life in London sets one on this process of wondering where else it is possible to live, where else to have the intellectual activity but also be able to feel alive, part of our natural world? As a European I don't think I should live outside of Europe without an invitation, so I keep coming back to thinking of how to make a life in Switzerland. I'm not interested in its clean streets and vile banking system but I am interested in its natural landscapes. Perhaps it is because of my childhood there but there is little to compare to swimming in mountain lakes, jumping in rivers that flow through city centres and walking in mountains. Perhaps this will be 'my escape', this is where I've felt the 'natural world' at its most enchanting – ancient, dangerous, beautiful, invigorating. With Deepa's injuries perhaps this is where I can take the children on walks, jumping into flowing rivers, skiing, snow shoeing? Maybe it's the Himalayas where Deepa is from? Our child will be from both places! I'm not sure. But the mountains is where I feel most at home and most energised; the storms, the potential danger from cliffs and avalanches, the reminder of our existence around every corner? It's where you would take a day off to watch the snow, or make sure you take your holiday so as not to miss jumping in that river or walking through mountain meadows. Wonder if it will happen or if London's 'weather dome' of seductive intellectual possibility and constant clashes will trap us, hold us here even longer?

Lunch

Lunch was amazingly early again today, though I do enjoy the banter with the 'hot plate lads' whatever time of day it is! Always up for a swimming joke and also legal advice etc. It's a burst of energy – short and sharp. Good guys. Like the guys on B Wing. Real characters. Somehow 'cause you see them twice a day you feel like you know them. Latest advice was to contact my MP urgently if I'm not given the home curfew tag. They also made a joke to make sure it's waterproof so I can swim LOL! Brilliant!

Marxism Church

This morning many want to go off to Christian services, most to the RC service. Throughout the week Sikh, Hindu, Muslim and Jewish services are held. I wonder what it would take to have Marxism services? Considering how religious in nature his arguments are and how so many follow him in such a religious manner, surely it could be possible? What would it need to be registered as a religion to hold services in prison? Could it be a way to get his ideas across in prison? Could there be a two-hour sermon and then religious classes each week? What does it take to be a registered church and able to hold services in prison? Would it be possible? Something I will research later, when 'out', and see if I can start to hold services! I will be like most priests/ministers – a non-believer and actually arguing for something else but coming across as a pious Marxist LOL!

Without a doubt the last two weeks have been very difficult for me in here! *Love and Capital* has brought up a great many issues for me: personal, political, tactical. It has been quite a confronting and unsettling time! I have always been quite apprehensive about Marxism for two main quite anti-intellectual reasons. Firstly, I could never reconcile how so many entirely ineffectual bourgeois 'academics' and hangers-on openly called themselves Marxists and how enthusiastically the middle classes took to it, whilst most workers of the world have been and remain sceptical. And secondly, how religious it all seemed; in its request for sacrifices now and promises of salvation 'possibly tomorrow, but certainly in the future'. And how its leaders considered themselves smarter, more advanced; if only the masses were woken up; no longer ignorant and unaware of their situation.

Having read the book it has helped me understand why Marxists have never come to the defence of the world's indigenous peoples, who they somehow consider as backward and their destruction a sad but necessary sacrifice (murder) on the long march of 'progress' and salvation. I've found it difficult, very difficult, to have some of my most unpleasant uncertainties confirmed. It is the opposite of what I was wishing for and has been, as a result, hugely unsettling. I've not done much but read this book and spend hours in contemplation. I'm not sure I have written any letters for a week, possibly two. I'm not feeling very well.

Reading *Love and Capital* has been like trying to take a much looked forward to bath and finding out the plug is missing. I had been hoping the hot and cold waters would combine, fill the bath right up to the top so I could soak in it, relieving my pains, allowing myself time to reflect and hoping that I would step out of it clean, calm and revitalised. Without a plug I expelled significant energy trying anything that would cover the hole; even using my own hands to cover the hole, hoping the waters would rise. There came a point when I realised there was no way to plug the hole and I had to let the water from the tap just drain away, making the most of the situation by splashing some of the warm water onto my body. It has also, as I wrote the other day, been very difficult to read how so much tragedy can take hold of just one family. I have had no choice but to wonder what impact this lens on life Deepa and I embody will end up having on our own family. Does it have to be such a tragedy? Is tragedy a result of being like this?

Trenton Oldfield

It has also been difficult to read that Marx thought it was entirely okay to have a nanny/housekeeper and other domestic staff most whom worked day and night just 'for board'. And, in the end, that Marx had a child with their long suffering 'housekeeper' – not unlike similar power imbalances that slave owners were taking advantage of in other parts of the world around the same time. The child was cast out from the house and hidden from the rest of the family until much later. What 'revolutionary of the workers' has a nanny alienated from her own family in order to clean his house, cook his meals and raise his numerous children and at the same time force her to expel and alienate her and his own child from the home? Such practices only encourage an already critical eye to question even more.

How can you not be unsettled by Marx's time–consuming, adolescent attacks on anarchists and anarchism? How can you not feel perplexed by his continual arguments for and assurance in the idea of nation states, in parliaments? How could I not feel deeply uncomfortable and hurt by his paternalism towards 'peasants' and workers – and his disinterest, often opposition, to indigenous peoples' existence? Why aren't people deeply sceptical about an idea that suggests some people are more advanced and thought to have 'progressed' more than others? How could the concept of 'progress' capture him and thousands since … when even if they used their own ideas of 'scientific measurement and evidence' it doesn't compute; it doesn't reconcile. There may be more different technology but this has only increased the levels of violence whilst increasingly removing the perpetrator from being present or getting blood on them. How can you not become concerned about a man that never once took to the barricades despite being in very close proximity to them on several occasions? How can you not be critical of a man that constantly tells those on the barricades that they got their timing wrong, that their deaths and jail sentences have been for nothing, that they are fools? How can it be that people can uncritically accept 'deliverance' arguments inherent in Marxism that are so similar to leaps of faith like Christianity though couched in science? How isn't there more unease with an idea, an argument, that promises salvation only if 'a' then 'b' then 'c' happens?

In the end it's no surprise to me that the 'middle–class intellectual' took to Marxism so willingly. Like those that have studied theology sincerely, at a certain point you surely come to know it's all a complete load of bollocks? You know that there will be no second coming, that god doesn't exist and that no utopia will appear as a result of the pursuit of scientific 'progress'. With this knowledge you are safe to replace 'the good books' with other/whatever books that help you keep that view out over the people from that Ivory Tower. In the case of priests, you can do anything you like because you know there is no hell! Having studied religion or Marxism sincerely surely you learn it can't possibly be anything more than seductive ideas that play off people's worst biases and the entirely, ENTIRELY unforgivable promise of a delayed justice and a delayed paradise?

It's been interesting to read that both Marx and Jenny came from quite religiously active families. My speculation, stuck in this cell, without any way whatsoever to substantiate it, is that if you have studied both you would probably see that Marx picked up many of his 'best lines' from religions. However you also probably know there are many emotional and financial perks to perpetuating a myth that you can regularly become the centre of and are seen as an oracle into 'truths' that could potentially be humankind's (or part of humankind's) saviour. You know a Marxist utopia/second coming will never happen but instead of calling it out, you've become used to and enjoy people herding to you, seeking your wisdom at times of crisis (every 3–5 years for priests due to regular natural disasters around the world but every 15–25 years for Marxists as they can't claim natural disasters, only wisdom into economic disasters – at this stage LOL!). Sheesh, it's been a tough two weeks but it's the sort of sauna/sweat lodge I had been hoping might happen from these books and from being in here!!

Thursday 29 November 2012
Another set of books

There must be 10 books that haven't made it through despite the policy that says it's okay to have books delivered. I'm worried these wonderful gifts will be lost to the system. Deepa sent across the policy and it says books are 100% okay and if not can be deposited with my other items in reception if not passed through. Why they have to be destroyed seems like pure madness to me – even if they could possibly include drugs as suggested to me. One screw has told me books that have been sent via Amazon are okay as they will have been checked by sniffer dogs for drugs! This is the madness I will never understand – how is it that a global corporation that has managed to pay no tax in the UK, has destroyed independent bookshops and so on and which most people consider to be 'criminal', is seen as 'ethical and lawful' enough to check for drugs. They probably run part of the global drug business! Who better than a delivery company prisons think is ethical and lawful!

Computer says 'no'

As it becomes apparent that I will be released on the 4th December, I'm starting to remember how frustrating things could be 'on the outside', those frustrating 'computer says no' moments. When x can't happen until y happens. Imagine what it is like for people in here who think x or y will happen but the form has gone missing, the pre-sentence report hasn't been done, the judge is ill, the forms can't be found in America or alike. Spoke with a guy I thought had left the prison. Said they brought him back because the trial couldn't be held because no report had been done by x team. He states his innocence and really thought he would have been home today. However, because he is on remand, he had to come back here. He now has to wait, here in prison, for the end of January for the trial to start. He could well be here for months. The trouble is he just got custody of his seven-year-old daughter in America. He has only been able to call her a few times as it took weeks for the prison staff to agree the phone number and place it on the system. His ex-wife is dead. His daughter is staying with a foster family (which we know are not great places for young girls to be). Remand should only be used as the very last resort and for very particular crimes, it's much too damaging on the individual and their family. Today and yesterday we've had 'association' for just 20–30 mins. There is always a line for the phone – people have just five minutes before it cuts off after a few beeps. With hundreds of people and just six phones it's always difficult to actually get on the phone. I heard his conversation with his daughter – he repeatedly told her she wasn't abandoned, he would be coming for her. The time difference mid-west America and school times etc mean it's almost impossible for him to contact her. It's eating him up. I've not seen someone walk as he does to get to the phone before others. Yesterday the phones weren't working due to the rain apparently. He was distraught.

In here small clerical errors, delays (probably increasing due to funding/staffing cuts) have huge impacts on people's lives – huge. People lose family, businesses, livelihoods and months, years of their lives. It's very serious. No doubt people think if they are criminals they don't need 'the system' to work for them – they are the worst of the worst, why wouldn't we abandon them? There is no doubt in my mind that any part of the 'justice system' should be highly tuned, effective and entirely focussed on the prisoner. I'm sure people that know nothing of classism and racism would be shocked if they found themselves in here. It's fundamentally important prisoners are treated with dignity and as full citizens. Everything should be done to have people out of prison as the greatest impact is not on the prisoner but those 'at home'. There is no reason for loved ones to suffer, is there? I can't think of a reason. The prison system must work for the prisoner and their families.

HMP Wormwood Scrubs

Speaking with someone today from the 'threes' who has been in and out of prison for the last 20 years he said HMP Wormwood Scrubs is by far the worst in London – said it's always at the bottom of the ratings. Said he's trying to get transferred as soon as possible – can't stand it here. I asked him what and why. He said food, quality of cells, access to training and that screws here are always the most ignorant. Said there is a weird culture here from the main governor down! Oh man.

Cooking

As someone that enjoys food but has never taken it seriously as most people I know do, it's a joy for me to have food ready twice a day! It's always been important to staying awake and alive but I've never gone for the 'food culture' that most peers seem very into - some even taking pictures and setting up blogs on the topic! That doesn't mean I'm not over the moon when great food comes my way, particularly Deepa's cooking OMGoodness! I wonder how many in here are the same? Cooking is one of the routines I've found the most frustrating outside. It's the time it takes to collect, prepare, cook and clean. I've always wanted to spend less time on food and more time working, reading and doing things! I never went for the 'foodies' who seemed much more interested in food than people. However I'm wondering if it might be worthwhile teaching cooking in here? Might take away the concern and the banality of meals I'm sure many experience 'on the outside'. I've enjoyed not having to think about, collect, prepare and clean up for each meal – which can take so very much time. Collecting my food twice a day has allowed me significantly more time to read and write. I'm very grateful for the removal of what I consider to be a humdrum or over romanticised part of life – for me. I'm sure others would feel differently but for me, it's been brilliant! Though I do feel deeply terrible that Deepa is in ill health and stress, has had to look after herself, undertake this humdrum stuff herself – even though she doesn't consider it as such.

TV

Two things I've noticed from TV – maybe I'm projecting? (1) There is a strangely high number of people wearing suits and very conservative suits – waistcoats etc. Gary Barlow, some boy band, guests and even hosts of naff trivia shows! Nothing tells me suits are 'finished' more than Gary Barlow wearing one on X Factor! Is this the pre–crash 1920s again? Should we see this as a sign? How deeply conservative and sheepish have we become? (2) Today TV adverts and shows seem to be showing women chasing men! There was no way this was the case when I was growing up! Men needed to learn how to be of interest to women to even capture their attention. On TV ads as a kid it was without doubt men that needed to chase women and there was much humour made at the expense of men trying to do this! Now women are shown to dress seductively etc in order to attract men! How should we be reading this shift? Is there a new wave of misogyny here or on its way?

I can't get over those Christmas adverts where women do absolutely everything and somehow feel good about it. How can companies promote such ideas? And I've mentioned it before but where is all this snow? When did the UK become Sweden? When did women start the chasing of men? That's crazy! When did that change? I can't believe in 2012/2013 women (mums) are the ones shown to be wonderful for doing everything, exhausted etc, but it's all okay cause people are smiling when the turkey or whatever is brought to the table! Is this the 18th century when such a slave was expected to be happy for making her slave master happy? These adverts, combined with the ones where women/girls chase men/boys, mixed with all those awful suits people are wearing, must signifying that we are not 'living in exciting times' but rather worryingly deeply conservative times. I've only seen one 'black' family also in these Christmas adverts – it's a Tesco ad. The woman is still the happy slave, though to her family! Phuck me this is a joke!!? Who the phuck makes these and who the phuck acts in them; allows themselves to 'act' in such adverts! The Lynx advert is a fucking disgrace; hundreds of semi-naked women walk in a trance-like condition to a man on a 'Noah's Ark'!

Saturday 01 December 2012

I've been manically writing letters. I'm not making lists; I'm just going through the piles of mail. I hope it will be okay. I hope I finish. It will be awful if I don't manage to write to everyone. Some letters and postcards don't have postal addresses so maybe I will make it through. I really hope so. I'm rushing as it seems I will be released on home detention on Tuesday. That's not much time to finish these letters, write in my diary, and try and read all these books LOL! I'm not sure it's possible! I also somehow want to take some time to think, to feel this place, to think of 'life on the outside'. Sun knows with a little one on the way life outside is likely to be quite different. Up until this point I have been fighting for my metaphorical children; the future generations. Things have just got a lot more serious. Now there is shape and form to the ideas I have been fighting for. I could never let my little ones face being indentured, enslaved, humiliated and without agency. If it means I'm back in prison again and again, it won't stop me from this fight for equality, dignity and justice for all. It's up to them! Put on the lens of equality in all you do, or expect me, expect us. We are not going away and you won't enslave me or even try to do it to my children. I don't care if you criminalise me, send me to your jails, that's on you. If I have to use my body again, then I will. Whatever it takes.

Monday 3 December 2012

If everything goes to as it should, and I have been told everything is in order, then I shall be released from this prison and put on home detention for another two months or there about. I will have to be in my apartment from 7pm and not leave again until 7am. Such is this life. At least I can be home and we can really start working on the festival! Someone will come tomorrow evening to slap a digital tag around my ankle. The tag sends a message to a box that will also be in my home – confirming that I am there. It's barbaric but such is this life! Someone told me it can be tracked anywhere as well and of course I am not surprised to hear this. While my 'crime' didn't happen in the home, most crimes do, so it seems odd to force people to be home. My 'crime' happened in the early afternoon so it seems odd to be on curfew in the evenings! I have a feeling the whole thing is really (1) an avenue for our politicians' friends in corporations like Serco, G4S and so on to keep the drain of money flowing from our treasury to them, and (2) a reflection on the over criminalisation of people – hoping we continue to feel disempowered and that society will continue to look down on us, be afraid of us. All it will do to me, I think, is ensure I'm even more focussed on the festival than usual LOL!

I've been frozen by the 'light, bright light at the end of the tunnel'. I have so much to write about my time in here and at the same time I am wondering if anything I write even matters as I know I won't forget a moment of this, any of the people in here. Maybe I should sleep? I'm not sure when I will have the chance to sleep in the middle of the day! Maybe I should read; when will I ever have the chance again to lie on a bed in the middle of the day and read the books I have wanted to read for years? If I don't manage to reply to everyone today, I will do so when I am out! Should I pack tonight? Is that bad luck? Is it a similar mistake as wearing a suit on sentencing day? There have been many wonderful aspects of being in here, I shall list them only today, as I must really unfreeze myself and get cracking on things:

- The chance to be absent from the piercing annoyance that comes from the noise (rarely actions) of all those fraudulent–pseudo–academics! Not having anything to do with their desperately low self-esteem issues has been amazing! I plan to not waste a minute of my time on their issues but I now have many clear ideas for tackling them in a much–needed conference and furthering most of the issues we started in TINAG in a book or blog.

- The chance to finally read some of the books I have always wanted to but never had the time to do.

- The chance to be free, entirely free, from the World Wide Web.

- The chance to correspond via letter with some of the most wonderful people on planet earth in a manner of robust honesty, thoughtfulness and sincerity. I will miss this more than anything. I will miss these people more than anything. I know it will change when I'm out – it's just not possible to correspond the same way, or about the same issues on email. I know I will have less time and my attention will be all over the place again. I know people will think, understandably, that everything is okay again when I am out of prison. It has been amazing though, a real gift!

- The chance to not be on any CCTV cameras! The chance to have disappeared from the five million+ CCTV cameras for two months.

- The chance to not have to deal with or think about everyday domestic practices like shopping, cleaning, cooking, laundry and so on and so forth.

- The chance to slow down, slow right down, enough to know the true time of a day. The chance to step aside from the rat race for a while. The opportunity to reflect. If only this could be built into our social welfare system, three months once every seven years?

- Most importantly, the chance to meet some truly wonderful people; good people. People in here care about each other, support each other. I have felt their solidarity with me, my actions. I hope they have felt my solidarity with them.

- Prison has made me 100 times stronger and clearer of mind, purpose and action. I feel more content than at any stage yet in regards to my actions. I had no choice but to do it. And I would do similar actions again, without hesitation. Maybe not the same action.

When I am out I want to make sure I write and talk about the following things:

- The urgent need for charities that will work on reforming judges and the judicial system. There is no doubt in my mind there is significant and urgent work that needs to be undertaken! If any group of people 'in' the justice system need reform and rehabilitation it is this minority group.

- How the fear of prison, 'the middle-class hell on earth' is unfounded and comes only from their own snobbery and their desire to have someone available to them to denigrate, step on. Through cultural mechanisms such as television, films, fiction and the news, 'prison' is heavily performed and full of cultural symbols. My guess is it's mostly to do with the ongoing attack by the middle classes on the/our poor and the 'black other' – the perpetuation of a 'vicious poor' for their own middle-class interests.

- I want to 'demystify' prison based only on my own experience – suggesting that the fear of prison is the greatest panopticon, the greatest control mechanism. The fear of prison might well stop us from taking many risks that are needed. No longer fearing it might be a very powerful moment.

- How neither prisoner nor prison guard could explain why we were in prison, what the point of our incarceration was, what was meant to happen as a result of us being here. How prisons seem to exist just because we think they have always existed. I want to write about how they couldn't possibly exist if we actually took a moment to consider them, what they are and what they do.

- The devastation caused to lives as a result of being held on remand and how class war against the poor is once again played out in this arena.
  How one must always carry £20 cash, the phone numbers of loved ones and a lawyer on a piece of paper. You never know when you will be taken and you need some money in prison straight away to start any chance of a decent defence in court and your own life.

- If there was no fear of the criminal justice system, prison and criminal records were discontinued, imagine what could be achieved, almost overnight. Not having a fear of prison would also mean they would finally lose their cultural meaning – probably closing down within a few years. The demise of prisons would also mean a significant shift had occurred in ideas of class and race also.

- How 'criminal records' and the bourgeois ideas of 'trustworthiness and respectability' are condemning tens of millions to an inevitable cycle of great difficulty by criminalising individuals and their families. Should prisons continue to exist, people should either 'do the time' or 'have a criminal record' for x period of time. Both should never occur. Prisoners shouldn't be demonised.

Before I step back into the streets that are on Google Maps, these are the stories I have torn out of newspapers in just the last few weeks – just to remind me of what that glorious life on 'the outside' means for the little one that will arrive this summer:

- British Government involved in detention without trial and extra–judicial extraditions of many people in its 'war on terror'.

- British Government holds its own citizens for 7 years without trial, extradites them without charge to America where three of the 5 have never set foot.

- British Government continues with its plans to establish Secret Courts. Parliament likely to give agreement.

- University fees cap (£9,000 pa!) could be eroded within just a few years due to planned ongoing funding cuts to education. Applications down at some universities by up to 25% – around 10% across England & Wales.

- British colonial government covered up massacre and targeted killings in Kenya.

- No plans to reinstate EMA despite significant impact on poorest.

- Owners of overcrowded slum–condition accommodation for cleaners 'imported' from 'eastern Europe' to clean Olympics are given 'all clear'.

- Report ordered on how people were tricked and forced to work on the Elizabeth Windsor's River Pageant weekend for free is yet to appear.

- Government goes ahead with 'highland clearance' laws which will cap housing benefits. London councils already moving claimants to areas in the north of England.

-

    Squatting of empty homes has been criminalised. New laws being introduced to criminalise the squatting of empty commercial buildings also.

- Undercover police revealed to have formed long-term relationships with 'activists'. Some married and even thought to have had children before suddenly disappearing.

- Leveson Inquiry establishes well-known unsavoury links between the mainstream media, politicians and police/judiciary – 'problematic' and 'in need of reform'. LOL!

- After people's inquiry, police confirmed to have conspired to cover up preventable deaths and manslaughter of over 96 people at a football match in Hillsborough in April 1989.

- Inquiry called to be opened on evidence that police conspired to manipulate and fabricate evidence against protesters at Orgreave Miners' Strike.

- Jimmy Savile is thought to have abused over 300 people. Five other people arrested and charged on similar offences. A separate paedophile ring is thought to been linked/controlled through the Houses of Parliament.

- Harry Windsor has been caught naked on camera with women in Las Vegas, America. Mainstream media think it's a hoot!

- 'Royals' are reported to have had numerous private meetings with cabinet ministers and are known to have vetoed certain laws and influenced policy.

- Energy prices have been exposed by a whistleblower to have been rigged, cartel style. Domestic energy prices have gone up significantly in recent years.

- Birmingham City Council has lost a court case where it knowingly discriminated against its female employees, most of whom did 'working class' jobs as cooks, cleaners and care staff – underpaying them around £757 million.

- Major banks, including the people who owned RBS, are confirmed to have rigged the Libor rate. They are fined a tiny, insignificant amount in comparison to the money they made as a result of rigging the rate.

- British economy is in triple dip recession (Depression) due to the same things tube delays are blamed on: wind, rain, snow …

- British government/British armed forces confirmed to have undertaken extra–judicial murders in Northern Ireland.

- Policeman acquitted of killing member of the public who was passing through a protest. Crown Prosecution Service doesn't drop trumped up charges against two student protesters, one who was nearly killed by a police baton.

Post Script

A WING STATEMENT OF PURPOSE:
To provide a safe, secure and productive environment by facilitating access to employment, housing, mental health and addiction services so that 'revolving door' criminals are given the support to live law abiding and healthy lives upon release.

This A4 'Statement' was laminated and pinned to a notice board on A Wing's 'seconds'. It was the only 'statement of purpose' I came across at any stage in any of the four wings of Wormwood Scrubs I was incarcerated within. This statement was of particular interest as the question I asked almost everyone I spoke to (screws, my fellow prisoners, gym instructors, education staff and so on) was "what is prison for, what is meant to happen to us as a result of being in here?" Their answers were as obscure as this meaningless official 'statement of purpose'. 'Prisons' were probably unexplainable at any period however their existence today and their subsequent construction of 'prisoners' and 'criminals' is perhaps one of the most striking indictors of not only a disquieting lack of imagination but a desire to propel and maintain the idea of 'savage poor', a criminal underclass, those that should be kept away from civilisation; an 'uncivilised'.

Visual Diary

Silvine

perfecto

WSB 0399018

Oṁ

THE BHAGAVADGĪTĀ

or

THE SONG DIVINE

(With Sanskrit Text and English Translation)

Gita Press, Gorakhpur

India

HM PRISON
SERVICE

PRISONER
NAME AND NUMBER

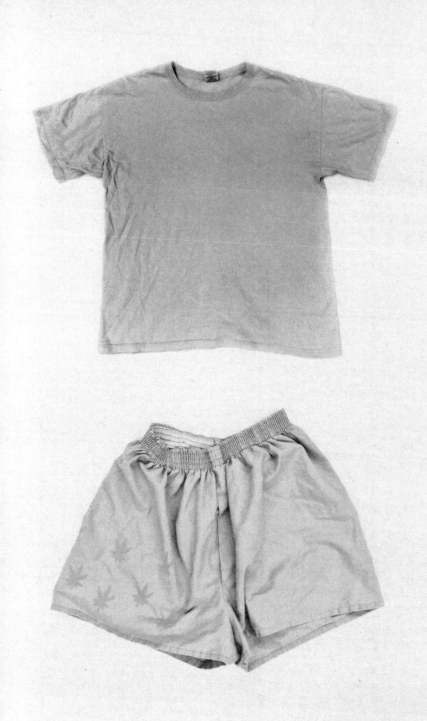

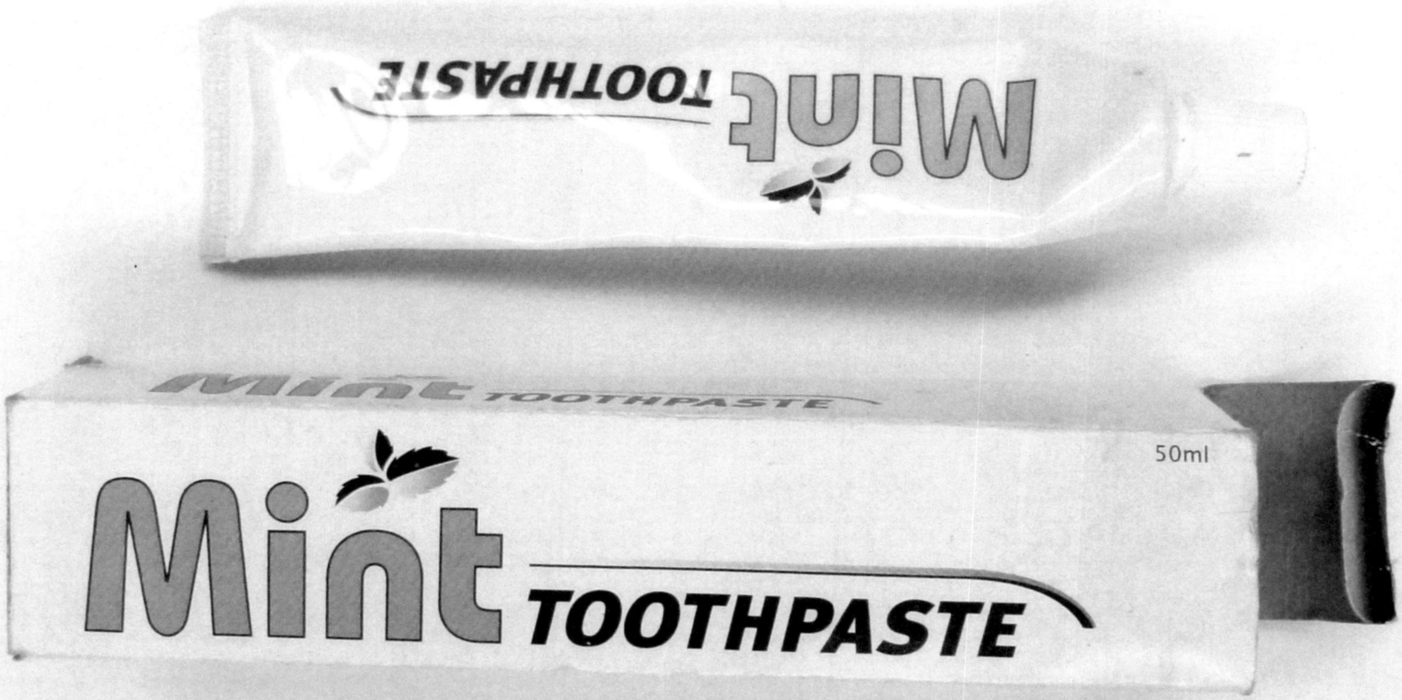
Mint
TOOTHPASTE
Mint
TOOTHPASTE
50ml

PAMPERED
ICE
BLUE
ANTI-PERSPIRANT

All day freshness
Long lasting protection

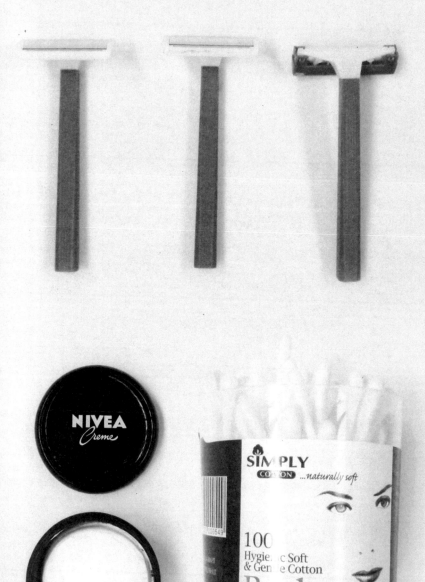

39p   39p

SPRING WATER
500ml ℮

CO REFILL PACK

97%
LESS PACKAGING WEIGHT

Red
Mountain

Medium
Roast

Rich & Smooth Coffee Granules

everyday
ginger
nuts
crunchy ginger biscuits
with a hint of lemon

a great tasting family favourite

150g

Hill everyday
ginger nuts

bebo
Light

MILK
CHOCOLATE
100g

55p
55p
55p

INDICTMENT

IN THE CROWN COURT AT ISLEWORTH

THE QUEEN - v - TRENTON OLDFIELD

TRENTON OLDFIELD is charged as follows:

STATEMENT OF OFFENCE

PUBLIC NUISANCE.

PARTICULARS OF OFFENCE

TRENTON OLDFIELD on the 7th day of April 2012, in the River Thames near Chiswick Eyot, caused a nuisance to the public by swimming into the path of The University Boat Race and causing it to be stopped.

Officer of the Court
14. 05. 12

URN: 01TX0074811

...ended on
...ntil
PREFERRED ON 14|05|12

In the Crown Court at ISLEWORTH

Case No: T20120506
Court Code: 475
PTI URN: 01TC0074812

Indictment
PSR
Antecedents
Psych reports
Other

Custody Officer NEIL JARMAN
(print name):
Date: 19/10/12
Time: 12 ш05 hrs

Order for imprisonment

Made under the Criminal Justice Act 2003

The defendant	TRENTON OLDFIELD (date of birth: 11-May-1976) was convicted of crime on 25-Sep-2012
	Details of the conviction and sentence are on the court record.
The Court ordered	on 19-Oct-2012 that the defendant serve a period of imprisonment, details of which follow.
Custodial sentences	The court ordered that the defendant be sentenced to 6 month(s) imprisonment.

An Officer of the Crown Court

Signed: MS STEF BRIDGES

Date: 19-Oct-2012

Associated Cases: None

H.M.P WORMWOOD SCRUBS RECEPTIONS INFORMATION SHEET

HM PRISON SERVICE

> Your Prison Number Is
>
> **A1010 CT**

THIS IS YOUR PRISON NUMBER. IT IS IMPORTANT THAT YOU REMEMBER IT IN ORDER TO COLLECT YOUR CANTEEN, WRITE LETTERS AND RECEIVE MEDICATION ETC.

What happens when prisoners first arrive at prison

There are a few procedures that take place when a prisoner first arrives at prison. These are done to make sure the prisoner has everything they need and to highlight any problems they may have such as a medical complaint.

The reception interview

Shortly after arriving at prison, you will have an interview with a member of the probation staff, or a personal officer'. A personal officer is a prison officer who has been allocated to individual prisoners. The reception interview is another chance for the prisoner to discuss any problems they may have. Prison staff are there to help if there is anything the prisoner does not understand or if they need any advice or support.

Prisoner's property / Full Searched

The first thing that happens is that the prisoner's property is listed by an officer and put into safe-keeping. Some of the items can be kept by the prisoner, the rest will be returned to them when they leave prison. Items that can not be retained or stored will be destroyed for example lighters, alcohol, tobacco and tobacco tools and all food items. During process you will be full searched by two male officers.

Checking the prisoner's health

The healthcare team will also interview you. It is important that every prisoner is assessed so that they can be given the proper care that they need whilst they are in prison. All this information is treated as confidential - just like going to a normal GP.

First Night Centre

This is to help you settle into prison life, an induction session has been developed to explain how the prison works and what is your responsibilities. It also helps you to think about making the best use of your time in custody.

Ongoing support

Of course, from time to time, prisoners may have worries or problems that they might need to speak to someone about. Their personal officer or the officer in charge of their wing or unit are there to talk problems through with prisoners. In addition prisoners can talk to a prison 'buddy', chaplain or directly to the Samaritans. **Samaritans 08457 90 90 90**

Visits Booking Times & Telephone Contact Numbers
09.30 – 11.00am Monday
09.00 – 11.30pm Saturday
Visits gate close: 10.30am and 15.30pm
0208 588 3504 or 0208 588 3566

Canteen

Your canteen is usually allocated on a weekly basis and clearly displayed on the wing normally either outside the landing office or on a notice board. Post days are displayed in a similar fashion around the wing.

Decency

The Prison Service is dedicated to treating prisoners with decency in a caring and secure environment. This is a very important area of our work and requires our staff develop positive relationships with prisoners. We believe that by treating people with decency, they will be more likely to go on to live useful and law-abiding lives that will benefit them as individuals and society as a whole.

We are committed to ensuring that staff, prisoners and all those visiting prisons or having dealings with the Prison Service are treated fairly and lawfully, irrespective of their race, colour, religion, sex or sexual orientation.

HMP WORMWOOD SCRUBS, DU CANE ROAD
LONDON, W12 0AE

London North East and East Courts
London Collection and Compliance Centre PO Box 31092 London SW1P 3WS
Payments 0300 790 9901 www.direct.gov.uk/payacourtfine
Information 020 7556 8500 www.cao.latestinfo.co.uk AP 31715

Mr TRENTON OLDFIELD
Flat 24 Myrdle Court
Myrdle Street   809
London
E1 1HP

Division: 078
New account number: **12053639I** TH
Born: 11 May 1976

Notice of transfer of fine

The financial penalties shown below have been transferred to this court for enforcement from Isleworth
Crown Court. The total amount to be paid is £ **750.00**

Date of Transfer: 29 October 2012
Date of Conviction: 19 October 2012

Please read the enclosed information 'How to Pay' and use your **new** account number whenever you make a
payment or contact the court.

C Jennings

Designated Officer

Date: 29 October 2012

Offences and penalties

Date	Offences and Impositions		Amount £
19 Oct 2012	Cause a public nuisance.	Costs	750.00
Time to pay:	The total amount on or before **28 October 2013**.	Total: £	**750.00**

Mr TRENTON OLDFIELD   6 November 2012/FINOT_29_0/9747.13/1

HMP WORMWOOD SCRUBS JANUARY 2012

PHYSICAL EDUCATION PROGRAMME

COMMENCEMENT DATE – 29 JANUARY 2012

TIMINGS	07:30 / 07:45	07:45 / 10:00	10:00 / 12:00	11:30 – 12:00 / 12:30 – 13:30	13:30 / 16:00	EVENING PE 16:30 / 18:00
MONDAY	Fabric & Equipment Check Staff Meeting Class Prep	Accredited Coursework Over 50's Remedial Health Care	Accredited Coursework A WING (60) Remedial		Accredited Coursework C WING (40) IDTS/SDP E Wing (20 Prisoners)	E Wing (50) EMPLOYED Super Enhanced (10)
TUESDAY	Fabric & Equipment Check Staff Meeting Class Prep	Accredited Coursework A WING (60) Football	D WING (60) Football		Accredited Coursework C WING Football (60)	E WING EMPLOYED (60 Prisoners)
WEDNESDAY	Fabric & Equipment Check Staff Meeting Class Prep	Accredited Coursework Induction Prep Volleyball Squad Remedial	B WING (50) Volle-ball Squad	MASS MOVEMENT/ADMIN	Accredited Coursework EXERCISE REFERAL CIRCUIT CLUB (60) Comberre Gym (20)	E WING (50) EMPLOYED Super Enhanced (10)
THURSDAY (кое-что)	Fabric & Equipment Check Staff Meeting Class Prep	Accredited Coursework GYM INDUCTION Remedial Induction	INDUCTIONS C WING (60) Paperwork		Accredited Coursework B WING Football (40 Prisoners) A WING (20 Prisoners) IDTS/SDP	D WING (50) EMPLOYED Super Enhanced (10)
FRIDAY	Fabric & Equipment Check Staff Meeting Class Prep	Accredited Coursework A WING (20) B WING (25) Basketball	C WING (45) Squad		STAFF LUNCH — D WING (50) Super Enhanced	E WING (40) EMPLOYED
WEEKEND PE	08:00 / 08:20	08:30 / 10:00	10:00 / 12:00		13:30 / 16:00	To maximise Gym numbers extra spaces will be offered to wings on a Ad-Hoc Basis
SATURDAY	Fabric & Equipment Check Staff Meeting Class Prep	A WING	B WING		C WING	
SUNDAY	Fabric & Equipment Check Staff Meeting Class Prep	D WING	E WING		VOLLEYBALL MATCH or B WING	

11:30 – 12:00 MASS MOVEMENT/ADMIN

12:30 – 13:30 STAFF LUNCH

PRISONS THAT YOU MAY BE ALLOCATED TO FROM WORMWOOD SCRUBS

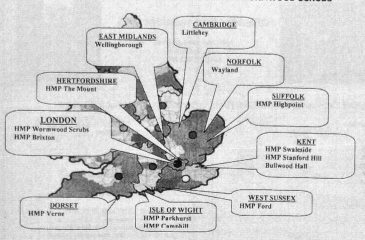

CATEGORY B	**HMP PARKHURST HMP CAMPHILL** NEWPORT, Isle of Wight, PO30 5NX Telephone: (01983) 554000		**HMP SWALESIDE** Barbazon Road, EASTCHURCH, Sheerness, Kent, ME12 4AX Telephone: (01795) 884100
CATEGORY C	**HMP BULLWOOD HALL** Road, Hickley, Essex SS5 4TE Telephone: (01702) 562800		**HMP THE MOUNT** Molyneaux Avenue, Bovingdon, HEMEL HEMPSTEAD, Herts, HP3 0NZ Telephone: (01442) 836300
	HMP THE VERNE The Verne, PORTLAND, Dorset, DT5 1EQ Telephone: (01305) 825000		**HMP LITTLEHEY** Perry, HUNTINGDON, Cambridgeshire, PE28 0SR Telephone: (01480) 333000
	HMP HIGHPOINT Stradishall, NEWMARKET, Suffolk, CB8 9YG Telephone: (01440) 823100		**HMP WORMWOOD SCRUBS** PO Box 757, Du Cane Road, LONDON, W12 0AE Telephone: (020) 8588 3200
	HMP WAYLAND Griston, Thetford, Norfolk, IP25 6RL Telephone: (01953) 804100		**HMP WELLINGBOROUGH** Millers Park, Doddington Road Wellingborough, Northants Telephone: (01993) 232700
CATEGORY D	**HMP STANDFORD HILL** Church Road, EASTCHURCH, Sheerness, Kent, ME12 4AA Telephone: (01795) 884500		**HMP FORD** ARUNDEL, West Sussex, BN18 0BX Telephone: (01903) 663000

DATE OF SENTENCE	CATEGORY	1ST REVIEW DATE	2ND REVIEW DATE	3RD REVIEW DATE

DATE OF NOTIFICATION	ISSUING STAFF MEMBER		COMMENTS	

Bail conditions from 23/05/2012 onwards

- Not to enter or remain within 100 metres of any road being used on that day for the passage of the Olympic Torch.
- Not to enter the City of Westminster on 04/06/2012, 06/06/2012, or 16/06/2012
- Not to enter the City of London on 05/06/2012
- Not to go within 100 metres of the River Thames on 02/06/2012 or 03/06/2012 except when travelling by underground rail service.
- Not to enter the Royal Borough of Windsor & Maidenhead at any time from 19/06/2012 to 23/06/2012 inclusive
- Not to enter South Oxfordshire District, Wycombe District or Wokingham Borough from 27/6/2012 to 02/07/2012 inclusive
- Not to Enter or remain within 100 meters of any existing or proposed Olympic competition venue within England and Wales, until 17th September 2012.

These amended conditions are sought to prevent the defendant committing further offences at the following events:

Olympic Torch Relay	19/5/2012 – 27/07/06
Diamond Jubilee Pageant on the Thames	03/06/2012
Concert at Buckingham Palace	04/06/2012
Thanksgiving service at St Paul's Cathedral	05/06/2012
Commonwealth Heads Community Lunch	06/06/2012
Trooping of the Colour	16/06/2012
Royal Ascot	19/06/2012 - 23/06/2012
Henley Royal Regatta	27/06/2012 – 01/07/2012
Olympic and Paralympic Games	27/07/2012 – 16/09/2012

How to pay

Please allow 5 days for any payment to reach your account.

Payments can be made 24 hours per day using credit or debit card (Visa, Visa Electron, Mastercard or Maestro) by telephoning:

0300 790 9901

or by going to the following internet address:

www.direct.gov.uk/payacourtfine

You will need to have your Division number **078** and Account number **12053639! TH**. Payments must be received on or before the date ordered.

If you would like any further information regarding your account please contact the court using the details located on the front of this document.

NOTE: Upon completion of your payment you will be given an authorisation number. You should keep this as proof of payment along with the date and amount paid.

The court will not issue you with a receipt. Any written request for a confirmation receipt would need to be accompanied by a stamped addressed envelope and directed to the address at the head of this letter.

Difficulty in making payments

If you cannot pay using credit or debit card, you did not submit a statement of financial circumstances to the court and cannot pay as instructed or if you can no longer pay as agreed due to a change in your financial circumstances please contact the Fines Team to discuss what options may be available.

If you require advice on managing your debt you can get free, confidential and independent advice by calling Community Legal Advice on 0845 345 4 345 or going to www.communitylegaladvice.org.uk

What should I do if I change my name or address?

If your name or address changes it is your responsibility to notify the court immediately with this new information using the contact details on the front of this document.

Offender Management Unit

HMP Wormwood Scrubs
Du Cane Road
London W12 0AE

HM PRISON SERVICE

WORMWOOD SCRUBS

Initial Categorisation & Allocation Information sheet for Offenders

Number:	A10 10 CT	Name:	OLDFIELD	Wing Location:	B3-46

You have been allocated to transfer to the following prison. Your move will take place once Population Management Section has allocated a vacancy to us.	You have been given the following security category:

				B	C	D

Category B Prisons

HMP Swaleside	
HMP Parkhurst	
Other * please specify location	

Category C Prisons

HMP Bullwood Hall	
HMP Wayland	
HMP Verne	
HMP The Mount	
HMP Highpoint	
HMP Bure	
HMP Huntercombe	
HMP Birmingham (Suitable for Overcrowding drafts)	
HMP Wormwood Scrubs (Further Charges)	WSEM
HMP Brixton	
Other * please specify location	

Category D Prisons

HMP Brixton	

*The Prison to which you have been allocated is only **provisional** and may be subject to change at any time.*

YOUR SENTENCE PLAN
(OASys)

❑ If you have been sentenced to more than one year but less than four years with a minimum 6 months to serve you will have a an OASys assessment completed within 8 weeks of your sentence start date. This "Sentence Plan" will set out your offending behaviour program and any other targets required to help you return to society better able to manage your life. This Sentence Plan will be reviewed every 12 months. Your categorisation will be reviewed at the date specified on your notification slip.

❑ If you have been sentenced to four years or more you will have a an OASys assessment completed within 8 weeks of your sentence start date This "Sentence Plan" will set out your offending behaviour program and any other targets required to help you return to society better able to manage your life. This Sentence Plan will be reviewed twelve-monthly and your categorisation will be reviewed at the same time.

❑ If you have any questions regarding your Sentence Plan / OASys or allocation you should contact the Offender Management Unit by application

Offender Management Unit Staff
SO D Bloor
Officer Anderson Officer
Officer Webster Officer Manton
Officer O'Callaghan Officer Cole
Officer Kirkham
Psych Assistants
Ms K Taunton
Mr A Elliot Ms J Haria
Ms S Hatcher Ms M Terry

Prisoners' Visits Booking Application Form

To book a visit you must complete the Visits booking application form. The forms are located on all residential units.

Failure to complete the application form correctly will result in the form being returned to you and you visit will not be booked.

Information required.

- Your name
- Number
- Location
- Date.

You will also be required to provide the following details for your **visitor(s)** and your preferred date and time you wish for your visit to take place.

- Name
- Address
- Date of Birth
- Relationship
- Three proposed dates for the visit

This information is required for each person (max of 3 adults) visiting including children

Applications must be completed and sent to the visits booking department a minimum of 7 days in advance of your preferred visit date/s, as identified on your application form

Once the application has been processed you will be sent a reference number on a "Confirmation of Social Visits Application form".

It is your responsibility to ensure your visitors are aware of the date the visit will take place and the reference number allocated. Failure to do so will result in your visitors being denied entry to the establishment.

Please also note it is your responsibility to ensure you have sufficient pin phone credit in you account to contact your visitor/s.

HMP Wormwood Scrubs Visits Booking Application Form
CONVICTED PRISONERS ONLY

Number .... Name .... Location.......... Date................

Failure to complete this application form correctly will result in the form being returned to you and your visit **will not** be booked.

Please note: Applications must be received a **minimum of 7 days in advance** of your Preferred visit dates, as identified below.

Please state 3 preferred times and dates that you are able to keep. We will endeavour to book your first request.

	Day	Date	Time (AM or PM)
Preference 1			
Preference 2			
Preference 3			

Check Landing notice for visits times

Adult Visitor Details

Please note that if you do not provide full details then your booking will not be processed.

Visitor 1		
	Surname	
	First Name	
	Address	
	Town	
	County	
	Postcode	Telephone Number
Relationship		
Date of Birth		

Visitor 2		
	Surname	
	First Name	
	Address	
	Town	
	County	
	Postcode	Telephone Number
Relationship		
Date of Birth		

Visitor 3		
	Surname	
	First Name	
	Address	
	Town	
	County	
	Postcode	Telephone Number
Relationship		
Date of Birth		

Children Visitor Details (All those aged under 10yrs)

Surname	First name
Address	
Date of Birth	Child Relationship

Surname	First name
Address	
Date of Birth	Child Relationship

Surname	First name
Address	
Date of Birth	Child Relationship

If there is a requirement for extra children names please use over the page

Chaplaincy Worship/Activities

> Please ensure you are ready and waiting to be unlocked for the act of worship.

	Time
SUNDAY	
Roman Catholic Mass	09.00/10.30
C of E Service	09.15/10.45

MONDAY

Somali Support Group	09.00
Sikh Service	14.00
Buddhist Meditation	14.00
Fatherhood Workshop	14.00
Bible Study (D & E)	18.00

TUESDAY

WEDNESDAY

Hindu Worship	14.00

THURSDAY

Islamic Class	09.00
MARK Time	14.00

FRIDAY

Sikh Class	09.00
Muslim Prayers	13.00

SATURDAY

COMMUNITY CHAPLAINCY

Settling back into the community after a prison sentence can also be stressful. If you require help ask for the Community Chaplain.

SSAFA

Soldier, Sailors, Airmen, Families Association. "One days pay, a life time of support".

Important Information

PHONE CALLS

Chaplaincy members are NOT allowed to make phone calls for prisoners.

RELIGIOUS FOOD

For special feasts and celebrations all food MUST be eaten at the place of worship and may not be taken onto the Wings.

ABLUTIONS

All registered Muslim prisoners are required to complete their ablutions in their cells before attending Friday Prayers. There are no suitable facilities in the prayer areas to complete your ablutions.

APPLICATIONS

Ask your Landing Officer for an Application Form. You can also ask the Landing Officer to phone the Chaplaincy Department.

FAITH FORUMS

The Wing Chaplain will lead Faith Forums at least 3 times a year.

FAITH COMMENTS BOOK

On each Wing there is a Comments Book for suggestions relating to faith matters. These are in the SO's Office.

PENFRIENDS

If you would like a Penfriend from outside prison (NOT a girlfriend), Give your name, prison number and the prison, write to: Penfriends, PO Box 33460, London. SW18 5YB.

RC CONFESSIONS

Please complete an application form if you wish to have your confession heard by a priest.

PRISON VISITORS

Having no one to visit you whilst in prison can be hard. Ask for a Prison Visitor with an application.

Chaplaincy Members

(B Wing/FNC/SEG Chaplain)
Helen Baly (RC/Coordinating Chaplain)
(D Wing Chaplain)
Ibrahim Mehtar (Muslim)
(C Wing Chaplain)
Kabir Uddin (Muslim)
(Conibeere Unit Chaplain)
Alethea Malcolm-Lamont (Free Ch)
(Health Care Chaplain)
Sr Gina Pizzey (CE)
(A Wing Chaplain)
Gagandeep Singh (Sikh)
(E Wing Chaplain)
Bhadresh Trivedi (Hindu)

Kabir Uddin (Muslim/Acting CC)
Yusuf Rawat (Muslim)
Dr Senevi Aturpana (Buddhist)
Melvyn Hartog (Jewish)
Rabbi Stern and Venitt (Jewish)
Fr Maxim Nikolsky (Orthodox)
Sue Flemons (Quaker)
Shibbin Ahmed (Muslim)
Peter Haughton (Jehovah Witness)
Ray Elliott (Prison Fellowship)
Judy Thomas (Prison Fellowship)
Sr Carmen (Volunteer)
Elizabeth Kellar (Volunteer)
Rev Rudi Pedro (Volunteer)
Roger Foster-Smith (Volunteer)
Christopher McLeod (Volunteer)
Pastor Suthesh (Tamil Volunteer)
Pastor Keneady (Tamil Volunteer)
Hazel Norbury (SSAFA)
Anthony Henry (Mormon)

*Members of the Chaplaincy pray daily
for all prisoners and prisoners'
families.*

"To enrich life through faith"

Chaplaincy

To: *Trenton Olfield*

Cell: X4. 5.

Religious Registration:

RELIGIOUS REGISTRATION
If your religious registration has been
recorded incorrectly, please inform the
Chaplain.

Chaplaincy can help in the
following areas:

- Religious Books
- Worship Materials
- Religious Instruction
- Pastoral support
- Relationship issues
- Spiritual Support
- Bereavement support
- Religious Dietary Needs
- Alpha Course
- Penfriend Scheme
- Prison Visitors
- Community Chaplaincy
- SSAFA

HMP Wormwood Scrubs
PO Box 757, Du Cane Road
London. W12 0AE

Tube: East Acton (Central Line)

Buses: 7; 70; 72; 272; 283

WORKSHOP 6 ALLOCATION
Resettlement Workshop

Name OLDFIELD
Number A1010CT
Cell A4-021

Dear

You have been allocated to the following course in shop 6.

12/11/12 - Job club

....

**This course will provide you with valuable skills, which will help you
when you come out of custody.
Previous students who have attended have received information and
guidance from trained staff.**

We look forward to meeting you in workshop 6 shortly.

Thank you

Workshop 6

Notice to Prisoners

FOR ACTION	FOR INFORMATION	ISSUE NUMBER
All Prisoners	All Prisoners	NTP 003/10

DATE OF ISSUE	IMPLEMENTATION DATE	EXPIRY DATE
8th February 2010	Immediate effect	

SUBJECT	CONTACT POINT
DISPLAY OF OFFENSIVE MATERIAL	Landing Staff

Display of Offensive SEXUAL Material

The following material will NOT be permitted in possession or on display in cells or any other area of the prison:

1. Fully erect penises
2. Urination or defecation
3. Ejaculation
4. Penetration: oral, anal or vaginal
5. Naked images of children, juveniles, persons who appear under age
6. Mutilation
7. Sexual acts which depict restraints, coercion or violence
8. Images of illegal activities, such as bestiality and necrophilia
9. Photographs of children, juveniles or naked images of persons who appear to be under age, if deemed exploitative or displayed against the best interests of those children, juveniles or persons.

Material suitable for possession, but NOT suitable for display:

1. Full or partial nudity, male or female
2. Images of genitalia, male or female
3. Images which have been altered, e.g. full or partial nudity where genitalia or nipples have been removed or covered by marker pens or other obstructions.
4. Topless pictures of any sort, male or female.
5. A picture or image of a person in swimwear or underwear can be displayed, providing the clothing is not transparent or see-through.

Banned Organisations material and publications are listed below (this list is not exhaustive)

- Rene Guyon Society
- North American man boy love association
- Child sensuality Circle
- Paedo- Alert Network
- Lewis Carroll Collectors Guild

- Minor Problems
- Cries
- Single Mothers
- Matchmaker International
- Pets Monthly

RACIST OFFENSIVE MATERIAL

The following are NOT permitted for display:

1. Any image, picture or article that incites racial hatred or violent acts, or is likely to do so.

2. Any image, picture or article that is perceived to be racist by any prisoner, visitor or staff

The following will NOT be allowed in possession:

1. Material which incites racial hatred or violent acts, or is likely to do so

2. Any material which promotes intolerance of any group of society, or is likely to do so

3. National flags.

Prohibited Organisations and Publications:
(This list is not exhaustive)

- Black Panthers
- Ku Klux Klan
- White Wolves
- Arian Nations
- UDA / IRA
- British national party (BNP)

- Combat 18
- Hammersteins
- Swastika
- Al-Qaeda
- National Front

OTHER OFFENSIVE MATERIAL

Under NO circumstances will material listed below be permitted
(This list is not exhaustive)

1. Any words or images that illustrate or depict any racist views or philosophies, any views or philosophies against specific religions or religious people, any sexist or Homophobic views or philosophies.
Any other slogans, symbolism or general remarks that could reasonably cause offence to any individual

2. Images or words that illustrate or depict any form of profanity (swearing), abusive or defamatory statements or language, and any other comment, statement or language that is intended to cause offence or humiliation to another

3. Any words or images that illustrate or depict killing, murder, gratuitous violence and/or glorifies violent conduct.

4. Any images or words that illustrate or depict any illegal substance, or type of substance misuse.

5. Any badges or tattoos that illustrate or depict any form of Racism, abusive or defamatory statements or language, and any other comment, statement or language that is intended to cause offence or humiliation to another.

Management by Staff of offensive Material.

All prisoners that are found to be in possession of any offensive material will be either given an IEP, or placed on report.

All staff have been instructed to remove all offensive material.

Phil Taylor
Governor

RELEASE DATES NOTIFICATION SLIP

WORMWOOD SCRUBS (HMP)

A-4-21

Name: TRENTON OLDFIELD

NOMS No: A1010CT   Prison No: G88604   Cell: WSI-B-3-046

Sentence calculated on: 22/10/2012

Sentence(s)

   1 /   1   19/10/2012   0 years 6 months 0 days

Number of days in sentence	: 182
Sentence Expiry Date	: 18/04/2013
Unconditional Release Date	: 17/01/2013
HDC Eligibility Date	: 04/12/2012
Licence Expiry Date	: 18/04/2013

22/10/2012 14:10

Calculated by : ....

Checked by : ....   Date : ....

Page 1 of 1
Version : 3.13

A 1010CT

A 4 21
OLDFIELD

- Insufficient information or details – all the sections must be completed concerning visitors
- Dates need for visits
- Visits Closed
- Not 7 days in advance – all visits must be booked for at least 7 days in advance
- Fully booked on dates requested

Thank you
Visits Booking Team

9/10/2012

		Date	Time (AM or PM)
Preference 1	SATURDAY	10 NOV 2012	PM - 3
Preference 2	SUNDAY	11 NOV 2012	PM - 3
Preference 3			

Check Landing notice for visits times

Adult Visitor Details

Please note that if you do not provide full details then your booking will not be processed.

Visitor 1	Surname	NAIK		
	First Name	DEEPA		
	Address	FLAT 24, MYRTLE COURT MYRTLE ST		
	Town	LONDON		
	County			
	Postcode	E1 1HP	Telephone Number	020 7247 0166
Relationship				
Date of Birth				

Visitor 2	Surname			
	First Name			
	Address			
	Town			
	County			
	Postcode		Telephone Number	
Relationship				
Date of Birth				

Visitor 3	Surname			
	First Name			
	Address			
	Town			
	County			
	Postcode		Telephone Number	
Relationship				
Date of Birth				

Children Visitor Details (All those aged under 10yrs)

Surname	First name
Address	
Date of Birth	Child Relationship

Surname	First name
Address	
Date of Birth	Child Relationship

Surname	First name
Address	
Date of Birth	Child Relationship

If there is a requirement for extra children names please use over the page

Date. 16/11/12

Parcels

Number. A101OCT   Name. OLDFIELD

Location. A4 -21   Delivery Number. _____

The following items were received in a parcel. They have either been
issued to you as in possession property or have been placed in
reception for storage. Should you wish any property which has been
placed in reception you must make an application to reception.

Cash / Postal Order / Cheque   amount £
All monies are processed and given to finance for crediting to your account.

The following Items have been issued to you.

1.   2.

3.   4.

5.   6.

Seal Number WSB

The following items have been placed in Reception

1. POSTERS   2.

3.   4.

5.   6.

7.   8.

Seal Number WSB   4204416

Post Room Staff

Name	LHM WSGR
Signature	

Copy to Prisoner / Reception / File

MEMORANDUM   HDC OFFICE   HMP WORMWOOD SCRUBS

To: A1010CT/OLDFIELD

Location: B3-046

Date: 25/10/2012

Re: HDC

Please find attached the HDC2 in respect of Home Detention Curfew (HDC).

1. If you wish to be assessed for Home Detention Curfew please complete the first page of the HDC2 making sure you have included your proposed HDC address and contact telephone number in the space provided near the top of the page. When the form is fully completed please sign and date the bottom of the page before returning it to the HDC office.

2. If you do not wish to be considered for Home Detention Curfew please complete the section at the bottom of the second page of the HDC2 and return it to the HDC department as soon as possible.

3. If you are unable to propose an address for the home detention curfew scheme, it may be possible for the Bail Accommodation and Support Service (BASS) to provide you with accommodation for the duration of the HDC period. BASS is mainly shared small houses or flats within the community. **Please note if you are ineligible to claim housing benefit it would be your responsibility to meet any rent payments.** Additionally BASS have a support only service if you have an address.

If you wish to be considered for accommodation or support through BASS please complete the section below and return this form to the HDC office as soon as possible.

I do not have a release address and I wish to apply for accommodation/support through BASS for my HDC assessment.

Signed _____ Print name _____ Date _____

1

The information which you give on this form will be used when the Governor decides if you should serve part of your sentence in the community on Home Detention Curfew in advance of your automatic or conditional release date.

You should provide details on this form of a suitable home address to which you can be curfewed. The details you provide will normally be passed to the probation service. It may be necessary for a member of the probation service to visit the address to discuss with other residents there the possibility of curfewing you to this place.

A suitable home address does not guarantee that you will be released on Home Detention Curfew. All prisoners will also have to pass a risk assessment.

Please read the following notes before completing the form.

Guidance for completion of the form

1. The proposed address must be within England, Wales or Scotland. It is not possible for prisoners to be curfewed to other areas.

2. The proposed address must be connected to an electricity supply in order for the monitoring equipment to function. You should also provide details of whether the accommodation has its own telephone. If no telephone connection exists, a telephone can be installed by the monitoring contractor. This can only be used to contact the monitoring company and the emergency services. It will not allow you to make calls to other people, and will be disconnected at the end of the curfew. You will be unable to use your line if it only allows incoming calls, or has an answerphone, fax, internet connection or call waiting. Please indicate if you have any of these facilities.

3. If there is another adult resident at the proposed curfew address who has responsibility for the property you must give their name. It would be helpful if you could also indicate the most convenient time for a member of the probation service to call at the address to make any enquiries necessary.

4. If you will be the only person living at the proposed address and you do not own the property, please provide the name of the landlord and an address and telephone number where they can be contacted.

5. You will need to provide the name and age (if under 18) of all other people who will be living at the proposed address and their relationship to you. You must also disclose whether you have been convicted or cautioned for any offence involving those resident at the address or living in neighbouring properties.

6. If, after you have competed this form, the address you have provided becomes unavailable you will need to supply details of an alternative address as soon as possible.

7. If you do not supply a release address, you will not be considered for release on Home Detention Curfew, and will only be released at your automatic or conditional release date (at the half way point of sentence). In this case you should sign in the box below.

I do not have a release address / I do not wish to be considered for Home Detention Curfew.

Prisoner / YO Signature _____ Date _____

HMP WORMWOOD SCRUBS
PIN TELEPHONE SYSTEM
NUMBER REQUEST

Prison Number	Name	Unit

The telephone numbers you submit will only be allowed on the understanding that the recipient is willing to accept your call.

CERTIFICATION

I am requesting that the names and telephone numbers listed on this form be added to my list of telephone contacts.
I certify that all the numbers listed are to persons willing to accept my calls and that the telephone calls made to those persons will be made for the purposes allowed under Prison Rules.

Signature	Date

Wing Staff. I confirm that this form has been fully completed and that the information provided is sufficient to enable the appropriate checks to be made.

SIGNED: _____ DATE: _____

Date forwarded to PIN'S _____

Date arrived at PIN'S _____

(PIN'S)	Not subject to Public Protection Measures
Public Protection Measures apply YES/NO	Signed: _____ Print: _____

LEGAL TELEPHONE NUMBERS TO BE ADDED

Number (Including Area Code)	Name of Contact	Company Name Town/City	Approved by PIN'S OSG YES/NO (Sign/Print/Date)

FAMILY & FRIENDS NUMBERS TO BE ADDED

Number (Including Area Code)	**Full** name of Recipient	Relationship to Prisoner	Address	Approved YES/NO (Sign/Print/Date)

NUMBERS TO BE REMOVED

Number (Including Area Code)	Name of Recipient	Relationship to Prisoner

11. You must not conduct a conversation on a PIN phone that contains any of the following:

- plans or information which would assist or encourage any disciplinary or criminal offence
- escape plans that might jeopardise the security of prison;
- information that might jeopardise national security;
- information associated with the making of any weapon, explosive, poison or other destructive device;
- obscure or coded messages;
- material which would create a clear threat, or present danger of violence or physical harm, to any person, including incitement or racial hatred, or which might place a child's welfare at risk; and/or
- material which is intended to cause distress or anxiety to the recipient or any other person, such as messages which are indecent or grossly offensive, or a threat, or information which is known or believed to be false.

12. **FAILURE TO ABIDE BY THESE CONDITIONS MAY RESULT IN WITHDRAWAL OF ACCESS TO THE TELEPHONE AND DISCIPLINARY ACTION UNDER PRISON RULE 51 (YOI RULE 50).**

LETTERS – TERMS & CONDITIONS FOR WRITTEN CORRESPONDENCE

1. Prisoners must include their name, number and establishment address on any outgoing correspondence. Any legally privileged mail must be marked.

2. A maximum of up to 5% of the correspondence sent and received on a daily basis by prisoners is subject to monitoring. **All mail, except legally privileged or to a confidential access organisation, may be opened to check for illicit enclosures and may be subject to monitoring.**

3. Letters can be read in the following cases:
   - prisoners in High Security establishments or any unit which holds Category A prisoners;
   - prisoners who are on the Escape (E) list;
   - prisoners who are identified as posing a risk to children;
   - prisoners remanded for, or convicted of, an offence under the Protection from Harassment Act 1997, or subject to a restraining order or injunction. Routine reading must continue while an order/injunction is in force, and subsequently if deemed necessary;
   - information has been received that the prisoner presents a risk for the intimidation of victims/witnesses.
   - prisoners remanded for, or convicted of, an offence of sending or attempting to send obscene mail

4. The exception to 2 and 3 is that correspondence that is legally privileged (Prison Rule 39 or YOI Rule 17) or to / from a confidential access organisation, will not normally be opened or read. However, it should be recognised that it may be opened accidentally or in error if it is not clearly marked as either 'Rule 39', 'YOI Rule 17' or 'Confidential Access'. If staff suspect that a letter marked 'Rule 39' or 'confidential access' may contain an unauthorised item, they may, on authority of the Governor, decide to open it in your presence. In exceptional circumstances, the Governor may be so concerned about the contents of the correspondence that they decide to read it in your presence. This would be because they think it may endanger the security of the prison, or someone's safety, or that the letter is intended to further a criminal purpose.

5. Prisoners may write their letters or receive letters in the language of their choice, but letters not written in English and which are subject to reading may be subject to delay while they are translated.

6. Correspondence must not contain the following:

   a. material which is intended to cause distress or anxiety to the recipient or any other person, such as messages which are indecent or grossly offensive; or a threat; or information which is known or believed to be false;

   b. plans or material which could assist or encourage any disciplinary or criminal offence (including attempts to defeat the ends of justice by suggesting the fabrication or suppression of evidence);

   c. escape plans, or material which if allowed may jeopardise the security of a prison establishment;

   d. material which may jeopardise national security;

   e. descriptions of the making or use of any weapon, explosive, poison or other destructive device;

   f. obscure or coded messages;

   g. material which is indecent and obscene under Section 85(3) of the Postal Services Act 2000;

   h. material which, if sent to, or received from, a child might place his or her welfare at risk;

   i. material which would create a clear threat or present danger of violence or physical harm to any person, including incitement to racial hatred or which might place a child's welfare at risk;

   j. material which is intended for publication or use by radio or television (or which, if sent, would be likely to be published or broadcast) if it contravenes the guidance in PSI 49/2011and PSI 01/2012.

A WING HMP WORMWOOD SCRUBS
GENERAL APPLICATION FORM

USE THIS FORM TO ASK OR REQUEST ANY GENERAL QUESTIONS OR
CONCERNS THAT YOU HAVE. ONCE COMPLETED GIVE TO YOUR
LANDING STAFF WHO WILL DEAL WITH YOUR REQUEST

NAME......................... NUMBER...................

DATE.......................... CELL No...................

To be completed by Prisoner
Explain as fully as you can what your application is:

Landing Officers response:

Tear off and return to the prisoner

Your application for:................................. Received on (date:)...................

Has / Has not been approved:...

Senior Officer...

LEO Employment Application LOG NUMBER ___/___/___

NAME _____ NUMBER _____ LOCATION _____

Status (Remand, Sentenced, LR, JR etc) _____ Release Date (If known) _____
Do you have any medical issues or disabilities which may effect where you work? Y / N
(If yes, please specify) _____

> PLEASE STATE BELOW WHICH AREA YOU WOULD LIKE TO BE EMPLOYED. FOLLOWING RECEIPT OF YOUR
> APPLICATION, A RISK ASSESSMENT WILL BE CARRIED OUT; YOUR IEP LEVEL, HISTORY SHEET AND SECURITY
> INFORMATION WILL ALL BE LOOKED AT AND A DECISION MADE ON YOUR RISK LEVEL. BASED ON THESE
> DETAILS A DECISION WILL BE MADE AS TO WHERE YOU WILL BE ALLOCATED EMPLOYMENT.

TICK ONE OPTION ONLY

ON WING WORK TICK HERE	OFF WING WORK TICK HERE
Examples: Hotplate, Cleaner, Kit Store, Painter	Examples: Workshops, Laundry, Kitchen, Off-Wing Cleaner (Visits, Reception etc) Shop 6 (Business Enterprise/Banking/Graphic Design)
ON WING Specialist TICK HERE	OFF WING Specialist (LOW RISK ONLY) TICK HERE
Examples: Foreign National Rep, Insider, Toe by Toe, Learning & Skills Rep	Gardens, Works, RED BAND (If applying for RB, be aware that extensive checks will be carried out)

Please tell us if you have any relevant qualifications or experience in any areas, which
will help your application.

Is the activity you've applied for part of your Sentence Plan? Yes____ No _____ don't know _____

SIGN	DATE

Now hand this form to your Landing Officer who will pass it on to LEO

LEO OFFICE USE ONLY Book Number _____ Edu Level _____ Application Number _____
Date received_____ Date to Security_____ R/A Level H   M   L Ethnicity ____
Accept/Reject (If rejected, state why)_____
ALLOCATED TO _____ AM/PM/BOTH START DATE _____
SIGNED   Name   Date

- -

Name _____ Number _____ Loc _____
Your application has been received by LEO and is currently being processed.
You will be notified within 14 days of the decision and allocated employment if suitable

**PLEASE DO NOT REAPPLY ONCE YOU HAVE RECEIVED THIS SLIP, AS THIS WILL DELAY YOUR
ORIGINAL APPLICATION**

> Landing Staff, please complete reverse of this form before forwarding to LEO

LEO

EMPLOYMENT SUITABILITY ASSESSMENT

OFFICIAL USE ONLY

MUST BE COMPLETED BY WING/LANDING STAFF FOR <u>ALL</u> EMPLOYMENT APPLICATIONS

GENERAL BEHAVIOUR	IEP LEVEL	COMPLIANCE TO REGIME
(circle one)	(circle one)	(circle one)
EXCELLENT GOOD ACCEPTABLE CAUSE FOR CONCERN	ENHANCED STANDARD BASIC	EXCELLENT GOOD ACCEPTABLE CAUSE FOR CONCERN

Has the prisoner completed his Education Assessment (see Activities on PNOMIS)

YES / NO

Do you believe the prisoner is sufficiently trustworthy to be left unsupervised?
YES / NO
For example, do they comply with the landing regime? Have they been left unsupervised before?
_____

In your opinion, does this prisoner have the temperament to work safely and without causing disruption?
YES / NO

Are there any other issues you are aware of that the LEO should be aware of in deciding on suitable allocation? (e.g. Risk of self harm, bullying issues, health, mobility)
_____

Further comments
Do you think the prisoner is suitable for employment in the area(s) he has applied for? And if no, why not?_____
_____

_Finally, how long has this prisoner been known to you?_____

SIGN_____NAME_____DATE_____
-------------------------------DO NOT WRITE BELOW THIS LINE-------------------------------

THANK YOU FOR COMPLETING THIS FORM

FORM HDC(5)   NOTIFICATION OF PROVISIONAL ACCEPTANCE FOR HOME DETENTION CURFEW

4 - 21
REC 28 NOV 2012

SECTION ONE: PRISONERS DETAILS

Surname **Oldfield**			Forename(s) **Trenton**				
NOMS Number: **A1010CT**			Date of Birth: **11/05/1976**				
Prison Number: **G88604**							

Proposed date of release on HDC **04/12/2012**

Proposed address of curfew:

FLAT 24
MYRDLE COURT
MYRDLE STREET
London
E1 1HP

Curfew hours:

Start			End		
Mon	19:15		Mon	07:15
Tue	19:15		Tue	07:15
Wed	19:15		Wed	07:15
Thu	19:15		Thu	07:15
Fri	19:15		Fri	07:15
Sat	19:15		Sat	07:15
Sun	19:15		Sun	07:15

Curfew hours on day of release:
19:00 until 07:15

You have provisionally been assessed as suitable for release on Home Detention Curfew, subject to the continued availability and suitability of the address given above. This decision may also be reversed should your subsequent behaviour or any new information demonstrate that you should no longer be considered suitable.

This information will be disclosed to the electronic monitoring company responsible for monitoring your whereabouts. They may contact others at the above address in advance of your release.

If for any reason the proposed curfew address given above becomes unavailable, you must immediately inform a member of staff. You may be asked details of to provide alternative address.

Once released on Home Detention Curfew you may be liable to be recalled to prison if <u>any</u> of the following happen:

(i)   You fail to remain at your curfew address during any part of your curfew hours, or otherwise fail to comply with your curfew conditions.
(ii)   The curfew address can no longer be electronically monitored.
(iii)   It is decided that you pose a serious risk to public safety.
(iv)   You are charged with a further offence while on Home Detention Curfew.

If you are serving a sentence of one year or over, or you are a young offender you will also be subject to other licence conditions and will be supervised by the Probation Service. You will be given a licence to sign before you are released which will give details of the licence conditions which will apply to you.

Signed: _CMMWG_   Name: _CMMWG_

Grade: _PSMC_   Date: _23/11/12_

COMP 1A FORM

PROTECT

**PRISONER'S APPEAL AGAINST
THE RESPONSE TO A FORMAL COMPLAINT**

Serial N°: ....

Read these notes first

1. This form is for you to appeal against the response to the written complaint which you have made.
2. Say why you are not satisfied with the response to your complaint. Be brief and to the point.
3. When you have completed the form, sign it and post it in the box provided.
4. If you are still not satisfied, you have the right to refer your complaint to the Prisons and Probation Ombudsman.

Your details (use BLOCK CAPITALS)

Surname:	First name(s):
Prison number:	Location:
Original Complaint Log Number:	

Your appeal: say why you are not satisfied with the response to your complaint

Signed: ....

PROTECT

Date: ....

VF012A Printed By HMP Wymott

Wormwood Scrubs

Note: Available Spend Cannot Be Manually Amended

V 1
For Deliveries From 19/11/12
Expiry End 16/02/13

Price	Item	IC	Qty	Price	Item	IC	Qty	Price	Item	IC	Qty
	PHONE & STAMPS			£4.07	Hair,Scalp &Skin Oil 237ml	094596		£1.75	Roast Salted Cashew 75g(V)	102524	
£1.00	Phone Credit	PC		£0.35	Hair Comb	100254		£1.15	Peanuts & Raisins 350g	126906	
£0.60	1st Class Stamp	096207		£0.99	Hair Brush Vented	102294		£1.59	Tropical Fruit&Nut 350g(V)	126930	
£0.50	2nd Class Stamp	096208		£1.00	Afro Comb	093358		£1.49	Almonds 150g(V)	103582	
£0.10	10p Postage Stamp	125683		£1.32	Cyclax Apricot Face Scrub	093403		£1.00	Bk Sweet Popcorn (H.V)	135153	
£0.01	1p Postage Stamp	125678		£3.99	Palmers Coco Butter Lotion	093244		£0.69	Caramel Peanuts 90g (V)	098009	
	TOBACCO			£1.99	Nivea Crème 50ml	288071		£0.59	Bombay Mix 80g (V)	102522	
£3.87	Amber Leaf 12.5g	108859		£1.89	Johnsons Baby Lotion 200ml	770520		£1.75	Soft Pitted Dates 375g	131774	
£3.39	Ashford Gold 12.5g	133562		£1.00	3 Blade Disposs Razors 5s	120616		£0.75	Peperami Hot Sgl	746230	
£3.90	Cutters Choice 12.5g	535903		£2.19	Gillette Blue II Fixed 5's	698901			**DRINKS**		
£3.45	Turner Tobacco12.5g	092678		£7.29	Gillette Mach3 Blades 4s	131039		£1.09	Red Mountain Coffee Pouch	121063	
£4.19	Golden Virginia 12.5g	355158		£7.50	Gillette Mach4 Razor	085770		£3.79	Nescafe Orig 150g (V,H)	124363	
£2.44	Red Bull Tobacco 12.5g	063138		£1.00	Matima Shaving Gel 150ml	128229		£0.13	Nescafe Orgi 1 Stick(V,H)	131758	
£7.57	Amber Leaf 25g	974940		£1.92	Shave Cream Tube 100g	098205		£1.00	Typhoo Eco Pack 40s	108598	
£8.16	Golden Virginia 25g	481937		£4.59	Gillette Shave Balm 100ml	097944		£1.29	PG Tips 40's	107746	
£1.75	HMP Golden Virginia 5g	094783		£0.95	Cotton Wool Balls 100's	100183		£0.69	Economy Tea Bags 80's	116022	
£0.96	Hamlet Cigar	429307		£0.99	Cotton Buds 100's	100166		£1.69	Green Tea Lemon 50's	100902	
£3.66	B & H Gold 10's	047222		£0.99	Face Cloth	125967		£1.39	Red Berries Tea 20's	125117	
£3.69	L A B King Size 10's	302075		£0.60	Soap Box	112525		£1.39	Citrus Tea 20's	125106	
£0.20	BBrand Rolling Paper Green	128632		£0.29	Shower Cap	113213		£1.39	Peppermint Tea 20's	125113	
£0.20	BBrand Rolling Paper Red	128618		£1.01	Toe Nail Clipper	102948		£2.96	Cbury Choc Instant 280g(V)	585596	
£0.25	Rizla Papers Green	026316		£2.61	Multi Vits Tablets 60s(V)	095742		£1.49	Coffee Mate 200g(V)	748681	
£0.69	Borand U/Slim Filter Tips	116394		£4.07	M/Vit Tabs with Iodine(VE)	108915		£0.29	Cadbry Highlight Sachet(V)	121654	
£0.75	Lighter Child Resitant	081883		£1.90	Cod Liver Oil Tabs 90s(GF)	097672		£2.19	Marvel Dried Milk Skimmed	007393	
£0.75	Economy Safety Match (box)	051909		£1.29	Johnsons Baby Oil 200ml	446820		£0.55	Economy UHT Semi-Skim(V)	989150	
£2.19	Swan Rolling Machine	084561		£1.79	Johnsons Baby Powder 200g	328369		£0.51	Economy UHT Skimmed(V)	989140	
	BATTERIES			£1.69	Imperial Leather Talc 300g	350512		£0.59	Economy UHT Milk Whole(V)	989170	
£1.75	Duracell +C Battery (1's)	965420		£1.79	Savlon Antiseptic Cream00g	207050		£0.99	Soya Milk Unsweet 1Ltr(VE)	092989	
£0.75	Panasonic Battery C(1's)	098197		£4.07	E45 Cream 125g	130628		£1.49	Juice Summer Fruits 2 Ltr	063375	
£0.87	Duracell AA Battery (1's)	045554		£1.49	Lypsyl Original	121064		£0.55	Eco NAS Apple&Black 1L(V)	117363	
£0.50	Panasonic Battery AA(1's)	098195		£0.50	Economy Box Tissues	109756		£0.88	Eco Lemon Squash 1L (V)	072014	
£0.37	Panasonic Battery AAA(1's)	098196		£1.00	ES Wet Wipes	121975		£0.65	Eco Orange Squash 1L (V)	061752	
	TOILETRIES & HEALTH				**SWEETS & SNACKS**			£0.85	Economy Orange Juice 1ltr	120026	
£1.13	Branded Toothbrush	066219		£1.00	Haribo Starmix Bag (GF)	099107		£0.65	Economy Tropical Juice 1L	126032	
£2.03	Aquafresh T/Paste 125ml	985099		£1.00	Haribo Tangfastics Bag(GF)	099122		£0.75	Economy Apple Juice 1ltr	126027	
£2.96	Colgate Advance 125ml	126548		£1.00	Foxs Glacier Fruit Bag(V)	126772		£1.29	Rubicon Mango Juice 1ltr(V)	111995	
£2.89	Sensodyne T/Paste	137425		£1.39	Werthers Sugar Free (V)	113925		£1.15	Pineapple Juice 1L	101250	
£1.69	Mcleans Whitening 100ml	102722		£0.50	ES Milk Chocolate 100g	114953		£0.49	Economy Cherryade SF 1Ltr	120474	
£2.71	Kitsilver T/Pasta 100ml(VE)	099904		£0.50	ES Plain Chocolate PM50	133578		£0.49	Economy Cola 1lt	120475	
£0.83	Eucryl T/Powder Freshmint	108544		£1.99	MooFree Chocolate 100g(VE)	124720		£0.49	Economy Lemonade 1Lt	120478	
£3.01	F/Mint Mouthwash 500ml	104705		£0.58	Yorkie Standard (V)	124302		£0.49	Economy Orangeade SF 1Lt	120452	
£1.99	Dental Floss Sticks	132575		£0.56	Boost Bar (V)	180706		£1.71	Pepsi Regular 1.5Ltr	089468	
£1.39	Steradent Tablets Org 30s	060336		£0.54	Bounty Milk Std	057011		£0.75	Coca Cola Can (VE)	282574	
£1.29	Dettol Antibac Bar Soap x2	124366		£0.55	Cad Double Decker Std(V)	264811		£0.75	Coke Diet Can (VE)	282673	
£2.09	Palmers Coco Btr Bar Soap	099205		£0.54	Kit Kat 4 Finger(V)	048905		£0.75	Fanta Orange Can(V)	282707	
£0.73	Dove Soap Bar	707415		£0.60	KitKat Chunky Peanut Buter	127524		£0.49	KA Ginger Beer 330ml	133392	
£0.66	IL Soap 100g	126649		£0.51	Mars Bar Std(V)	090164		£0.49	KA Sparkling Fruit Punch		
£0.81	IL Roll On Deodorant 50ml	099899		£0.49	Snickers Bar Std(V,K)	090168		£0.70	Im Bru Can	408395	
£2.93	Dove Stick Invisible 40ml	094741		£0.51	Twix Twin Bar Std(K)	563064		£0.75	Sprite Can(VE)	242030	
£1.50	Vaseline Roll-On 50ml	112978		£0.13	Sw Refreshr Bar S/Berry	105173		£0.45	ES Energy Orange 380ml	125548	
£2.34	Lynx Stick Africa 50ml	094729		£0.13	Swizzels F/Gums Mini P/Mix	211551		£0.60	Walley Still Water 1.5Ltr	094369	
£3.56	T Marine Stick Deodrant(VE)	127493		£0.47	Polo Original Std(V)	573000		£0.39	Economy Water 500ml	100570	
£0.75	Economy Shower Gel 250ml	099082		£0.72	Halls Mentholyptus SF	159831		£0.99	Yazoo Banana Milk(V)	074809	
£2.58	Redox Shower Gel 250ml	276121		£0.47	XXX Mints Extra Strong	097499		£0.99	Yazoo Strawberry Milk(V)	074804	
£2.49	Lynx Shower/Gel 250ml	516070		£0.49	Seabrook Salt/Vinegar (V)	134504			**CARDS**		
£1.09	Enliven Shampoo App&Raap	094861		£0.49	Seabrook Sea Salt (V)	134489		£0.65	I Love You Card	103408	
£1.09	Enliven Conditioner A&R	094865		£0.49	Seabrooks Prwn Cocktail(V)	134505		£0.65	I Miss You Card	103415	
£2.79	H/Shoulder Shampoo Classic	126808		£0.49	Walkr Chse&Onion Std Bag(V)	126808		£0.65	Thinking Of You Card	103422	
£2.50	Palmers Coco Oil Condition	093414		£0.20	Space Raiders BBQ(V)	111119		£0.65	Just To Say Card	103427	
£4.24	African Pride Shamp/Cond	094606		£0.20	Red Mill Tangy Tomato	115723		£0.65	Blank Card	103444	
£3.57	F/Nature A/Vera Cond(VE)	093645		£0.29	Doritos Chilli (V)	100641		£0.65	Female Birthday Card	103444	
£3.87	G/Fruit A/Vera Shamp(VE)	093406		£0.75	Jalapeno Pot Stick 90g(V)	092929		£0.65	Male Birthday Card	103464	
£0.59	Hair Gel Firm 250ml	071567		£1.74	Pringles Texas BBQ 180g(VE)	122772		£0.65	Chld Birthday Card Boy	103468	
£3.06	Dax Pomade	084902		£0.65	Salted Peanuts 50g(V)	107524		£0.65	Child Birthday Card Girl	103476	
£3.06	Dax Short & Neat Tin	093236		£0.65	Dry Roasted Peanuts 50g(V)	107528		£0.65	Mum Birthday Card	103478	

V - Vegetarian   Ve - Vegan   H - Halal   Fl - Fair Trade   Gf - Gluten Free   Sf - Sugar Free   Ho - Healthy Option   K - Kosher

Price	Item	IC	Qty
£0.65	Daughter Bday Card Child	103484	
£0.65	Daughter Bday Card Adult	103486	
£0.65	Sister Birthday Card	103490	
£0.65	Wife Birthday Card	103496	
£0.65	Dad Birthday Card	103502	
£0.65	Son Birthday Card Child	103506	
£0.65	Son Birthday Card Adult	103509	
£0.65	Brother Birthday Card	103513	
£0.65	Open Anniversary	103529	
£0.65	Get Well Soon Card	103535	
£0.65	New Baby Boy Card	103537	
£0.65	New Baby Girl Card	103539	
£0.65	Sympathy Card	103543	
£0.65	Congratulations Card	103545	
£1.35	EID Card 8 Pack	100436	
	CHILLED		
£1.00	Economy Mild Cheddar (V)	118468	
£2.45	P/Choice Mature Cheddar(V)	058092	
£1.75	Philadelphia Reg (V)	129332	
£1.25	DLea Cheese Portions(V)	133135	
£0.50	ES Buttery Spread 250g(V)	114003	
£1.15	Flora S/Flw Spread 250g(V)	112190	
£1.59	Suma Sunflower Spread(VE)	126418	
	BISCUITS & BAKERY		
£1.00	Economy Custard Creams	120919	
£1.00	Economy Bourbon Creams	114368	
£0.85	HS Jam & Cream Rings(V)	127789	
£0.85	Economy Coconut Rings(V)	128614	
£0.79	Economy Fruit Shortcake(V)	128567	
£0.85	Economy Rich Tea (V)	126490	
£1.00	Econ Milk Choc Dig (V)	120902	
£0.59	Economy Choc Chip Cookies	104805	
£0.85	Economy Ginger Nuts (V)	126495	
£0.99	Economy Jaffa Cake	089294	
£1.80	Milk Choc Hobnobs (V)	124829	
£1.29	Ritz Original Box(V)	130726	
£0.49	Eco Cream Crackers(V)	116439	
£1.00	McVities Taxi 6pack(V)	116518	
£0.55	GoAhead Fruit Bar (V)	124592	
£0.99	Chocolate Chip Muffin 5pk	133689	
£0.55	Raspberry Flapjack	327361	
£1.65	Mcv Syrup Cake (V)	126166	
£1.65	Mcv Jamaica Ginger Cake(V)	126156	
£2.99	Jamaican Sponge SpiceBun	120715	
£0.79	Plain Pitta Bread 6's	106404	
£0.89	Soreen Malt Loaf(V)	107687	
	GROCERIES		
£1.75	Harvest Muesli 1kg	125686	
£1.59	Ready Brek 250g(V,K)	131466	
£2.75	Kg Cornflakes 500g(V,K,H)	128782	
£2.55	Kgs CrnchyNut 375g(V,K,H)	089998	
£2.35	Kg FruitNFib 375g(VE,K,H)	087281	
£2.49	Frosties 500g(VE,K,H)	126368	
£2.09	Sugar Puffs 320g	116495	
£1.59	Weetabix 12s(VE,K)	090061	
£0.75	Superfast Oats 500g(VE)	035730	
£2.15	Shredded Wheat 12's(V)	065063	
£1.09	Granulated Sugar1kg(V,GF)	095442	
£1.29	Hermesetas 300's	031779	
£1.99	Econ Sqzy Honey(Y)	109755	
£1.99	Smooth Peanut Butter	126043	
£0.19	Nutella 15g Portion	105417	
£1.29	Economy Tuna Chunks Brine	111694	
£0.75	Economy Tuna Flakes Brine	124144	
£1.29	Economy Tuna Chunks Oil	797770	
£1.55	Mackerel Fillet in Oil	142949	
£1.55	Mackerel Fillet Tomato	101303	
£1.05	Sardines in Oil	633933	
£1.05	Sardines in Tomato	633827	
£1.35	Genuyk Pilchards Tomato	033956	

Price	Item	IC	Qty
£2.69	Corned Beef 340g	834481	
£2.59	Corned Beef 340g(H)	100668	
£1.15	Hot Dogs 400g	834432	
£1.59	Beef Hotdog 400g(H)	098884	
£1.09	Chicken Sausages 400g(H)	103596	
£1.29	Pork Luncheon Meat 198g	105200	
£2.59	Stewed Steak 392g	142681	
£1.59	Princes Hot Chicken Curry	126106	
£1.09	Westlers Beans & Sausages	136103	
£1.45	Minced Beef/Onion&Gravy	834374	
£0.43	Go Crunch Chicken Noodle	135352	
£0.35	Inst Noodle Chicken C/Mein	092653	
£0.35	Instant Noodle Mushroom(V)	092659	
£0.35	Instant Ndle Spicy Tom(V)	092666	
£0.35	Instant Noodle Beef	092652	
£0.35	Instant Noodle Curry (V)	092655	
£0.35	Instant Noodle Prawn (V)	092664	
£0.43	GoC n Hot&Spicy Noodles(V)	092667	
£0.50	Noodle Pot Snack Chic&Mush	102336	
£0.50	Ndle Pot Snack Curry	102337	
£0.59	Smash Original (V)	872180	
£1.29	Nap Pasta Shells 500g(V)	076056	
£0.69	Economy Ketchup 470g(V)	118375	
£1.00	Economy Mayo 250ml (V)	133563	
£1.00	Econom Salad Cream 445g(V)	133964	
£1.00	Sqeezy Brown Sauce 470g(V)	130963	
£1.25	HZ BBQ Sauce	126246	
£1.29	Heinz Hoisin Sauce	128247	
£1.25	Heinz Chilli Sauce 360g	128248	
£0.99	Colmans Mustard Tubes 50g	447193	
£1.99	Encona Hot Pepper Sauce	073046	
£1.89	Pataks Bengal Pickle 305g	133333	
£1.99	Mango Chutney 375g	109076	
£0.95	Cup a Pasta Chicken Sgl	113165	
£0.95	CupaPasta Tom&Herbs Sgl	113173	
£1.75	Cup A Soup Chicken 4s	125653	
£1.75	Cup ASoup Golden Veg 4s(V)	125083	
£1.75	Cup A Soup Tomato 4s(V)	125654	
£0.55	Cock Soup 50g	128254	
£0.89	HZ Baked Beans Tin(V,GF,K)	269581	
£0.35	Economy Baked Beans	118833	
£1.36	HZ Ravioli Tom Sauce 400g	101984	
£0.75	Macaroni Cheese Tin	128593	
£0.75	Economy Sweetcorn Tin	129117	
£0.55	Sea Isle Chick Peas 400g	091862	
£0.79	Mandarins in Juice 298g	631958	
£0.39	Pineapple Slices in Juice	089919	
£1.19	Fruit Cocktail Syrup 420g	936001	
£1.25	Pear Hlvs in Juice415g	936509	
£0.95	Peach Slices in Syrup 227g	062331	
£1.99	Carnation Cond Mlk(V,H)	529872	
£0.89	Carnation Evapo Milk (V,H)	185031	
£0.65	Angel Delight Chocolate(V)	125213	
£1.05	Ambrosia Custard Tin (V)	134917	
£1.05	Ambrosia Crmd Rice Tin (V)	134918	
£0.72	Table Salt 750g	114023	
£1.00	4 in 1 Herb Selection Mix	126918	
£0.85	All Purpose Seasoning 100g	092752	
£0.85	Tropical Sun Grn 500g	092755	
£1.48	Bisto Gravy Grans 170g (Y)	005363	
	SUPPLEMENTS		
£1.15	Nrich Banana (V)	128138	
£1.15	Nrich Chocolate (V)	128139	
£1.15	Nrich Strawberry 400g	128142	
£1.15	Nrich Vanilla 400g(V)	128143	
£6.10	Creatine Mondhale 180g(V)	094723	
£0.87	Elite Protin Pwd Banana(V)	094724	
£0.87	Elite Protin Pwd S/berri(V)	094725	
£7.75	Only Whey(Whey protein)(Y)	106527	
£1.00	BActive Dairy Drink 4P'k	131492	

Price	Item	IC	Qty
	STATIONERY		
£0.40	DL Envelopes 10 Pack	105167	
£0.59	First Post Writing Pad A5	088772	
£1.19	SE A4 Refill Pad 80 Sheets	125836	
£0.19	Rubber Tipped Pencil	092227	
£0.30	BIC Cristal Black Med Pen	041126	
£1.49	Coloured Pencils 24k	126455	
£0.19	Metal Pencil Sharpener	093768	
£0.19	Eraser	093782	
	RELIGIOUS ITEMS		
£2.99	Prayer Perfume Frag 27	115977	
£2.99	Dakkar Prayer Perfume	111928	
£1.42	Prayer Beads-Tasbesh/Subha	094567	
£1.95	Simple Prayer Booker	136114	
£5.16	Prayer Mat	094554	
£1.11	Prayer Hat (Topi)	098793	
£0.56	Plain Tooth stick (Miswak)	098795	
	GENERAL ITEMS		
£2.99	Sport Shaker Bottle 700ml	131022	
£1.00	Non Bio Soap Powder	107394	
£1.00	Economy Fab Conditioner	115999	
£3.19	Bold Bio 2in1 8 Tablets	105713	
£2.59	Ariel Handwash 960g	799990	
£1.99	Lenor Fab Conditioner	126049	
£0.60	Economy Wash Up Lqd 500ml	127344	
£1.00	All Purpose Cloth 4s	131534	
£1.05	Econ Toilet Tissue Twn Wht	114083	
£1.00	Incense Sticks 20s	133650	
£1.29	Alarm Clock/Needs AA Batt	114383	
£2.54	Addis 3 piece seal tight	065506	
£1.32	Latte Mug 34cl	122717	
£1.99	Flip Flops Size 8-11	059046	
£1.00	Playing Cards	126317	
£1.05	Table Tennis Ball 6pk	115759	
£7.99	Safety Flat Sheet White	124288	
£13.99	Safety Duvet Cover SkyBlue	125726	
£2.99	Pillowcase Sky Blue	129312	
£13.99	Safety Duvet Cover Lemon	136196	
£2.99	Pillowcase Lemon	136202	
£22.99	Safety Sgl Quilt 9 Tog.	123996	
£9.99	Safety Single Pillow	124287	
£2.95	Neoprene Wrist Support	096103	
	SPECIAL OFFERS		
£3.45	Valentines Cards Various	092945	
£3.65	Valentines Cards 2013	136464	
	Offer 1		
	Offer 2		
	Offer 3		
	Offer 4		
	Offer 5		
	Offer 6		
	Offer 7		
	Offer 8		
	Offer 9		

Total Number of Items Ordered _____ Total Cost _____

A4.21

14 DAY RULE NOTIFICATION SLIP

Date Received ...8.|11.|12................. Expiry Date22.|11.11.12..............

Prisoner Number ..A.1910.C.T......... Name ...OLOFIELD.................

You have received an item in the post via an unauthorised source. The items are listed below.

1. 1x. Guardian.. Weekly....   2. 1x. copy Home Dentention curfew

3. ....   4. ....

Unless you make an application to either post the item/s out at your expense or to hand them out on a visit within the next fourteen days they will be disposed of and destroyed.

Please return this slip to stating how you wish to dispose of the item / s

I wish to hand it /them out on my next visit   Date of next visit ....

I wish to pay for the item / s to be posted out at my expense and attach a cash dispersement form to that effect

Signed ....   Name ....

EDUCATION DEPARTMENT
HMP WORMWOOD SCRUBS
EXTENSION: 3360

To: OLDFIELD   Number: A1010CT   Location: A4. 021

1st freeflow
(workshop)

From The Induction Team
Re: CLASS ALLOCATION NOTIFICATION

Date: 16-11-12

You have been allocated to the following class in Education:

Days	Class	Time/session _Delete as required_		Start Date	Teacher	Room Number
		AM 08:45- 11:15	PM 13:45- 16:00			shop
Monday to Friday	1T		13:45- 16:00	19-11-12	Tnoria	6

PLEASE BRING THIS SLIP WITH YOU ON YOUR FIRST DAY

Failure to attend Education after allocation will result in NO PAY.
We look forward to seeing you - Welcome to Education.

Earn as you Learn

Education Assessment Results:
Literacy:
Numeracy:

TEA

Choice	THURSDAY - TEA	Codes
A	Halal Lamb Burger In Gravy	(Lamb) (Halal)
B	Cauliflower Cheese	(Veg) (Vegetarian)
C	Pasta in tomato sauce	(Veg) (Vegan) (Healthier)
D	Corned Beef Pasty	(Beef)
E	Pork Faggot x 2 In Gravy	(Pork)

Choice	FRIDAY - TEA	Codes
A	Chicken & Mushroom Pie	(Poultry) (Halal)
B	Cheese & Tomato Pizza	(Veg) (Vegetarian)
C	Butter Bean Lasagne	(Veg) (Vegan) (Healthier)
D	Battered Fish	(Fish) (Halal)
E	Chicken Tikka Pie	(Poultry)

Choice	MONDAY - TEA	Codes
A	Chilli Minced Beef	(Beef) (Halal) (Healthier)
B	Sweet & Sour Vegetables	(Veg) (Vegan) (Healthier)
C	Chick Pea Curry	(Veg) (Vegan)
D	Chicken & Vegetable Pie	(Poultry)
E	Minced Beef Curry	(Beef) (Healthier)

Choice	TUESDAY - TEA	Codes
A	Beef lasagne	(Fish) (Halal) (Healthier)
B	Vegan vegetable Pie	(Veg)
C	Vegetable Soya Chilli & kidney b...	(Veg) (Vegan) (Healthier)
D	Meatballs in Chilli Sauce	(Poultry)
E	Beef lasagne	(Beef) (Healthier)

Choice	WEDNESDAY - TEA	Codes
A	Lamb Pie	(Lamb) (Halal)
B	Vegetable Curry Pasty	(Veg) (Vegetarian)
C	Mixed bean salad	(Veg) (Vegan) (Healthier)
D	Turkey & Ham Pie	(Pork) (Poultry)
E	Savoury Mince Beef & Dumpling	(Beef) (Healthier)

SWEET

Choice	THURSDAY - TEA SWEET	Codes
X	Vanilla Sponge & Custard	(Vegetarian)
Y	Yogurt	(GM) (Healthier)
Z	Fresh Fruit	(Veg) (Vegan) (Healthier)

Choice	FRIDAY - TEA SWEET	Codes
X	Fruit crumble & custard	(Vegetarian)
Y	Yogurt	(GM) (Healthier)
Z	Fresh Fruit	(Veg) (Vegan) (Healthier)

Choice	MONDAY - TEA SWEET	Codes
X	Jam sponge & Custard	(Vegetarian)
Y	Yogurt	(GM) (Healthier)
Z	Fresh Fruit	(Veg) (Vegan) (Healthier)

Choice	TUESDAY - TEA SWEET	Codes
X	Ginger Sponge & Custard	(Vegetarian)
Y	Yogurt	(GM) (Healthier)
Z	Fresh Fruit	(Veg) (Vegan) (Healthier)

Choice	WEDNESDAY - TEA SWEET	Codes
X	Eve's Pudding & custard	(Vegetarian)
Y	Yogurt	(GM) (Healthier)
Z	Fresh Fruit	(Veg) (Vegan) (Healthier)

MAKE YOUR CHOICES IN THE GREY BOX

ON THE OTHER SIDE

KEY TO SYMBOLS

- ☺ : Healthier Option (Lower in Fat & Sugar)
- ● : Vegan Option (Also Vegetarian and Halal Option)
- ☯ : Vegetarian Option (Also Halal Option)
- ☪ : Halal Meat, Poultry or Fish
- ⌘ : May Contain Genetically Modified Foods
- Main Ingredient: Veg/Fruit/Grains/Beans/Cheese
- Main Ingredient: Fish
- Main Ingredient Poultry (Chicken/Turkey/Egg)
- Main Ingredient: Pork / Bacon
- Main Ingredient: Beef
- Main Ingredient: Lamb
- Main Ingredient: Goat

All dishes are subject to availability and may change without prior notice
All medical dietary needs must be reported to the kitchen through the Medical Officer / Doctor

Pre-select Menu Week 3			LUNCH		week commencing:	06/12/2012

Choice	THURSDAY - LUNCH		CODES	
1	Beef Sausage Roll		☪	
2	Vegetable Samosa		☯	
3	Soya Cottage Pie		●	☺
4	Minced Beef Pie			
5	Sweet & Sour Turkey			☺

PRISON NUMBER : ....

NAME : ....

CELL : ....

① **Circle Your Choice**

Choice	FRIDAY - LUNCH		CODES	
1	Tuna Baguette		☪	
2	Cheese Baguette		☯	
3	Peanut Butter Baguette		●	☺
4	Beef Baguette			
5	Tomato Soup & Baguette		☯	

LUNCH

THURSDAY	1	2	3	4	5	6
FRIDAY	1	2	3	4	5	6
MONDAY	1	2	3	4	5	6
TUESDAY	1	2	3	4	5	6
WEDNESDAY	1	2	3	4	5	6

Choice	MONDAY - LUNCH		CODES	
1	Beefburger in gravy		☪	☺
2	Cous Cous Salad		●	☺
3	Mixed bean stew		●	☺
4	Bacon Chop			
5	Beefburger in gravy			☺

TEA

THURSDAY	A	B	C	D	E	F
FRIDAY	A	B	C	D	E	F
MONDAY	A	B	C	D	E	F
TUESDAY	A	B	C	D	E	F
WEDNESDAY	A	B	C	D	E	F

Choice	TUESDAY - LUNCH		CODES	
1	Turkey Fricasse		☪	☺
2	Potato Au Gratin		☯	
3	Soya bolognaise		●	☺
4	Battered Chicken Steaks			
5	Jumbo Pork Sausage In Gravy			

SWEET

THURSDAY	X	Y	Z
FRIDAY	X	Y	Z
MONDAY	X	Y	Z
TUESDAY	X	Y	Z
WEDNESDAY	X	Y	Z

Choice	WEDNESDAY - LUNCH		CODES	
1	Savoury Lamb Mince & Dumpling		☪	☺
2	Vegetable Casserole		●	☺
3	Vegetable Sausages in Tomato Sauce		●	☺
4	Breaded Fish		☪	
5	Ox Liver Casserole			☺

TURN OVER FOR TEA CHOICES

Notification of discharge from prison

This person has been
discharged from prison.
We have advised them to call
at your office to make a claim

- To claim benefit or apply for Pension Credit when you are discharged, contact your Jobcentre Plus office, Jobcentre, social security office or Pension Centre.
- To find your nearest office, look in the telephone directory under Jobcentre Plus, Jobcentre or Social Security or look at our website www.jobcentreplus.gov.uk
- If you or your partner are aged 60 or over, you may be entitled to Pension Credit. To apply for Pension Credit please contact 0800 99 1234.
- Please say when you claim if you have claimed benefit using any other name or address or if you have claimed at another office. This may help us deal with your claim more quickly.
- You do not need an address to claim benefit.
- Please bring this form with you when you make your claim

Surname	Oldfield
Other names	Trenton
Date of birth	11 / 5 / 76
National Insurance (NI) number	Letters Numbers Letter
Prisoner number	A1010CT
Address on discharge	Flat 24 MYRDLE Court Myrdle Street London Postcode

Date custody began	19 / 10 / 12
Date of discharge	4 / 12 / 12
Amount of discharge grant	£ 46.00
Any other money on discharge	£ 4.00
List of any clothes issued on discharge	

Prison contact (BLOCK CAPITALS)	CUSTODY OFFICE
Phone number	020 8588 3200
Date	4 / 12 / 12.
HM Prison stamp	H.M. PRISON WORMWOOD SCRUBS P O BOX 757 DU CANE ROAD LONDON W12 0AE

LICENCE

Criminal Justice Act 2003

WORMWOOD SCRUBS (HMP)
Telephone – 020 8588 3200

A1010CT

Surname:
OLDFIELD
Forename(s):
TRENTON
DOB:
11/05/1976

Name: **Trenton Oldfield**

NOMS No: **A1010CT**   CRO No. **284489/12E**   Date of Birth: **11/05/1976**

Prison No: **G88604**   PNCID No: **12/173365X**

1. Under the provisions of section 246 of the Criminal Justice Act 2003 you are being released on licence and must comply with the conditions of this licence.

2. You will be subject to a Home Detention Curfew. The objective of the Home Detention Curfew is to help you manage your return into the community.

3. Your Home Detention Curfew commences on **04/12/2012** and expires on **17/01/2013** unless this licence is previously revoked.

4. The address(es) to which you are subject to curfew is:
   FLAT 24
   MYRDLE COURT
   MYRDLE STREET
   LONDON
   E1 1HP

   Details of curfew times are shown below at paragraph 6.

5. On the day of your release, you will be subject to curfew at your curfew address from **19:00** until midnight. The contractor will visit you at this address during this time in order to fit you with the tag. On your last day of curfew the contractor will visit you to remove the tag and monitoring equipment. This will take place in the last two hours of your last curfew period between 10pm and midnight.

6. After your day of release, you are required to remain at your place of curfew during the following hours:

Monday	from	19:15	Hrs each evening until	07:15	Hrs the following morning
Tuesday	from	19:15	Hrs each evening until	07:15	Hrs the following morning
Wednesday	from	19:15	Hrs each evening until	07:15	Hrs the following morning
Thursday	from	19:15	Hrs each evening until	07:15	Hrs the following morning
Friday	from	19:15	Hrs each evening until	07:15	Hrs the following morning
Saturday	from	19:15	Hrs each evening until	07:15	Hrs the following morning
Sunday	from	19:15	Hrs each evening until	07:15	Hrs the following morning

7. Your compliance with the conditions of the Home Detention Curfew will be monitored by the electronic monitoring contractor. You must provide the contractor with access to the curfew address to install and check the monitoring equipment and electronic tag. Such visits will be made during your curfew hours but not between midnight and 6.00am. However, the contractor may visit the curfew address between midnight and 6:00am in order to investigate a reported violation.

8. The monitoring equipment will usually operate via the mobile cellular network and will only need a dedicated telephone line to be fitted if the mobile signal is poor at the curfew address. You will be responsible for meeting the cost of the small amount of electricity used by the monitoring equipment at your curfew address. It is your responsibility to ensure that there is an electricity supply available during your time on curfew.

LICENCE

Criminal Justice Act 2003

WORMWOOD SCRUBS (HMP)
Telephone – 020 8588 3200

Name: **Trenton Oldfield**

NOMS No: **A1010CT**   CRO No. **284489/12E**   Date of Birth: **11/05/1976**

Prison No: **G88604**   PNCID No: **12/173365X**

9. In the event of a dedicated telephone line needing to be installed you must agree to the installation at your curfew address for use by the supplier. The supplier will notify you of a time and a date and you must be present, and provide access to, the curfew address at the notified time to allow installation to take place. The installation will normally take place during standard working hours and is fully paid for by the supplier.

10. While on Home Detention Curfew you may be liable to recall to prison if you breach the condition of this licence relating to the curfew. You will be in breach of this condition if:

    i.   You are absent from your curfew address during the specified curfew hours;

    ii. You commit violence against or threaten the contractor or any of his staff with violence;

    iii. You damage or tamper with the monitoring equipment;

    iv. You withdraw your consent to the monitoring arrangements.

11. **It is a condition of your release on licence that you are well behaved, do not commit any offence and do not do anything which could undermine the objectives of your early release from prison.**

12. In addition, you may be recalled to prison if your whereabouts can no longer be electronically monitored at the specified address.

13. The contractor may authorise your absence from your place of curfew in clearly defined circumstances, which you will be informed about by the contractor in writing. You must contact the contractor in advance of any such absence to seek authorisation where this is possible. If it is not possible to contact the contractor in advance, you must contact them as soon as possible thereafter. Absence for any other reason other than these clearly defined circumstances will constitute a breach of your curfew condition.

14. If you need to seek a permanent change to your curfew conditions (for instance because of the requirements of a new job), you must contact the Prison Service establishment from which you were released. A contact number is attached at the bottom of this licence.

15. Your sentence expires on **18/04/2012**.

Contact Points

Monitoring Supplier: **London & Eastern (Serco)**   08080 965 124

Releasing establishment: **WORMWOOD SCRUBS (HMP)**   020 8588 3200

LICENCE

Criminal Justice Act 2003

WORMWOOD SCRUBS (HMP)
Telephone – 020 8588 3200

Name: **Trenton Oldfield**

NOMS No: **A1010CT**　　　　CRO No. **284489/12E**　　　　Date of Birth:**11/05/1976**

Prison No: **G88604**　　　　PNCID No: **12/173365X**

Signed:　　　　　　　　　　　Status:　PSM F

Date:　3/12/12

for the Secretary of State for Justice

This licence has been given to me and its requirements have been explained.

Name: **Trenton Oldfield**

Signed:

Date:　4/12/12

Bringing service to life

serco

Curfew Monitoring
As an Alternative

Electronic Monitoring Subject Guide

You have been made subject of a curfew order by a Court or other Authority.
(Hereinafter called the "Authority")

What this book tells you about

This tells you about the requirements of the curfew and the equipment which is used to monitor that you are keeping to your curfew. It also tells you who to contact if you have any problems, how "Tagging" works and tips on what you must do and must not do to make sure you complete your curfew.

What is a curfew?

It means that you must stay indoors at a set place during times that have been given to you by the Authority.

What is electronic monitoring?

It is the official wording for "tagging". It means that you will wear a tag and have a box installed at the place you must stay at during the curfew. The box and the tag will check that you are where you should be and immediately let Serco know if you break the curfew conditions

When does the curfew start?

Usually on the day it is given to you by the Authority. You must be in during your curfew times.

What does it mean to me?

An officer from Serco Monitoring will meet you at your curfew address at some point during your curfew period, to install the tagging equipment. Make sure you see their identification card.
The tagging equipment comprises of a waterproof tag which is usually lifted to your ankle and a box called a Monitoring Unit which will be placed into your curfew address.

For the box to work it must be connected to the electricity supply at all times. It will report information regarding your compliance with your curfew to the Monitoring Centre using a telephone system. You may be required to allow Serco to install a telephone line into your curfew address. If you do not let this happen you could be returned back to the Authority for action

Serco Monitoring will only install the equipment once you have been correctly identified, therefore please ensure you have available any paperwork given to you by the Authority and photographic ID or ID with a signature on it.

You will be reminded about your times and boundaries of your curfew. This usually means you cannot go outside your front door or back door or into any rooms that can only be accessed externally

It is quite possible that you may get telephone calls any time during your curfew which must be answered. This will be the Monitoring Centre trying to get in touch with you about your curfew

1

Warnings and Violations

Your curfew has been made by the Authority and you must keep to your curfew times and place set by them
If you go out during your curfew you may receive a warning letter or be sent back to the Authority for action
You can also be sent back if you or anyone else damages any of the equipment.
You could be held responsible for the damage

Action will be taken if you or anyone else threatens or assaults any Serco Monitoring staff.

If you keep to the curfew times and your equipment does not get damaged then you will have little contact with the monitoring officers

Visits and Telephone Calls

Monitoring officers will visit or phone at various times during your curfew.

■ When you are first put onto the system.

■ At any time during the curfew hours if you do not keep to your curfew or tamper with the equipment

■ Occasionally to check or service the equipment

■ Monitoring officers may also be seen outside your place of curfew checking to see if you are keeping to the curfew

■ To carry out a subject satisfaction survey, to ask questions about how your curfew is going.
You must always answer any calls made by the Monitoring Centre and allow entry to your place of curfew if they wish to check any part of the equipment.

Hints

■ Always allow plenty of time to get home before the start of your curfew. Take into consideration heavy traffic, delayed busses etc.

■ Use the clock on the monitoring box; this is correct. Set your watch by it

■ Make sure you have plenty of food etc to see you through to the end of each curfew period.

■ If you have an electricity meter, make sure you have enough coins or cards

■ Arrange your family needs and commitments around your curfew

If you have a medical appointment or a meeting with another agency (Job Centre, Probation etc.) which will affect your curfew times make sure that you tell them that the Monitoring Centre will phone them to check that you have been there.

If you have to change the address or the times of your curfew, you must gain permission from the Authority before doing so, failure to do this will result in you being sent back to them for action. Make sure you notify the Monitoring Centre **before** any changes happen.
If there is anything you are unsure of, just phone the Monitoring Centre on the free phone number provided.

2

Absences you know about before they happen:

If you tell us know 24 hours before any of the following absences we may be able to give permission for a one-off absence

- For a job interview
- To attend a wedding or funeral ceremony of a family member (but not the reception it in curfew hours)
- For attendance at court as a witness/defendant
- A one-off medical appointment
- Other circumstances where the Authority has agreed that an absence may be authorised

For any of the 5 reasons you must telephone the Monitoring Centre 24 hours before it happens. You will have to send Serco Monitoring written confirmation about where you have been. If you do not get the appropriate permission and miss part of the curfew you may be reported to the Authority who may take action against you. Our officer may visit you to find out the reason and ask for written evidence of that reason.

What to do in an Emergency

There may be a time when you need emergency medical treatment. If this happens you must telephone the Monitoring Centre during the absence or at the latest, within 12 hours after your visit to the doctor or hospital has ended. We will check with the place where you received treatment that you have attended, who the patient was and whether it was urgent.

Telephones

A telephone system will be provided at no cost to allow us to contact you during your curfew.

The Monitoring Centre is always open and you can speak to one of our staff at any time of day and night. If you are away from home the free phone number of the Monitoring Centre is on the tag.

**The freephone numbers are: 08080 965124
08080 152369**

Important – All calls to and from the
Monitoring Centre may be recorded.

How tagging works:

1. The tag is fitted to the ankle, and a monitoring box is put in the place of curfew. This box picks up a signal from the tag that says when the tag leaves the place of curfew. You will be expected to stay indoors and not go outside

2. If the tag leaves the place of curfew or if it gets damaged, it tells the monitoring box which tells the Monitoring Centre

3. The Monitoring Centre will quickly telephone you to find out what happened

4. A monitoring officer may visit you to find out what has happened, at any time during the curfew even after midnight

Monitoring requirements:

The following refers to
Early release from custody on Licence / Sentence from Court / order given by other Authority

(Hereinafter called the Authority)

I know that I have been given a curfew when I will be monitored electronically.

I must reside at:

My curfew boundaries are:

I also agree to follow these requirements during the times of my curfew.

1. I will wear an electronic tag 24 hours a day until my curfew requirements end or I am told otherwise by the Authority or Responsible Officer. (The Responsible Officer is another way of saying – the tagging company).

2. I know that my curfew starts now and ends on _____ at (time).
   (date)
   My curfew times have been explained to me. If I am not at my place of curfew without good reason during my curfew hours it is a breach of my curfew and I may be sent back to the Authority for action. I also understand that I will have to explain why I was not at my curfew address when I should have been.

3. If I must leave my place of curfew because of an emergency I will try to telephone the Monitoring Centre immediately. If I cannot do this, I will call the Monitoring Centre as soon as I can afterwards, to explain what has happened. A free telephone number is printed on the tag. If I break my curfew requirement for any reason at all, I know I will have to explain or give other evidence of the breach. That evidence may be shown to the Authority.

4. I am fully responsible for all the monitoring equipment and trying to take off or damage any of the equipment by me or anyone else, without good reason will be discovered immediately. If anybody else interferes with any of the equipment I could still get the blame. Any interference with the equipment may be taken as a violation of my curfew requirement and I might be sent back to the Authority for action. I understand that if this happens I will have to explain the violation.

5. If I receive an instruction to remove the tag or otherwise damage or move any of the electronic monitoring equipment I will contact the Monitoring Centre first to confirm that instruction. Only if the operator confirms the instruction should you remove or touch any part of the electronic monitoring equipment. Failure to comply with this may result in breach proceedings being taken against you.

6. I give permission to fit a new telephone line, if one is needed at the curfew address to be used for my curfew. I also agree to let the monitoring company find the telephone line provider into my place of curfew so that they can fit, maintain and take out any telephone or electronic monitoring equipment that is needed for my curfew. I will not have to pay for the telephone line or calls that are made while the line is used by the monitoring service. I know that I must not do anything to damage or remove the telephone line, or telephone, such as unplugging the cable or leaving the phone off the hook. I will make sure the householder and other persons present know about this.

7. I know that I must always provide a continuous supply of electricity for the monitoring equipment.

5

8. I must always answer any call made to the monitoring unit. I may also get visits by Monitoring Officers at any time during my curfew hours so that they can inspect the equipment. They may also visit me to check where I am if there is a suspected violation of the curfew. I understand that if I do not let the officers into the curfew address during my curfew periods for these reasons it may result in breach proceedings being started against me.

9. I have been told that the local police may be able to ask about how I have been during on my curfew order. If at any time they have cause to believe that I may be suspected of another offence.

10. I hereby give permission to any third party to answer any enquiry from Serco about any appointment or visit. I have made during the curfew hours. Serco acknowledge that any information received will be treated in strictest confidence.

11. If for any reason I cannot stay at my curfew address, the Monitoring Centre as soon as reasonably possible to tell them why. I will also apply to the Authority for the curfew address or times of the order to be changed as soon as is reasonably possible, preferably 24 hours before the changes happen. If I change my address without contacting the Monitoring Centre and the Authority, then it may result in breach proceedings being taken against me.

I understand that if I break any of the above requirements I will be reported to the Authority who may take action against me.

Staff Safety

Although the employees of Serco Monitoring are visiting your home, they are still entitled to work in a safe and smoke-free environment and we ask for your co-operation.

- No abuse or threats against our staff will be tolerated
- Ensure that any animals are locked away
- Do not lock doors or obstruct any exits which confine Serco Officers
- Please do not smoke or allow others to smoke when the officer is present

If you, family members or friends are unable to do this, Serco Monitoring staff have the right to leave the site and report the matter to the Authority.

You should be aware that each employee has a support team monitoring their safety and if they do not report in, assistance will be dispatched to their location.

You may receive a telephone call at some point asking you to answer some questions about your curfew. The information gained will help us improve the service we desire to you.

Confirmation

I confirm that I have had explained to me the terms and effect of all the guidelines I agree to comply with these guidelines throughout the whole of this order

Name: _____

Signed: _____   ID _____

Field Officer ID _____   Date _____

6

7

Guidelines:

You Must

- Stay at the place of curfew during the times you have been given.
  You must not go out, unless the Authority has already given you permission.

- Always answer the telephone as it will be the Monitoring Centre trying to talk to you about the curfew.

- Tell the Monitoring Centre immediately if you have any problems with your telephone, electricity or monitoring equipment.

- If you hear a loud noise when you are on the phone, please finish the call and start the call again a few minutes later. The noise will be the computer contacting the monitoring box.

- Always replace the handset onto the monitoring box and press the end call button after you have finished the call.

You Must Not

- Arrive late at, or leave the place of curfew during the time that you have been given.

- Try to break or remove the tag or allow anyone else to do so. You will get the blame if it is damaged. The Authority may be told about it and action will be taken against you.

- Unplug the electricity supply or the telephone. The box will still record your curfew events and alert the Monitoring Centre about the electricity or telephone being unplugged and that you may be breaking your curfew.

- Open or move the monitoring box. The Monitoring Centre will be alerted if it is moved in any way.

- Put anything on the monitoring box such as books or towels. Do not even dust it!

Information for Others

Please respect that the person on curfew has restrictions that they have to comply with. If there are any problems with the curfew please contact the Monitoring Centre.

Complaints

If you have any complaints about the way your curfew is being monitored please call our Monitoring Centre to tell us about it, they may be able to look into your problem immediately.

If it cannot be sorted out over the phone please write to:

The Responsible Officer
Serco Monitoring
PO Box 45
Norwich
Norfolk NR3 1BF

If you live in East Anglia or Greater London telephone 08080 965124

If you live in the West Midlands or Wales telephone 08080 152099

Your complaint will be investigated and you will be told about the result within 30 days.

IF YOU HAVE ANY PROBLEMS WITH YOUR CURFEW, YOU CAN TELEPHONE US AT NO COST

TELEPHONE CALLS MAY BE MONITORED AND RECORDED.

Serco Monitoring Centre Assistance
London & Eastern: 08080 965124
West Midlands & Wales: 08080 152369

we are here to help you
if you need us - just call !!

 **CRIMESTOPPERS**
0800 555 111

- Your call is free
- You do not have to give your name
- You may receive a reward

CHILDLINE
Free 24-hour
help line
0800 1111

SAMARITANS
0845 790 9090
- Totally confidential
- Can be totally anonymous
- Available 24/7
jo@samaritans.org

 nacro
changing lives
reducing crime

Nacro, the crime reduction charity

Nacro's Resettlement *Plus* Helpline

0800 018 1259

 jobcentreplus

0845 377 1002

Talk to FRANK
A-Z of Drugs • Advice • Help
0800 77 66 00
frank@talktofrank.com

Al-Anon Family Groups
Disturbed by someone else's drinking?
For a confidential Helpline Ring 020 7403 0888 10am-10pm

 European Union
European Social Fund
Investing in jobs and skills

Central London Community Healthcare **NHS**
NHS Trust

Barnet ‖ Hammersmith and Fulham ‖ Kensington and Chelsea ‖ Westminster

Offender Healthcare
HMP Wormwood Scrubs
Du Cane Road
London
W12 0AE

04 Dec 2012

Mr Trenton Oldfield

Date of Birth: **11 May 1976**

This gentleman has been under the care of Central London Community Healthcare NHS Trust Specialist Services Team.

If he needs to register with a GP will you please assist?

Please find attached his recent summary of care.

Should you require any further information please do not hesitate to contact us.

Mental Health Team	**020 8588 3382**
Substance Misuse Team	**020 8588 3655**
Primary Care Team	**020 8588 3449**
Pharmacy Department	**020 8588 3390**
General Practitioners	**020 8588 3392**

Regards,

The Healthcare Team

HMP Wormwood Scrubs
Education Department

kcc.ac.uk
Kensington and Chelsea College
West London Campus

INITIAL ASSESSMENT INFORMATION BOOKLET

Name: _OLDfield   TRENTON_

Prison Number: _A1010ct_   ULN: _____

Location: _____

Enclosed are the results of the assessment you have taken and information about the educational opportunities available to you while you are here.

ASSESSMENT RESULTS

Literacy	Numeracy	Computer Skills	Financial Capability
L1+	L1		

This document is important, you will need it as proof of assessment and levels obtained for allocation to education, training and employment.

What do your results mean?

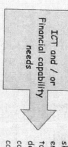

Pre entry to Entry 2

You will be referred to courses in the education department to further develop your skills. You can also get help from Toe by Toe in the wings. Additional learning support is available to help you to progress and achieve.

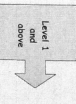

Entry 3

You will be referred to courses in the education department to further develop your skills. You may also engage in part-time employment.

Level 1 and above

You can engage with work in any area of the prison.

There are some courses delivered at level 2 through education.

You can also apply for distance learning or Open university, if you are sentenced.

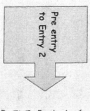

ICT and / or Financial capability needs

If you don't have any computer skills or they are basic, you may enrol in IT classes from beginners to Level 2. If you need help in dealing with financial matters, you can get help through attending education or being referred to other agencies for support.

The Learner's Charter

As a learner on our courses you can expect:

- good advice on how to improve your skills that lead to employability.
- a report with your initial assessment results
- an individual learning plan
- a programme of learning relating to the national standards that match your aims and aspirations
- full involvement in planning and reviewing your learning
- feedback and support on your progress
- flexible forms of learning that suit your needs and preferences
- advice on progression routes to other education, training or employment opportunities

All students on education are expected to:

- abide by Education rules
- undertake all work assigned by the tutor and work to the best of their ability
- not to misuse or remove furniture, equipment or resources and respect everything that is provided for your use
- not to leave the classroom unless agreed by the tutor
- co-operate fully with staff and act cordially towards staff and other learners
- Attend education punctually and provide valid reasons when not to attend
- comply with rules and regulations applicable to the use of the computers
- not bring tobacco or smoking products the education department and the library, which are non-smoking areas

What is on offer?

I.T. Learning how to use computers on your daily life. You can start your journey from the very beginning with ICT functional skills entry level or you can work towards an OCR Level 1 CLAIT modules on file management, creating spreadsheets, E publications, OCR Level 2 is also available which comprises of an additional 5 modules. Also available is the European Computer Driving Licence (ECDL).

Budgeting and Money Management: This course aims to enable learners to improve their knowledge on personal financing. Very useful if you want to start a business or simply manage your day to day finances.

Preparation for Work: This course aims to enable learners to obtain the skills and knowledge needed to gain training or employment.

Literacy Entry level 1, E2, E3 you can work towards the OCR Functional Skills exam. The class covers speaking and listening, grammar, punctuation, spelling and writing skills. You can also get help from the additional learning support tutors.

L1 and L2: You can carry on improving your basic literacy skills through a range of subjects. i.e. Employability and Life skills, Pathways to journalism, creative writing and writing skills, radio production, business start up. You will develop skills that allow you to write clearly and coherently, to interpret texts and to present your ideas and opinions make use of more structured and sophisticated language.

Numeracy Entry leve 1, E1, E2, E3 The aim of numeracy classes is to help you build upon your understanding of mathematical concepts and to apply these to practical situations. You can achieve a OCR functional skills accreditation.

L1 and L2 you will be taught mathematical concepts that help you to identify situation or problems and apply a range of mathematical methods needed for solving them. You can aim at achieving OCR Functional Skills as well as Adult Numeracy accreditation.

Employability and Life Skills: You will need to obtain level 1 in both Literacy and or Numeracy in order to apply for this programme, it supports the development of social and life skills by providing learners with opportunities to improve upon their levels of skills, knowledge, personal awareness and self esteem.

These courses aim to improve your employability skills, making you more able to acquire a job and sustaining it. It can also help you with managing your behaviour, attitude and relationships.

You will gain access to **Virtual Campus,** where you can look for real job opportunities on release.

Art: No previous experience is needed to join the Art Class. It is more important that you are enthusiastic and committed. You will be expected to study both drawing and painting, working towards a national qualification. .

Esol: This course is for foreign nationals who want to communicate better in English. All skills are covered; speaking, listening, reading and writing.

There are further information in other languages in the department. If you know someone who need help because of their lack of command of English language, please refer them to KCC.

KITCHEN

If you choose to work, you will have a range of vocational training to undertake. We will also offer you help with any learning needs you may have, in your work place.

GYMNASIUM

Laundry

Individual Learning Plan

The results of the initial assessment will be used to develop an individual learning plan (ILP) for you.

The ILP will be drawn up and agreed between you and your course tutor. Your tutor will meet with you regularly to discuss your progress towards identified learning goals with SMART targets to help you achieve.

The Education Department is a safe environment where

We respect one another as individuals.

Racist, sexist, inappropriate and homophobic language will not be tolerated.

Accept people's differences and learn to co-exist.

Provide advice, care and support appropriate to the needs of the individual.

Bullying will not be tolerated.

To manage difficult situations in a professional and calm way.

Staff will not discriminate against any individual or groups of individuals because of gender, racial group, sexual orientation, disability, religion, age, or any other factor.

We will tackle unacceptable behavior or address concerns as soon as they arise.

DRUGS AND ALCOHOL

ATTITUDE, THINKING & BEHAVIOUR

CHILDREN & FAMILIES

RESSETLEMENT PATHWAYS

FINANCE DEBT & BENEFIT

ACCOMODATION

MENTAL & PHYSICAL HEALTH

EDUCATION, TRAINING & EMPLOYMENT

ATTITUDE, THINKING & BEHAVIOUR

If your needs can not be met through the education department, we will refer you to other departments that will be able to support you.

Kensington and Chelsea College
Education Department
Wormwood Scrubs
Du Cane Road
London
W12 OAE

General enquries:3358

Induction Office:3360

You can **EARN** as you **LEARN**:
Students receive a wage for attending
education. classes.

Wormwood Scrubs

GYM USER

Name... Oldfield

Eth W9

No. A101901

Card No. 21540

In the Crown Court

at Isleworth

Case No: T20120506

Court Code: 475

Trenton Oldfield
c/o H.M.P.

Notice of costs order

In the case of Regina v OLDFIELD

the defendant Trenton Oldfield

Date of birth: 11/05/1976

was convicted on 26 September 2012.

On the 19 October 2012 the defendant was ordered ;

To pay £750.00 towards the costs of the prosecution;

PAYMENT is to be made to HMCS at the address below
within 12 months

Her Majesty's Courts Service,
London Collection Compliance Centre
Po Box 13093
LONDON
SW1P 3WT

An Officer of the Crown Court
Date: 19 October 2012

(5018)

Your pocket
guide to
Moving On.

Your Case Manager is:

RAJ KARIM
07814 462 961

ANGELA REEB
07791 029 782

FOR MR TRENTON
_____

ON THIS CARD ARE
THE CONTACT DETAILS
OF YOUR COMMUNITY
CASE MANAGERS

Articles &

Documents

End the Criminalisation of Protest

/

Press release issued by Defend the Right to Protest on 16 October 2012

On the 7th of April 2012, Trenton Oldfield undertook a direct-action protest at the Oxford and Cambridge Boat Race. The aim of his protest was to focus attention on the long-standing and entirely unjust inequalities in British society that are being severely exacerbated by government cuts and reductions in civil liberties. Trenton chose the Oxford and Cambridge Boat Race because it is a symbol of class, privilege and elitism in Britain.

An astonishing 70% of the cabinet in the current government are Oxford or Cambridge graduates. This government is protecting the privileges of the wealthy while cutting the essential necessities of the majority and the poor and reducing people's rights and freedoms. In the three days before Trenton's protest, the coalition government (1) received royal assent for its bill to privatise the NHS, (2) introduced the Communications Data Bill to legalise surveillance of all digital communications of UK subjects, and (3) called on people to 'shop their neighbours' if they suspected they might protest at the 2012 Olympic Games.

Trenton's protest aimed at drawing attention to these injustices. He swam into the course of the boat race. The race was halted and restarted 25 minutes later. The action was seen by an international audience but it affected just 18 rowers and a handful of event organisers on a closed river, on a long weekend. The direct-action protest was wholly consistent with Trenton's decade+ work in London on addressing this city's unnecessary poverty and inequalities. The audience for the free event experienced a minor delay of 25 minutes. The BBC coverage ended at its pre-scheduled time-slot. Not a single complaint was received from the public by either the Metropolitan police or the BBC.

Trenton was initially charged with Section 5 of the 'public order act'. Hansard reports reveal that government ministers asked the police commissioner to increase the charge so that a custodial sentence could be achieved. On the morning of his first court appearance (23 April 2012) Trenton's charge was significantly increased via the ancient common law charge of 'public nuisance' under which conviction can result in life in prison. On the 26 September 2012 Trenton was found guilty of causing 'public nuisance' for undertaking his protest.

The recent conviction and sentencing of Russian feminist rock collective Pussy Riot to two years in prison for their protest was rightly met with shock and anger for the lack of tolerance towards dissent under Putin. The very same lack of tolerance towards dissent seems to be happening in Britain as Trenton waits for sentencing on the 19th October 2012.

Defend the Right to Protest

Defend the Right to Protest and the signatories below extend our solidarity to Trenton and wholeheartedly believe that he should not have faced criminal charges for exercising his right to protest. We are concerned about the change in the original charge seemingly due to political and media pressure. To us it is clear that this protest against inequality and elitism does not warrant a custodial sentence, least of all possibly years in prison. Defend the Right to Protest are also alarmed that this charge might be levied against protesters in the future. The only motive we can see for the CPS selecting this outdated legislation is that it offers courts the chance to hand down sentences up to life in prison.

List of signees:

Adbusters, *Culturejammers*

Agnieszka Mlicka

Aidan Mosselson

Aisha Gill, Human Rights Law

Alberto Duman

Alberto Toscano, *Goldsmiths*

Alejandro Colas, *Birkbeck College*

Alessandro Columbano, *Birmingham City University*

Alf Guedeney

Alice Lobb

Alison Lloyd

Ama Menec

Ana Kutlesa, Ivana Hanacek, Marijana Manic, *BLOK Zagreb*

Ana Pedrosa, *Manobras no Porto*

Anastasia Kavada, School of Media, Arts & Design, *University of Westminster*

Andrea Gibbons

Andreas Lang, *public works*

Andrew Crowe

Aneta Szylak, Curator

Anja Marie Kirschner

Anna Maierski

Anna Minton, *Ground Control*

Anna Plyshtera

Ashley Wong

Atakan Mercan

Auro Foxcroft, *Village Underground*

Barbara Murray

Barbara Van Dyck

Ben Eastop

Ben Pritchett

Ben Watson

Benedict Seymour, *Mute magazine*

Brenna Bhandar

Brian Ashton

Campaign Against Criminalising Communities (CAMPACC)

Cany Ash

Cara Crewdson

Carolina Susaeta-Ball

Caroline Day, *Save Leyton Marshes*

Catarina Portugal, Urban Designer

Catherine Harty, Socialist Party Activist Ireland

Cathy Ward, Artist

Charlie Charman, *Games Monitor*

Chris Vavlekis

Christina Mitrentse

Claire Reddleman

Clare Odgers

Clemens Apprich, *Leuphana University*

Counterolympics

Cristobal Bianchi

Dale Farm, *International Romani Union*

Dan Hind, *The Return of the Public*

Daniel Lowe, *SOAS*

Danny Dorling, *Inequalities: Why Social Inequalities Persist*

Dave Zirin, *Bad Sports: A People's History of Sports*

David Boulogne, Photographer

David Burgess, *Activist 2003 'No*

War' Sydney Opera House
David Cannon
David Rosenberg, Educator
David San Millan, Photographer
David Vannen
David Wearing, Department of
Development Studies SOAS
Defend The Right To Protest
Doreen Massey, *World City*
Dr Bernadette Buckley, *Goldsmiths*
Dr David Dibosa, Academic
Dr Libby Porter, *Monash
University*
Dr Nick Thoburn, *University of
Manchester*
Dr S.Szczelkun, *University of
Westminster*
Dr Sebastian Kraemer
Dubravka Sekulic
Ed McKeon, Music Producer
Eduardo Cassina
Ellen O'Hara
Emma Davenport
Esther Johnson, Artist
European Alternatives
Evi Peroulaki
Fadi Shayya, *Discursive Formations*
Fanny Malinen and Steve Rushton,
Bread and Circuses
Fran Tonkiss
Francisca Santos
Franco Berardi Bifo, *The Soul At
Work*
Gabriëlle Schleijpen
Gary Clark, Football Coach
Ger Duijzings, *UCL*

Gloria Morrison, *Joint Enterprise
Not Guilty By Association*
Hamja Ahsan, Civil Liberties
Campaigner, Artist and Curator
Harald Hugues
Helen Wyatt
Hugo Moline, Architect
Ilan Wall, *Critical Legal Thinking*
Isabel Simons
James Leadbitter, *The Vacuum
Cleaner*
Jimini Hignett, Artist
John Carlos, Writer and
Activist 1968 Olympics Black
Power salute
John Cussans
John Pilger, *The Rulers of the
World*
John Roberts - Prof. Art
& Aesthetics, *University of
Wolverhampton*
Jonas Ranson
Jonathan Rokem
Joon Lynn Goh
Josephine Berry Slater, *Mute
magazine*
Jowan Mohmod
Julia Bard, Journalist
Julian Dobson, *Urban Pollinator*
Julie Sumner, *Life Island Campaign*
Julien Cheyne, *Games Monitor*
Justin McGuirk, Journalist
Kate Rich
Katherine Stanley, *Occupy Times*
Kathrin Bohm, Artist
Kris O'Donnell, *Occupy London*

Lasse Johansson

Laura Braun, Photographer

Laura Colini, *INURA*

Laura Hunton

Laura Lumachi Hunton, Teacher

Lavendhri Arumugam, Artist

Les Levidow, *Campaign Against Criminalising Communities*

Lia Ghilardi

Libby Porter, *Monash University*

Licia Cianettie

Lina Gudmundsson

Lise Autogena, Artist

Liz Adams, Architect

Lorenza Casini, Manchester

Lucia Caistor-Arendar, *Young Foundation*

Machteld Elize Speets, *Anti-capitalist Initiative*

Mara Ferreri

Marc Herbst, *Journal of Aesthetics & Protest*

Marc McGowan, Artist

Marc Perelman, *Barbaric Sport: A Global Plague*

Marcus Kern

Margareta Kern, Artist

Maria Isabel Botero-Hernandez

Marianne Mulvey

Marina Vishmidt, *Queen Mary*

Marisa Gonsalez, Artist

Marta Braun, Professor Art History

Marte Mortinez

Matt O'Connor, *Fathers 4 Justice*

Matthew Fuller, *Goldsmiths*

Matthew Hyland, *Mute magazine*

Maureen Ward, *Manchester Modernist Society*

Max Steckelmacher

Merlin Carpenter

Michael Edwards, *University College London*

Mike Davis, *Evil Paradises: Dreamworlds of Neoliberalism*

Mike Wells, *Games Monitor*

Mira Mattar, *Mute magazine*

Montse Seco

Nadine O'Connor, *Fathers 4 Justice*

Nanna Nielsen, Filmmaker

Nerea Calvillo, Architect

Nick Blomley, *Simon Fraser University*

Oliver Pohlisch, Journalist

Othello De'Souza-Hartley

Paul Philippou

Paula Marie Hildebrandt

Pauline van Mourik Broekman, *Mute Publishing*

Pocina Persina

Pragna Patel, *Southall Black Sisters*

Rafa Prada

Rainer Knupp, *Feldenkrais Practitioner*

Ramya Nair

Randa Lamirza

Raymond Obedencio

Rehan Jamil, Photographer

Romeo J De la Cruz

Rosalind Laura Gray

Rowena Hay

Saika Alam, Solicitor

Samur Berrak

Sandra Valencia

Sara Thor

Saurabh Vaidya, *UCL*

Sean Dockray, *The Public School*

Siddharth Nandakishoran

Silvija Stipanov

Simon Brackenborough

Simon Hardy, *Anti-capitalist Initiative*

Simon Worthington, *Mute magazine*

Siraj Izhar, Activist

Sonia Mehta

Space Hijackers

Spencer Ball

Stacey Hunter

Stanislava Pinchuk

Stefan Dickers, *Bishopsgate Institute*

Stephanie Braun

Stephen Graham, *Cities Under Siege*

Steve Dowding, *Games Monitor*

Steve Wright, *Monash University*

Stuart Croucher, Urban Designer

Tauri Tuvikene, *UCL*

Tijana Stevanovic

Tim Hart

Tim Mitchell, Artist

TJ Constable Taylor

Torange Khonsari, *public works*

UK Uncut

Vicky Sholund, *Save Leyton Marsh*

Victoria Jackson Wyatt

Vladimir Tatomir, *Association of young museologists Kontraakcija*

Wende Anne MauderWendy Davis, *Women's Library*

Yolanda de los Bueis

When Protest Is a Public Nuisance, the Public Should Worry

/

Julian Dobson

Next week Trenton Oldfield, the campaigner who disrupted this year's Oxford and Cambridge boat race, will be sentenced for causing a public nuisance. This catch-all common law charge allows the courts to impose any sentence up to life imprisonment.

The original charge was under section five of the Public Order Act. A conviction for disorderly behaviour can be imposed by magistrates and carries a maximum fine of £1,000. But after media and political pressure, the charge was changed.

So for disrupting the boat race and causing injury to nobody (the person most at risk was himself) it is possible that Trenton Oldfield may share a similar sentence to a man who made 1,000 obscene calls to women over the space of two weeks, and was jailed for nine years; to a man who persistently stalked a female police officer and got 30 months; or to somebody who obsessively made hoax 999 calls, and was eventually jailed for eight years.

Previous convictions[1] for public nuisance suggest that significant factors in sentencing should include either the intent to cause harm or recklessness about the consequences of one's actions. Disrupting a sporting event might be inconvenient and antisocial, but it's neither harmful nor malicious.

But if public nuisance legislation is to be used as a way of stifling protest we are in very different territory. It turns the judiciary into a political tool to be used against a government's opponents, outlawing opposition that doesn't use approved channels.

The UK has a long history of allowing public spaces to be used for all sorts of campaigns and demonstrations. Most have passed without incident; others have caused major inconvenience. For the most part, those who take part are allowed to make their point.

At the turn of the millennium hundreds of lorry drivers and farmers took part in one of the most disruptive protests this country has seen, blockading fuel depots and restricting supplies to hospitals and supermarkets. The Institute of Directors put the costs at more than £1 billion. Yet William Hague, leader of the Conservative Party at the time, called the protesters "fine, upstanding citizens"[2]. Nobody was jailed for the disruption they caused or for the danger they might have caused.

So why should Trenton Oldfield be singled out? You could argue that he spoiled a lot of people's fun. But some would say that the ban on smoking in public places has spoiled a lot of people's fun. Most weekends in Britain the rain spoils a lot of people's fun. We live with it.

You could argue that his protest offended the establishment. It clearly achieved that, even if it was unlikely to achieve much else. But we have TV shows and newspapers that lampoon the establishment every day. They don't get prosecuted.

You could argue, as the prosecutors did, that Trenton Oldfield was putting himself and possibly the rowers at risk. But that risk was minimal and no harm was done. If it is now the job of the courts to prosecute people for what might have been, then all our lucky escapes may come back to haunt us.

So it seems the law of public nuisance is being used selectively and disproportionately in this instance to criminalise protest - and only two years after the Law Commission mooted proposals[3] to simplify or abolish the offence.

It doesn't matter whether you approve or disapprove of this particular protest, any more than it matters whether you think the lorry drivers were right to make their point about fuel prices or not. A healthy democracy champions the right to dissent, and to do so visibly and publicly. If protests cause harm, then judges have all the artillery of criminal law at their disposal; if no harm is done, they should leave well alone.

The irony of the story is that if the police had simply sent Trenton Oldfield away with a caution, the incident might have been quickly forgotten, appearing perhaps as an obscure pub quiz question in years to come. As it is, the courts are likely to give his cause more publicity than he can ever have hoped.

* This article posted on 11 October 2012 in the *Huffington Post*, http://www.huffingtonpost.co.uk/julian-dobson/trenton-oldfield-protest_b_1953799.html.

1. http://www.cps.gov.uk/legal/s_to_u/sentencing_manual/public_nuisance/
2. http://news.bbc.co.uk/1/hi/uk/928701.stm
3. http://lawcommission.justice.gov.uk/docs/cp193_Simplification_Public_Nuisance_Consultation.pdf

Julian Dobson

The criminalisation of protest is part of the elite's class war

/

Nina Power

What price the preservation of the spectacle? Trenton Oldfield, who disrupted the annual Oxford-Cambridge Boat Race in April this year to protest against inequality, was sentenced to six months in jail for the offence of "public nuisance". Although the race was restarted 25 minutes later, Judge Molyneux made[1] it clear that Trenton had disrupted the smooth running of things, and for that he must go to jail: "Thousands of people had lined the banks of the river to enjoy a sporting competition. Many more were watching at home on live television." The message is blunt: if it's on TV and aristocrats are involved, then the state can deprive you of your liberty for as long as it likes.

In a period where many people have died following benefit cuts[2], Oldfield's protest against elitism and inequality is timely and symbolic. Astonishingly in the judge's ruling today, Oldfield was accused of "prejudice" in relation to the rowers, but the judiciary don't see fit to accuse themselves of the same thing – 78% of judges are Oxbridge-educated[3]. As solicitor Matt Foot stated today:

"The judge has sentenced on her view that this protest against prejudice amounted to prejudice. By that rationale the protests at cricket matches in the 1970s against apartheid were equally prejudiced. This sentence can only help undermine dissent."

Oldfield's sentence is clearly designed to deter others from protesting, and there is evidence that the use of the charge of public nuisance (which carries a maximum sentence of life) was upgraded under government pressure and precisely because of the varied spectacles of 2012. In a home affairs select committee discussion in April this year, the head of the Met police, Bernard Hogan-Howe[4], was asked by Conservative MP Michael Ellis:

"Do you think that Olympic security arrangements or diamond jubilee security arrangements need to be reviewed in the light of [Oldfield's Boat Race protest]? I particularly also want to ask you about the penalties available, because I notice from media coverage that the individual who disrupted the Boat Race appears to have been charged with a section 5 offence under the Public Order Act 1986, which is one of the most minor offences in the book, carries no custodial penalty option at all and usually only results in a small fine. Do we need to look at available offences?"

Hogan-Howe replies that the CPS are looking into a "more serious" charge, and indeed that's what they did – but would Oldfield's action have been punished so severely in a non-Olympic year, or if it had taken place at an event not attended and populated by members of the ruling class?

Nina Power

Oldfield has repeatedly made his motivations for protesting at the Boat Race very clear: "As inequalities increase in Britain and across much of the world, so does the criminalisation of protest; my solidarity is with everyone everywhere working towards more equitable societies." This principled stance against the severe and increasing inequality of life in Britain, nowhere more on symbolic display than at the Boat Race, is widely shared, and there is widespread shock at the severity of Oldfield's sentencing. The world was rightly outraged at the recent imprisonment of Russia's Pussy Riot[5] for playing a song in church, but Oldfield's jailing comes as part of a long series of heavy sentences for UK protesters, from the imprisonment of 60 mainly Muslim protesters following a 2009 protest against Israel's attacks on Gaza[6], to student protesters who went to jail for months for throwing a flimsy banner stick during the fees protests, to the people who got years for setting up joke riot Facebook pages or imprisoned for stealing water worth a few pounds[7].

So who, in the end, is the public on behalf of whom Oldfield is being punished? Is it the public sector workers who will march in their thousands[8] tomorrow against austerity, or is it the "public" represented by the judge, worried that protesters are "prejudiced" against those who have everything and yet want more? A key 1957 case of public nuisance stated that: "A nuisance is a public nuisance if, within its sphere, which is the neighbourhood, it materially affects the reasonable comfort and convenience of life of a class of Her Majesty's subjects." In Oldfield's case, unfortunately for him and for everyone else, the class whose "comfort and convenience" must be protected at all costs is, here and elsewhere, all too obvious.

* This article was first published on Friday 19 October 2012 in the *Guardian* Comment Is Free, http://www.guardian.co.uk/commentisfree/2012/oct/19/boat-race-protest-class-war.

1. http://www.judiciary.gov.uk/Resources/JCO/Documents/Judgments/sentencing-remarks-r-v-oldfield.pdf
2. http://blogs.mirror.co.uk/investigations/2012/04/32-die-a-week-after-failing-in.html
3. http://www.suttontrust.com/news/news/the-educational-backgrounds-of-500-leading-figures/
4. http://www.publications.parliament.uk/pa/cm201012/cmselect/cmhaff/1929i/120417.htm
5. http://www.guardian.co.uk/music/2012/aug/17/pussy-riot-sentenced-two-years
6. http://www.guardian.co.uk/world/2010/mar/05/gaza-protest-harsh-jail-terms
7. http://www.telegraph.co.uk/news/uknews/crime/8695988/London-riots-Lidl-water-thief-jailed-for-six-months.html
8. http://www.guardian.co.uk/commentisfree/2012/oct/19/march-saturday-against-cuts-fight

Political pressure criminalises protest

/

Steve Rushton

Today Trenton Oldfield, who interrupted the Oxford Cambridge boat race for 25 minutes, was sentenced to 6 months in jail for causing a Public Nuisance.

The Law Commission has proposed to scrap this law that it describes as "unacceptable" to "modern democracy". Mr Oldfield's action aimed to highlight the destruction of public services, the growing inequalities in British Society and establishment's attacks on the right to protest. He was originally charged with a minor Public Order offense. This was increased to Public Nuisance, after a Government MP asked for a custodial sentence.

In a Home Affairs Committee, ten days after the boat race on 17th April 2012, Michael Ellis MP expressed his concern over the boat race incident and how "one idiot" could cause such disruption. He requested that Bernard Hogan-Howe, Metropolitan Police Commissioner, seek a strong sentence and complained how the sentence the police originally charged Mr Oldfield with "Carries no custodial penalty option." The Commissioner responded, "I do know that the CPS are reviewing whether a more serious charge is possible, given the circumstances."[1]

Two years ago the Law Commission proposed to scrap the 12th Century crime of Public Nuisance. Asserting that it is vague, outdated, often conflicted with European Rights Law and potential offences were covered by other laws. When expanding these critiques, they warned how it could be used to criminalise anything that the establishment disliked, especially protests.[2]

With expectations of prison, prior to his sentencing, Mr Oldfield asserted, "Most nation states work very hard at creating and maintaining untrue myths about themselves. Great Britain has convinced many it is the home of democracy and the "gauge" for civilisation. Anyone that lives here today or who has experienced even a moment of their attempts at colonisation knows Britain, particularly England, is a brutal, deeply divided class-ridden place. Let there be no mistake, there has long been a deficit of democracy. Today it is at breaking point. It is time for a revolution."

Judge Anne Molyneax [sic] passed this sentence today in Isleworth Crown Court. Incidentally she used to be a corporate lawyer working within the City of London for Masons & Sprecher Grier Halberstam.[3] Many see the City of London as a key cause of a great deal of the inequality. For instance, despite the austerity cuts this year Chief executive pay in the top FTSE 25 rocketed by more than 41 per cent.[4] Within the verdict, the Judge mentioned how the swim, "spoiled the race", that afterwards it took 25 minutes to restart it. She complained, "No one will ever know the outcome of what would have been if you had not acted as you did."

Judge Molyneax asserted that Mr Oldfield made five wrong decisions. She claimed that he acted "disproportionately" and that it was unclear "what your views actually were"; secondly, "There was no immediate or instant need to act as you did"; also that his "actions were dangerous"; further that he stopped people enjoying watching a sporting event and that he "did nothing to address the inequality by giving yourself the right to spoil the enjoyment of others". Finally, she went on to suggest by targeting the participants he acted with "prejudice".[5]

Analysing Judge's Molyneax's verdict it is hard not to draw comparisons with Russia's Pussy Riot and their incarnation. It seems deeply hypercritical that British Foreign Office Minister, Alistair Burt, expressed his "deep concerns" about the treatment Pussy Riot, for an "an expression of political belief."[6] Another parallel with Pussy Riot is the political involvement of Putin, who was criticised for trying to influence the decision and calling for a custodial sentence of the punk band. This is exactly the same as Michael Ellis MP did using his position on the Home Affairs Committee.

It is also difficult to discern any logic from Judge Molyneax's verdict. There seems a blatant disregard for the European Convention on Human Rights, which protects the right to protest. She suggested disrupting the race was disproportionate in regard what the protest aimed to highlight. Mr Oldfield noted in the statement, which was released after the swim, how: the government had just been given royal approval for their bill that would begin privatising the NHS; would legalise the surveillance of all British email communication and they were calling on people to tell the police if they suspected anyone of planning protests against the Olympics. His statement also explained the protest aimed to highlight the deep inequalities in Britain, the devastating austerity measures and focused on a symbol of elitism. How the judge can argue a rowing race is more important than these issues is beyond my understanding.

The Judge's second point was that these problems were not crucially important, and do not need immediate remedy. Possibly they do not affect her on her salary. Although I think it would be fair to say many people are deeply concerned about these issues, and stopping the Conservative Government continue on its policy of austerity, privatisation, working on behalf of corporations and removing the right to protest. Judge Molyneax's third point was that his actions were dangerous: that by putting his life in risk he endangered the health and safety of others. Putting your own life at risk is not a crime. The judge then suggested that Mr Oldfield did not have the right to spoil the event and that it did nothing to address inequality. I would suggest this is incorrect. The right he had is enshrined within the European Convention on Human Rights, Article 10. In terms of addressing the problem, protests are often there to highlight problems, not many protestors expect to solve them the same day.

Judge Molyneax however, saved her craziest point for last. She said Mr Oldfield was prejudice against the elites by aiming a protest at them. "That no good ever comes from prejudice." I guess that environmentalists are prejudice against polluters, peace campaigners are prejudice against arms manufacturers, and so on... On this ruling, almost any political action could be banned. You could also argue the establishment are prejudice against the masses, which seems a valid point and the point of Mr Oldfield's protest.

Historically, many people have celebrated political actions that stand up against inequality. Not least, the suffragette Emily Davison, who martyred herself by throwing herself in front of the King's horse in the Derby. By this Judge's reasoning and logic I think she would have jailed the activist Ms Davidson, if she had survived. Judge Molyneax would probably criticise her for spoiling the Derby. The former corporate lawyer would have claimed that she acted disproportionately and that it was unclear to anyone, who saw jump in front of the horse, what her views were. The Judge might continue that there was no pressing need for her to act at that very precise moment, continuing that her actions were dangerous, that she did nothing to address feminism within her act and that it was prejudice. Prejudice against the King and against the domination of men over women.

Steve Rushton is a political writer, researcher and activist. He writes for *Occupy News Network* – more of his research is collated at www.steve-rushton. co.uk

This article was first published on 19 October 2012 in Occupy News http:// occupynewsnetwork.co.uk/political-pressure-criminalises-protest/

1. Home Affairs Committee – Minutes of Evidence: HC 1929-i http://www.publications. parliament.uk/pa/cm201012/cmselect/cmhaff/1929i/120417.htm.

2. The Law Commission, Consultation Paper No 193, Simplification of Criminal Law: Public Nuisance and Outraging Public Decency, March 2010 http://lawcommission.justice.gov.uk/ docs/cp193_Simplification_Public_Nuisance_Consultation.pdf.

3. Anne Molyneux – Circuit Judge (crime), Judicial Appointment Commission, "is a former partner (property litigation) in a City law firm." http://jac.judiciary.gov.uk/1506.htm. These city law firms include Masons & Sprecher Grier Halberstam. Steve Hoare, Property team quits Masons for Sprecher, *The Lawyer*, 19 May 2003, http://www.thelawyer.com/property-team-quits-masons-for-sprecher/100669.article.

4. Steve Rushton, Global Noise: a wake-up call for the world to reject austerity, Public Services Europe, 12 October 2012, http://www.publicserviceeurope.com/article/2584/global-noise-a-wake-up-call-for-the-world-to-reject-austerity.

5. http://www.judiciary.gov.uk/Resources/JCO/Documents/Judgments/sentencing-remarks-r-v-oldfield.pdf.

6. Foreign Office Minister deeply concerned at Pussy Riot verdict, Foreign Office, 17 October 2012, http://ukeu.fco.gov.uk/en/news/?view=News&id=801235082.

The Criminalisation of Political Dissent: Huckstering the Law

/

Brenna Bhandar

The subversion of law begins with the reduction of politics to a crime.[1]

What is never questioned is the bourgeois state of law upon which modern capitalism depends. This remains the sacred cow that even the most radical critics from the likes of Occupy Wall Street and the World Social Forum dare not touch.[2]

On October 19th, Trenton Oldfield was sentenced to six months in prison for his protest against elitism that saw him disrupting the Oxford Cambridge boat race. He was found guilty of causing a public nuisance.

Many others have remarked on the outrageousness of a prison sentence for this act of protest, this act of political dissent. It is entirely disproportionate, and reflects a perceived increase (more on that below) in the criminalisation of political protest by a state bent on punitive austerity measures that are affecting the poor, the unemployed, working peoples, peoples with disabilities, single mothers, and other vulnerable and marginalised communities entirely disproportionately.

The fact that the judiciary is comprised of 78% of Oxbridge graduates has been pointed out, drawing attention to a serious and well entrenched problem, the lack of what is obliquely referred to as "diversity" on the bench, and the interests that this majority of white elite men ultimately serve. The epistemological questions related to the capacity of judges to understand the life experiences, not to mention the political and legal consciousness of the subjects who appear before them has led to a globalised field of judicial (re)-education programmes and academic projects that re-write judgments from feminist and anti-racist perspectives as a way of imagining a judicial system that would be more representative and democratic. These projects are important and their value in realising change should not be underestimated.

However, I want to focus here on something else. I want to focus on the relationship between the right to protest, political dissent, and private property (or, the bourgeois state of law). In my view, Zizek has a good point. The right to protest and to not be criminalised as a result of said protest needs to be articulated as opposition to a legal system whose raison d'être is to protect a system of private property. Private property here is understood as being inclusive of many different things, including the properties that attach to individual ownership and wealth. These properties are affective and intangible and yet, have the most material of consequences. The sense of entitlement, privilege, security and power that attach to actual relations of ownership constitute the régime of private property that our current system of law works to uphold in manifold ways. As Bentham put it so well, the primary purpose of law is to provide security for private property interests.

So, this struggle to stop the criminalisation of political dissent, our outrage at sentences such as the one handed down today,[3] cannot only be about the right to political protest itself, and the desire for a more just system that does not come down so viciously on people protesting the rise in student tuition fees, austerity, the war in Gaza, police brutality, etc. While that would certainly be welcome, there is something rather more rotten in the state of the law itself. The very substance of the laws used to criminalise political dissent require a robust anti–capitalist, anti–racist, feminist critique that was once par for the course in both critical legal scholarship, critical race theory, and political activism.

Let's take the crime of public nuisance as an example. It has its origins in a private law action for interference with one's property, and then drifts into the public sphere as a means of criminalising improper conduct (along with interference with private property). This is not only a matter of Justice Molyneux having misconstrued who constitutes the "public" in considering who suffered the harm in this case. Nor is it solely about a judge upholding the interests of the elite who were engaged in a sporting event, over the rights of Trenton Oldfield to express political dissent of myriad forms of inequality and injustice. The crime of public nuisance has its origins, and remains in essence, a law concerned with protecting private property and notions of propriety. For this reason and others, the crime of public nuisance should be abolished.[4]

The crime of public nuisance has an interesting history. The word itself, spelt 'nusance' until the 18th century, "originally meant no more than 'harm'.[5] Theft contaminates its etymological roots, lawyers having stolen the term "from ordinary speech, assigned [it] a technical meaning, and then accused the man in the street from misusing [it]."[66] Nuisance originates during the feudal era as a private law action in tort, to protect individuals from any interference with their property short of actual dispossession. The tort of nuisance grows as a type of action between neighbours, but as early as the end of the 13th century, the private concern with property had drifted into the concept of public nuisance. The main concern was with the common benefit and the obstruction of highways by agricultural waste and effluence. It is not until the 16th century that, in the local criminal courts of the King, what are now considered to be 'public welfare offences' come to include a wide range of actions considered to be harmful to the community.

If words like "common benefit" and "community" are making you feel warm with nostalgia for a bygone era, please wipe that notion out of your head. Included in the list of 'public welfare offences' was the punishment of "common scolds." A common scold was by definition a woman, an angry, troublesome woman who would disrupt the peace in her neighbourhood. Punishment was by ducking, a form of torture reserved for women, exemplary of the kind of misogyny that the law once sanctified. By the 18th century public nuisance begins to be used to discipline all sorts of behaviour, including blasphemy, indecent behaviour, publishing obscene books, and even selling unwholesome food.[72] The array of conduct covered by public nuisance, a category that was treated as infinitely expandable, more elastic than any other common law doctrine is simply staggering. The category becomes a catch–all for any crimes not covered under any other existing offences. Spencer notes that by the early 19th century, "the expression 'public nuisance' is used more or less to describe the power of the King's Bench and it's successors to punish any behaviour, whether previously thought criminal or not, which is felt to be harmful to the public."[8]

The crime of public nuisance was used prolifically in the colonial context. And while there has been an intensification in the length of prison sentences handed out to those involved in the riots of August 2011, and the student protestors, the criminalisation of political dissent in the UK has a long history elsewhere, a history in which the colonies functioned as a legal laboratory for methods of suppression and subjugation. Michael Anderson notes that after 1870 in India, public nuisance crimes "represented the most frequent and systematic application of police power under colonial rule."[9] If we want to think, historically, about the perversion of the term "public interest" one need only look to the colonial context. It is in colonial India, as in Mandate Palestine (and in present day Israel/Palestine), that land, water, resources, and thus the livelihoods of people were and are routinely appropriated in the name of the "public" interest and for "public use". The concept of the "public" in colonial settler contexts is as tainted as the concept of sovereignty that represents settler interests at the expense of indigenous ones. When we think about the propertied nature of whiteness that endows particular communities with such a strong sense of entitlement to economic, social, cultural and political privileges over others, colonial histories and histories of slavery that have been fundamental to the development of English law and capitalism can only deepen our understandings of contemporary judgments about what the interests of the "public" are and conceptualisations of public space.

If the 18th century was a time when the crime of public nuisance punished behaviour deemed to be improper, lacking in the propriety expected of loyal subjects, the 19th century witnesses a coupling of the disciplinary dimensions of public nuisance with the use of this offence to protect private individuals from interference with their rights in real property. A private citizen, by the 19th century, could obtain an injunction against a public nuisance if it threatened physical damage to his property.

We have seen the effects of this use of public nuisance in recent injunctions sought to suppress political protest on campuses, and against the Occupy protestors at St. Paul's. Interestingly, and as a small corrective to Zizek's criticisms, the Occupy London protestors did attempt to disrupt and challenge the property rights of the City of London by asserting an indefinite right to occupy. Property rights are never indefinite, but exist as ascertainable periods of time, and thus by challenging the temporal framework of property the Occupy protestors attempted, albeit unsuccessfully, to alter the very fabric of property law.

Nearly if not all of the type of public nuisance offences that the law was historically intended to apply to have now been covered by statute. The profligate doctrine of health and safety breeds new rules and regulations daily it seems; and criminal law offences have become increasingly codified. What is left, after all of this content has been emptied out is a dangerously elastic form of criminal offence that can literally be applied to any sort of conduct. And with this, we arrive at Oldfield's sentencing hearing.

The Court found that Oldfield "decided that he had the right to stop members of the public enjoying a sporting competition which they had chosen to go and watch." Justice Molyneux tells Oldfield in no uncertain terms that "he did not have that right..." and that he had "given himself the right to spoil the enjoyment of others." Here the property interests at stake appear quite clearly. Oldfield is guilty of disrupting the rowers' sense of entitlement to carry on with their sporting event over and above his right to participate in direct political action, shored up by years of customary use, and rendering their right to use the river as they wish, according to their long-held tradition, insecure.

Oldfield not only violated and disrupted these long held privileges, but he is described as having "given himself the right" to do so. Oldfield is a lone individual who 'gave himself the right to protest', he is not a concerned individual expressing a political position that resonates with thousands upon thousands of people who have taken to the streets, who have written, who have rung their hands in the air, who have organised conferences, demonstrations, strikes, poetry readings, art installations, made films, all in order to protest government attacks on social services, education, and the politics of austerity generally.

Marx illuminated how the passage to a liberal democratic capitalist society essentially pulls a veil over actual inequalities in power and material wealth, leaving us with the illusion of equality between ostensibly sovereign individuals. The notion that Oldfield was 'prejudiced' (against the Oxbridge rowers) reflects a concerted effort to ignore the obvious differences in privilege and wealth of the participants in the race and those on whose behalf Oldfield was protesting. In the context of this public nuisance action, all parties are on equal footing, the rowers from Oxbridge and Cambridge as vulnerable to suffering the effects of prejudice as any other group of people.

Of course it would be just if the State were to stop criminalising political protestors, and this is necessary, at a minimum. But political transformation lies in challenging the nature of private ownership that pervades the very form that law takes. In the Economic and Philosophic Manuscripts of 1844, Marx writes that the "huckstering with landed property, the transformation of landed property into a commodity, constitutes the final overthrow of the old and the final establishment of the money aristocracy." Huckstering, Marx tells us, is what defines the very essence of ownership (whether it's feudal or capitalist, of land or money).

Perhaps huckstering is also an apt and analogous term for the use of law to criminalise political dissent. What we are being offered here (what is being peddled) is a version of the law that deems it criminally improper to disrupt the entitlement of the wealthy to enjoy sport, to assert a noisy, visible presence in public space, to challenge the increasingly private ownership of our universities. Perhaps one place to begin in reconceptualising a law of public harm is to imagine laws that are not tied to the protection of property in all of its glorious diversity, but conceives of public harm as that which damages the life chances of that majority living on the margins of socio–economic privilege.

Brenna Bhandar

Brenna Bhandar is Lecturer in Law, Queen Mary College, University of London

This article was first published on 22 October 2012 in Critical Legal Thinking http://criticallegalthinking.com/2012/10/22/the-criminalisation-of-political-dissent-huckstering-the-law/

1. K.G. Kannabiran,*Wages of Impunity: Power, Justice and Human Rights* (Delhi: Orient Blackswan, 2004).
2. Zizek, *Foreign Policy*, October 2012.
3. Or, to take another example, the sentences of up to two years of imprisonment meted out for those convicted of violent disorder after having taken part in political demonstrations against the war in Gaza in 2010; 78 young men were charged with violent disorder amongst other things, all but two of whom were Muslim.
4. Indeed, J.R. Spencer argues that the case for abolishing the crime of public nuisance is strong because of its tremendously vague and "infinitely extensible" character. J.R. Spencer, "Public Nuisance: A Critical Examination" in *Cambridge Law Journal* 48(1) March 1989, 55 at 83.
5. Spencer, at 56.
6. ibid.
7. Spencer, at 61.
8. ibidat 63.
9. Michael Anderson, "Public Nuisance and Private Purpose: Policed Environments in British India, 1860–1947" in SOAS School of Law Legal Studies Research Paper Series, available at www.soas.ac.uk/law/researchpapers.

Boat race protester: 'disturbing similarities' between Trenton Oldfield and Pussy Riot cases

/

Tim Ecott

in conversation with

Deepa Naik

TE: Hello, you're listening to the Voice of Russia. I'm Tim Ecott and this is 'In Conversation'. On the 7th of April the Oxford Cambridge boat race had just started on the Thames when a swimmer was spotted in the water. His name was Trenton Oldfield – a 36 year old Australian who said he was protesting at inequality and elitism in British society. He is now serving a six month prison sentence for public nuisance. Oldfield's treatment has prompted allegations that his jail term was disproportionate to the crime. Deepa Naik is Trenton's wife and one of the co–founders of the urban activist group This Is Not A Gateway. I asked her if she understood why people were annoyed that he disrupted the boat race which is a fixture on the sporting and social calendar in British society.

DN: Every single direct action protest will cause a disruption – that's the very nature of the act. So, of course I understand that people were upset about the disruption. What Trenton tried to do was a direct action protest in which he caused the least amount of damage but had the widest amount of potential coverage so

that his ideas and politics would be explored. The boat race, as you know, was temporarily delayed for 25 minutes; no one was harmed; no one was injured; there were no complaints made to either the police nor the BBC. So, I think it was an effective protest in that sense.

TE: It's a very emotional thing though – I guess you can imagine that for a lot of British people it is something that is filled with history and tradition and it seemed like here were young men in the peak of their physical powers, doing something which was fun but was a sporting competition and Trenton's actions – though be it politically motivated – caused them distress and effected something that they had been training for for years in some cases.

DN: Trenton's original charge was for causing distress to exactly what you've explained – the rowers. His charge was then changed to that of 'public nuisance', which was about causing a nuisance to the general public. As for the rowers – Trenton has stated his sympathy for them – he used to row himself and he understands what they might have felt. But the wider issues of cuts which are affecting the most vulnerable in this society – are, in this case, what Trenton has more sympathy for. Of course he knows that these athletes have trained and were disappointed – but they have also trained to restart races. And, historically that race has been restarted at different times. He understood that they would be – of course – upset, but they are top athletes that have trained to deal with obstacles and that is essentially what they did. They went back – we watched the footage and it was very calm in fact – they went back, they restarted. The decision to restart was made within two minutes and the race proceeded.

TE: Although psychologically it must have been very difficult for them to psyche themselves up again, presumably having had to stop.

DN: Yes, I'm sure.

TE: What about the danger aspect? A lot of people talked at the time about the fact that he could have been killed or he could have caused an accident in which others were injured. Do you reject that idea?

DN: There are two things I want to say about that. One, is that nothing about the charge that was levied against Trenton had anything about causing bodily harm or potentially causing bodily harm and neither did the judge's remarks. So, that wasn't an issue and was not why he was charged. And secondly, he didn't. And I would argue there wasn't a threat of danger or harm. Trenton is a very very strong swimmer; he knows that river very well; there is annual swim in that part of the river every single year – so people swim there all the time. As I said, he was a rower and he knows that the oars – in order to garner speed –don't dip very far into the water. So, he knew that he would swim towards the boats, duck under – essentially what you saw – and come out on the other end.

TE: If you'd been in London with him, would you have tried to stop him?

DN: Oh, no one has ever asked me that before. Umm... no.

TE: Why not?

DN: Because I think it's important that people – particularly now –

make sure that issues around first the erosion of civil liberties, which Trenton was trying to draw upon – and secondly, so-called 'austerity cuts' are discussed.

TE: What is the... I mean you have to speak for him in a sense – but you say you know his politics and presumably side with his opinions in some way or maybe not – tell me what was at the heart of his political protest that he wanted to make.

DN: Trenton was trying to draw attention to the culture of elitism, which is symbolised by the Oxford and Cambridge race. 70% if this current cabinet went to either Oxford or Cambridge; 78% of the judges went to either one of these schools. This culture of elitism sets one group of people apart and against the rest.

TE: Why do you believe it does that? I mean, if they treat people fairly once they rise up in society then why is that wrong?

DN: Unfortunately what we're seeing is that they don't do that. I mean, if they did, this obviously won't be a question but what is happening is that this government

is protecting the interests of the minority elite – of corporations, of banks, of very wealthy people at the expense of the working person, of single mothers, of people on disability, of other marginalised groups. They are the ones who are being cut and affected – university tuition as you know has trebled in this country; this is the first year were students will now pay £9,000. It's creating even more inequality. London now is one of the most unequal cities in the developed world.

TE: What do you mean by that?

DN: It has the widest gap between the rich and the poor.

TE: Let's go back to what happened to your husband, Trenton Oldfield, after the political protest or politically motivated protest in which he disrupted the boat race. He was initially charged with a public order offence but you have a theory that the powers that be, the establishment as you call it, set out to see that he was punished as severely as possible.

DN: Yes, it's not a theory, it's fact. What happened was Trenton was taken into custody on the

7th of April and charged with a
public order offence, in which
maximum fine would be £1000.
Ten days later, on the 17th of
April, Hansard reports showed
the conservative MP Michael Ellis
asked the police commissioner
what could be done about
Trenton's charge and could it be
increased in order to achieve a
custodial sentence. So, here we
have a member of parliament
interfering into the judiciary in
order to ensure that Trenton is, as
it were, 'hit with a bigger stick'.
And, that is essentially what
happened. The day that Trenton
went to court to plead guilty to his
first charge – public order – he was
told he was actually being charged
with an ancient law, it's from the
12th century, a law called 'public
nuisance'. When he asked 'why',
they said because the penalty
of the previous charge was not
high enough. Not that what he
did caused a public nuisance but
rather because it was based upon
the penalty.

TE: Someone official actually said
that?

DN: Yes

TE: Who said that to him?

DN: I don't have that information
– the lawyers have that
information.[1]

TE: The official explanation for
what the conservative MP Michael
Ellis did is that he raised Trenton's
case during a home affairs select
committee meeting where he
simply noted the penalty for what
he had done seemed relatively
minor for the disruption he caused
and other people have said that is
within the MP's rights – to raise
what is seen as a public issue – and
that is in fact what an MP
should do.

DN: It was my understanding
that the judiciary should
be independent of political
interference – so I completely
disagree with that. And, in
fact, in this country, when
it seemed that Putin had
interfered in a charge against
political protesters – the
group Pussy Riot – there
was outrage that a politician
should intervene into the
judiciary and yet the exact
same thing has happened here.

TE: Do you compare what
happened to Trenton Oldfield to
what happened with Pussy Riot?

DN: I think there are disturbing similarities unfortunately.

TE: Britain likes to hold itself up as a place where justice rules and where people are treated fairly – is that now not your view?

DN: I'm not sure that ever was my view. It's very interesting because as someone whose history has been marked by the British... you know, I'm of Indian descent, I grew up in Africa, I lived in Canada and now I am here. This is one map of the colonial and genocidal history. And yes, you're right; the British do like to present themselves as the gauge of civilisation and of democracy, which has shaped their foreign policy and was their justification of their so–called 'Empire'.

More recently, it is why they came out very heavily to rally behind the group Pussy Riot and their right to protest. Minister Alistair Burt spoke strongly about the disproportionate sentence for the right of political expression. But what we know – and what I've seen here first hand – is that there is a huge contradiction between their statements about other countries and their domestic policies – especially in relation to how protesters, in this country, are treated. This government, and the previous government, are criminalising protest. This idea that one has the right for political expression in other countries, this country will completely back, but how they treat dissenters in this country is very very different. I think there is a huge contradiction.

TE: You mention that you grew up abroad and have lived in other countries and lived here a relatively short time as an adult and Trenton, of course, is from Australia. Do you think that accounts perhaps for a lack of sympathy in British media and the British public towards you? Are you seen as 'outsiders'?

DN: I think anyone who disrupted the Cambridge and Oxford boat race would probably be going through something that Trenton is going through – they would find whatever they could to attack them.

TE: Do you think it irritated people even more that he was Australian rather than British?

DN: People did say 'you should go

back to your own country' and so on, which is quite a peculiar thing to say because if you see the world in terms of issues of justice and equality, you don't see them within nation state boundaries. An example I've spoken about before is Mahatma Gandhi, who was politicised in South Africa where he saw injustice and that is where he first became active before going back to his own country. Che Guevara, as we know, is an Argentinean, but a key figure of the Cuban revolution. There are also in our neighbourhood migrant workers that came mostly from Eastern Europe that fought for better conditions and are responsible for minimum working hours, fights for child labour laws, for minimum wage – so migrants contribute a great deal in terms of issues of equality.

TE: Do you compare Trenton to Gandhi?

DN: Absolutely not. I compare Trenton, if anything, to the migrant workers in our neighbourhood, that fought alongside so many working peoples – whether they were British or not – who were trying to fight in their own way for more equitable societies.

TE: Trenton is, as we know, Australian; he is well educated – what drives him to fight for social justice in this way?

DN: I think it's the core of who Trenton is and has always been – when he was in Australia he was very much part of the aboriginal rights movements. The core of Trenton is someone who is seeking to fight against injustice and to critically investigate how we might live in more equitable ways.

TE: Tell me a bit about This Is Not A Gateway – how would you describe that organisation?

DN: We formed the organisation in 2007. Trenton was working with local government on issues of poverty and inequality doing regeneration projects, he was on the boards of many charities and groups looking at issues of literacy, environmental issues and so on. On the side he was running independent art projects. Myself, I was working in academia curating exhibitions and also running projects on housing estates and in community centres. Trenton and I were both feeling frustrated – with our feet in these different terrains. There wasn't a forum where people could come together and discuss their work beyond 'professionalism', there wasn't a place to think through and discuss alternative possibilities around issues of social justice and equality. We started organising festivals, discussions and we publish books.

TE: Tell me a little bit about how you understand Trenton is coping with being in prison and what are the conditions like where he is living in.

DN: He's at Wormwood Scrubs – he's been classified as a section C prisoner, meaning that he will remain in a closed prison.

TE: Do you think that's too harsh?

DN: I do, yes. Trenton has no threat of escape, no threat of harming anyone, no prior convictions, he was proven to be a person of 'good character' – in fact the judge said, before her sentencing, that he has contributed more to this country then most British citizens. So, I do find it quite tough. The jury asked the judge for leniency before she

sentenced him and the probation report, which the judge is meant to base her sentencing on, recommended community hours. When Trenton received a custodial sentence it was very clearly back to the intervention of politicians who wanted to achieve a custodial sentence for him.

TE: Where you there in the court room when he was sentenced?

DN: I was.

TE: How did you feel when you heard he was actually going inside?

DN: Trenton and I were both very prepared – immediately, as soon as they changed the charge, we knew that this was the reason – they wanted to put Trenton in prison, to make an example of him. And, he is just one of many many people who are in prison for their political actions and beliefs against this government. We've seen student protesters who've been imprisoned for several months for taking a bottle of water at a protest – completely disproportionate. We've seen protesters in 2009 imprisoned for protesting against Israeli attacks on Gaza. It's consistent with how the British government treats protesters on its own soil.

TE: What do you think the experience of being in prison will do to Trenton and what will it mean for his beliefs?

DN: I think, if anything, it will strengthen his convictions. He's got a strong spirit and his concern is not for himself but how this law– 'public nuisance' law – might be used against other people. Two years ago the law commission wanted to scrap the law precisely because it's vague and it can be used for political purposes. It runs the gamut from a fine to life imprisonment – and as we've seen in this case, it's been used to serve a political agenda. That is where Trenton's thoughts are – to question the use of this law and the political intervention into sentences.

TE: Do you think that issue has been highlighted by (a) what he did on that day of the boat race and (b) what happened to him subsequently? Do you think people really care enough?

DN: It's interesting because when this all happened initially – you might remember, Trenton was

attacked and vilified – and since the sentencing there has been a shift, I think, with people, even if they don't agree with his way of protesting, they agree with his right to protest and agree that the sentence was over–the–top. Particularly when you look at other sentences – a week before Trenton was sentenced – a celebrity comedian received a few community hours for violently badgering his ex–girlfriend. When you see these kinds of inconsistencies, it reinforces exactly what Trenton was protesting against in terms of a two–tier culture, political and judicial system. I think the public has rallied around Trenton and these two issues are coming up more and more. One, the increasing inequality being exacerbated by government cuts and two, the criminalisation of dissent.

TE: Have you had any politicians come out in support of Trenton?

DN: Not that I know if, no. And organisations like Amnesty International who we know really rallied behind Pussy Riot, have not come out in support of Trenton. Neither have Liberty.

TE: Why do you think that is?

DN: I believe they are serving the government agenda here in this country.

TE: But the organisations you mentioned – Liberty and Amnesty – they are known as thorns in the side of the government, aren't they? They're known as people who are not afraid to say this is wrong.

DN: I think they serve the government's agenda, particularly in this case. And, I think in terms of rallying behind say Pussy Riot, it very much became an anti–Putin exercise. But, if you go to our website – on our homepage – we have hundreds of people who have lent their names in support of Trenton, from academics like Danny Dorling, Mike Davies, Marc Perelman to community groups like the fabulous Southall Black Sisters, The Campaign Against The Criminalisation of Communities..

TE: Is it possible they aren't supporting you because your ideals and Trenton's politics are a little too vague or hard to pin down?

DN: I think our politics are very clear. We are against these austerity cuts which are increasing inequality and negatively affecting the most vulnerable people in this society. Something I want to talk about is the Oxford and Cambridge boat race and this culture of elitism...

TE: What is it in London that upsets you so much about this perceived elitism?

DN: Let me go back to one point, a few weeks before the Oxford and Cambridge boat race there is another race on the river – it's called the Head Of The River Race. Three hundred boats compete, it is the National boat race in this country. There are everything from charity groups, small independent rowing clubs to top–notch clubs competing. It gets little funding, no media coverage – and the two teams that don't compete are Oxford and Cambridge. Instead, they self–isolate and form their own boat race apart from everyone else. That is the boat race, which people think is the 'elite boat race', with top rowers but it's not. If the Oxbridge athletes competed in the other boat race, they would lose because, if it was an equal playing field, there are other people who are much faster.

TE: I think people in the rowing world know that, I mean, they know that the Oxford and Cambridge boat race is really about the two universities and it is just a tradition; they don't set themselves up as the best rowers in the world. They are top level but it's actually about the tradition of Oxford versus Cambridge. It gets a lot more media attention and that is an example of the elitism you're highlighting?

DN: It's showing how one group self-isolates itself from everyone else, to create an 'elite' or 'top' event, to couch it as that when it actually isn't – it's a construct. And, if you carry this logic on when 70% of this government coming from those two schools, protecting the interests of the wealthy, corporations and banks.

TE: This is an old argument isn't it? It's the anti-capitalist argument. But we have a government and they like to be seen to be doing what they can to help the citizens of this country – they're not all from Oxbridge are they? And a lot of them fight very strongly for social equality and the upliftment of the poorest sections of this society.

DN: I don't think anyone in this government is doing that. 70% of this government come from Oxford or Cambridge ...

TE: Why is that wrong? If they are the top institutions where people can get an education?

DN: They're not the top institutions, which I tried to explain with the boat race example. It's a construct – they have cultural and social capital, which then creates a situation where they enter into influential positions. It's an unequal playing field. And, that is the problem with this country. It is ruled by a culture of elitism and self-isolation from the masses – the policies this government is pushing through are causing enormous detriment to the vast majority of people in this county and abroad. This government – it's important to note – was not voted in.

TE: What's Trenton going to do when he comes out of prison?

DN: Trenton and I will continue to do our work – we just recently published a book, before he was imprisoned. We're having a festival at the end of January –

we're continuing to pursue these questions around inequality, justice and the right for political dissent.

TE: How do you fund yourself?

DN: That was what I was doing in Jeddah – teaching to earn income. We're completely independent. We work on a very small scale.

TE: Trenton, having gone to prison is now notorious – is he going to capitalise on that?

DN: How do you mean?

TE: He's going to be a figure people now know – he's got an unusual name, he's been to prison, he did this high profile protest – is this the beginning of more protests?

DN: I think Trenton will continue the trajectory that his life has always been on, which is the pursuit of ideas around social justice, spatial justice and equality – whether it's writing books, which he's been doing, whether it's speaking at conferences – he'll continue doing what he has always done. This was never about careerising for Trenton at all.

TE: He's not a desperate publicity seeker?

DN: No, absolutely not. And, if you were to meet him, he is very soft spoken and thoughtful...

TE: What has he told you about being in prison?

DN: He said that people are treating him very well – the guards and fellow prisoners, there's a camaraderie and sense that perhaps he shouldn't be there. He is learning a lot.

TE: Learning in the academic sense or learning in the life sense?

DN: Learning in the life sense – it's a huge learning opportunity for him, and he's also taken loads of books so he's reading a lot. He has applied to sweep – he is going to try to garner as much from the experience as possible. As I said, his main concern is that no one else is put into this position – in which they are imprisoned for six months for a non–violent direct action protest exercising their democratic rights in this country.

TE: We haven't heard the last of him, it sounds like. And would you support him if he decides to do something high profile again?

DN: Of course, yes. I support Trenton – I trust him, I know his politics and I know his heart, he's a good person. Yes, absolutely.

This interview was first broadcast on 9 November 2012 on *Voice of Russia* radio http://ruvr.co.uk/radio_broadcast/73145563/94091638.html

1. The Crown prosecution informed Trenton's lawyers the reason for the charge being changed, was in order to achieve a higher penalty.

Appen–
dix

Trial

Tran–
scripts

IN THE CROWN COURT AT ISLEWORTH

Ref. T2012 0506

36 Ridgeway Road
Isleworth

Tuesday, 25th September 2012

Before

HER HONOUR JUDGE A. MOLYNEUX

R E G I N A

- v -

TRENTON OLDFIELD

MR L. MABLY(?) appeared on behalf of the prosecution
MR B. NEWTON appeared on behalf of the defendant

EVIDENCE OF TRENTON OLDFIELD

Transcribed from the official digital recording by
MARGARET WORT & CO
(Official Court Reporters)
Edial Farm Cottage, Edial, Burntwood, Staffordshire, WS7 0HZ

** *This transcript has been prepared without the aid of documentation*

EVIDENCE OF TRENTON OLDFIELD

TRENTON OLDFIELD, affirmed

(The judge addressed the witness)

Examined in chief by MR NEWTON

MR NEWTON: I am going to make it easy for you not to look at me by not looking at you. So you keep looking to my left. Could you give the court your full name please.

A. Trenton James Oldfield.

Q. How old are you, Mr Oldfield?

A. 36.

Q. Where were you born?

A. Sydney, Australia.

Q. And when you did you first move to Great Britain?

A. 2001, March.

JUDGE MOLYNEUX: Are you able to hear? (To the witness) Keep your voice right up and if anyone doesn't hear at any point, just wave your arms about so that Mr Oldfield knows that you can't hear.

MR NEWTON: So you moved to the UK in 2001, two months before your 25th birthday.

A. Yes, that's correct.

Q. Now, when you were growing up in Australia, just tell us a little bit about where you grew up and where you went to school.

A. Erm, I grew up in the north of Sydney - I'm sorry, I grew up in the north of Sydney--

JUDGE MOLYNEUX: Well, that's going to make you uncomfortable.

A. Shall I sit?

JUDGE MOLYNEUX: Sit down then. Because this court room was designed by an architect who hadn't really much experience of British courts, so there isn't a man or a woman or even a child alive for whom that microphone is at the right height. (Laughter)

A. Unless they jump around.

(Further discussion re: microphone)

A. I was born in the northern suburbs of Sydney and I went to a local primary school and er, had a very pleasant childhood, and then High School, I went for a small period of time to a boys' school in the centre of Sydney, and after that I went to a, I left after 4 years and went to another state school for the final 2 years of my studies.

Q. And what did you do between school and moving to Britain?

A. I did a erm, an undergraduate degree at the University of Newcastle in erm, social sciences, specialising in urban studies.

Q. That was Newcastle, Australia, not--

A. That's correct, Newcastle, Australia, 2 hours north.

2

Q. A bit warmer, I imagine.

A. Warmer and good surf.

Q. So why did you come to Britain?

A. Erm, I've always been fascinated in Britain. I was interested in the, at the time it was, it was a particularly interesting place, with erm, what was happening er, post-there was the election 2007, there was a lot of interesting work, a lot of interesting people--

Q. Do you mean 1997?

A. 1997. There was a lot of interesting work and er, people in the United Kingdom that - ancestrally I come from here as well, so it was an interesting place

to, to come.

Q. Going to skip on a little bit. You're married, are you not?

A. I am married, yes,

Q. Where did you meet your wife?

A. I met my wife at a talk. We, er, share a friendship and an association with an architectural firm. And er, we, I was commissioning them and Deepa was working

for them and they would hold talks on Friday evenings and people that were coming through the country that we could, erm, people would come and do a presentation on Friday evenings and it was quite a social thing, and I went along to

that and Deepa was there and we both had very similar interests, and that's how we met.

Q. And your wife sits in the middle on the front row, is that right?

3

A. That's correct.

Q. Now, before we move on to the interest you shared with your wife and what you went on to do work-wise - forgive me, what did you do when you first moved to the United Kingdom?

A. My very first job was in the, what's the museum that now has Darwin in it? Erm--

Q. The British Museum?

A. Not the British Museum, the Natural History Museum, that was very first job. I was a room attendant in the Natural History Museum, and then soon after that I started working in community development, which is erm, working in local neighbours to help or assist local people to make their area better, to work with central and local government to increase the services that they were getting, addressing issues around inequality and poverty, and erm, that was my first professional job here, if you like, or senior job.

Q. And who was that with?

A. That was with an organisation called Dalgarno SRB, which is Single Regeneration Budget and that was in North Kensington. And I did two, two posts there. First as a community development worker and then as a senior, as a senior project manager.

Q. After that?

A. After that I went erm, to the east of London and worked at an organisation called Cityside Regeneration which did the same thing but erm, in Tower Hamlets,

4

which is one of the most impoverished boroughs in the whole of the United

Kingdom. My job as a senior project manager was to work with these indices of

deprivation so people that have severe multiple indices of deprivation which

correlate with things like early death rates, low unemployment, erm, issues around

race, erm, gender, inequality, educational quality and standards, and my job was to

bring money in from Central Government to address those issues in the best

possible way.

Q. How long did you work there?

A. Erm, I think it was around 2-and-a-half years.

Q. So where are we up to now? What year are we on?

A. Erm, 2004.

Q. Where did you go to work then?

A. I, I went, my next job was er, I was employed as the coordinator for this

Thames Strategy, Kew to Chelsea, which runs from erm, well, it actually runs from

the Houses of Parliament to Kew Gardens, but it's called Kew to Chelsea, and just,

I think the name was better. My job there was to bring together all the competing

interests that exist along the river, such as the Port of London Authority, the

Environment Agency, the local boroughs, residents, erm, English Heritage, the list

is quite substantial, and my position there was to be able to bring these people

together, these different organisations and people together, to try and make the

river and it's environment erm, better, in that it was addressing the main issues

around the river to do with er, firstly, on a kind of philosophical level, the idea was to start with the river and move back to the land, so the river became the most important issue, so it was a lot of issues around development and--

Q. Just pause there for a moment. You're saying an awful lot and everyone is trying to take a note.

JUDGE MOLYNEUX: Never worry about me because I always complain. So if I get stuck you'll know. But if anyone is wanting Mr Oldfield to slow down please do say so.

MR NEWTON: Thank you very much, your Honour. (To the witness) Go ahead.

A. Yes, it was, it was an amazing job where it was 18 miles of river from, well, from the Houses of Parliament to Kew in West London and included all the catchment boroughs, so Hounslow and Kensington & Chelsea, Hammersmith & Fulham, Richmond, Wandsworth, and our aim was to, let's make the river and it's environment better than it had been. A lot of issues around kind of water quality, access to the river, there's a lot of areas that were blocked off so people couldn't get access to the river and make it a sort of a much more accessible environment for people.

Q. So how long did you work there for?

A. 4-and-a-half, possibly 5 years, I think.

Q. Practically speaking, what was achieved by that organisation in those 5 years?

A. Erm, I think we brought in a huge amount of - I mean, it's a relative term, I guess - but a huge amount of money into that erm, part of the river to address those issues so we could draw on money from Central Government, environmental

6

agencies, et cetera, to do that, and we, one of the main things was also to draw
attention to the river as well, so it didn't become the backdrop to London, it became
kind of a, the centre of, of London and the centre of how people understood
London and their relationship to it, and I believe and I'm speaking for myself and
others can, can confirm this, but I believe that we were quite successful at that.

Q. In 2009, did you carry on working for that organisation or did you do
something else?

A. No, I, no, I left the organisation erm, my partner Deepa and I decided to, as a
result of all our experience, Deepa's experience is in similar issues and sort of also
in erm, more kind of culture theory, things, we decided to form an organisation
together that we could address these issues beyond kind of er, statutory work, if
you like, on a more kind of philosophical level, we could influence policy through
that way and it's called, This Is Not A Gateway, and that organisation was formally
registered in 2007 but became active in 2009, and we, the aim of that organisation
or the type of things that we do is we organise talks, events, where different people
from different backgrounds, et cetera, can come together and discuss issues around,
to do with living in cities and sort of the main issues around inequality and poverty
that is so erm, prevalent in cities, and particularly in London, which has the highest
inequality in western, in the western world, if we call it that.

So London is er, the gap between rich and poor is 237 times that, it's, it's
kind of worse than in Dickens' time. I mean, we have shoes et cetera, but the issues
of inequality are much more dramatic than they've, they've been since all those

7

famous books were written about Tales of Two Cities et cetera, so we erm, set out as a result of both of that body of knowledge that we'd been working on to address those issues through this organisation. We do that with an annual conference where around 2,000 people come to it, and erm, contribute and it's very important that we bring a bottom-up approach with that, and it's, I think you've read some of the responses that people have said that have attended those conferences, about addressing those issues of inequality and...

Q. In addition to the conferences and the public speaking is there anything else your organisation does?

A. Yes, we publish books, a publishing arm called Myrdle Court Press--

JUDGE MOLYNEUX: Called what, sorry?

A. Myrdle Court Press.

MR NEWTON: M-y-r-d-l-e.

A. And it's erm, that was done to specifically er, to make sure that that body of knowledge that we are developing from people from all around the world could continue beyond just those conference moments, and they're, we were just, just had a good review about the work that we do (inaudible).

Q. Without wishing to be crass, do you and Deepa make much money out of this?

A. No, no. No. It's erm, no, we don't actually what, mainly what we do is we subsidise our work to do this work so erm, it can be, in the beginning I had savings as a result of my work with, over the previous 7 years, which I had been working towards setting this organisation up. For a period of time we lived off that and then

8

for the other period of time er, Deepa would go and work in erm, in another country to be able to fund this work. It's very much erm, er, a not-for-profit.

Q. Now, outside of your paid employment and This Is Not A Gateway, what else have you been involved with in the last 10 years?

A. Erm, yeah, this is, this could be difficult, right from the beginning coming to the United Kingdom, because I was so interested in this country and particularly the city, I was, I've been on a number of boards and organisations where I've volunteered my time. One period I was probably three nights a week at different organisations, such as the Westway Development Trust in North Kensington, which looks after the environment under the Westway between erm, Westbourne Park--

JUDGE MOLYNEUX: What's the name of this organisation?

A. It's called the Westway Development Trust, formerly the North Kensington Amenity Trust.

JUDGE MOLYNEUX: Thank you.

A. And that looks after - when the road was built, the community was concerned about the separation between the north and the south of Kensington because of the issues of inequality, so they decided to get together and take over the land underneath - and this is in the 1960s - take over the land underneath the roadway and make it for community use, so I erm, I was working in North Kensington, they heard of the work I was doing and invited me to join the board so I could help continue their work, which I was very pleased to do and it was, I really learnt a lot

9

in that organisation, and I was, I think I was on three boards there that - it was the arts committee, the finance committee, and the property committee - so for the first couple of years, that was one of the organisations I was involved in. I was also on the board of an organisation called Subtext, which was doing a lot around issues of literature in East London. So that organisation would go out and raise money to be able to do projects with young people to increase literacy and make education more accessible.

There are a number of other organisations which are probably not listed but it was one of the most important parts of my time being here was these extra aspects that I could contribute.

Q. Odd question to ask but I have to ask you, have you ever before 7th April this year been in trouble with the police in this country, have you got any convictions or cautions here or in Australia?

A. Never, in either country. Do you want me to talk about the other organisations? The Red Cross Refugee...

Q. Okay.

A. When I first came here, it was the Red Cross Refuge group in Westminster I first volunteered with, and at the time there was still a lot of people coming from erm, the former Yugoslavia with the wars in Bosnia. What we did was work with er, people that had just arrived to adjust them to London, give them shoes - we had a basement where there was shoes and clothes and things - and we would work with people there to - and then go to where they were staying. Often they were in

10

B&Bs and we'd spend time with them orientating them in the neighbourhood, letting them get to know the environment and pointing them, taking them to meetings with government departments, et cetera. I did that between 1 and 2 days per week for the first couple of years when I arrived.

Q. We all know that this is all leading up to an act of protest in April this year. The organisation you have described - This Is Not A Gateway - could it in any way be described as being a protest movement or a protest organisation?

A. No, erm, I, nothing that was involved with the protest was linked to that organisation. The organisation is, is a, is an organisation that's critical and does critical work, as in that it works on a kind of academic level so it doesn't take the status quo and celebrate the status quo, it kind of works towards how can we make society better, how can we make it more equal, how can we, how can more people have greater opportunity. Erm, whereas I was very clear that my protest wasn't associated with that. Even though the ideas are the same, there was no kind of er, opportunity to kind of promote the organisation or anything like that that...

Q. Was it on behalf of any other organisation?

A. No, it was myself as an individual.

Q. Now, we're not going to use your trial as a soapbox, so just in one or two sentences, why did you do that protest on 7th April?

A. Erm, in the 3 days leading up to the protest, the, the, the government, or the coalition government, which is, which was erm, not elected but was created, had been passing some very dramatic erm, cuts to the, our lives, and in the 3 days

11

before the, the, the bill had been introduced into Parliament or was suggested to be introduced into Parliament to, in simple terms, sell off the NHS. They had also introduced - actually, excuse me, it had been signed that week, that week, the NHS bill. The second issues was the--

JUDGE MOLYNEUX: Sorry, I missed what you said then. A bill was introduced to sell off the NHS.

A. It was actually signed and it had been given Royal assent that week.

JUDGE MOLYNEUX: Had been signed?

A. Yes. It had passed previously. There was very little in the press but erm, and the next issue was the, the erm, the government had suggested it was going to

introduce in the Queen's speech, and this happened, a bill that would allow the government and other agencies to snoop on er, Internet use or digital telephones et cetera. And the third thing that happened that week was the Olympics Minster

said that if you think your neighbour might be going to protest at the Olympics you should dob them in. I can't remember his name, a very tall chap.

But that was the kind of, the context of, of what was happening and that was, that was the level of - I'd just returned from erm, Canada where I'd been with my partner, Deepa, looking after her father who'd passed away from er, cancer in the previous month, so I'd come back to London in this very kind of erm, and the

level of poverty and the, the inequality that existed here became very, very sensitive, and with these levels of cuts that were happening to people, it, it became

clear to me that erm, something needed to be done on a protest level and, and

12

there's a long history in this country and other countries of, of those moments existing. And it, it was a, it was a, it felt an important thing to do.

MR NEWTON: Since the Boat Race, you've been under various conditions of your bail.

A. Correct.

Q. Have you engaged in any other form of protest since then?

A. No.

Q. Before the 7th April, had you ever done anything like that before?

A. No, nothing like that. I've been on all the marches.

Q. What kind of marches?

A. Well, anti-war march.

Q. But nothing similar to what we're dealing with here.

A. No, no.

Q. So that was the first and only time that you did it, when you got back from Canada.

A. Correct.

Q. Now, in relation to the actual events that day, we've seen it all, I'm not going to take you through it all, in a nutshell, how much preparation did you have to put into that?

A. It was quite spontaneous, I mean, these issues, particularly those three days with the massive changes to British society that was happening, erm, it, it's, (inaudible word) the next day I went and bought the wetsuit and the next day was

13

the Boat Race. So it didn't take much preparation. I mean, I think I knew, I knew the landscape quite well because of having worked in the area for so long. It was, you know, there was a momentum, it was a very quick decision.

Q. In the immediate aftermath of it, we've heard read evidence this morning that you were charged with a public order offence and released that night, bailed to Magistrates' Court. In relation to the rowers themselves, how do you feel about them?

A. I mean, I mean I chose or I mean it was that week so it became apparent that that was a good place to protest but to me I was trying to minimise the disruption as much as possible that could happen, particularly to workers that, there wasn't going to be an impact like if you'd done a protest on a railway or something or the NHS, that there was going to be no impact on, on workers. Erm, that was very important to me, and it was, it was important to chose the, the least possible er, disruption, you know, you know, 16 people erm, that was, that was important to me as well, and er, what was the question?

Q. How do you feel about the rowers?

A. How do I feel? I mean, I, I do, I do have sympathy, I mean I really have sympathy for the situation. I have myself done those kind of sporting events, I have actually rowed myself as well, and I know that incredible physical exertion, you know, it, er, exertion that you put into it, it's a very er, physical sport, so I do have a lot of sympathy for that, that level of erm, exertion that they do put in. What's interesting about that race erm, is 3 weeks before that race is a, is a race

14

called, Head of The River Race, where 403 boats race, and it's actually a national

event, where people from all over the country come together and race, and Oxford

and Cambridge don't participate in that race interestingly. I'm not sure if it's

because they might lose, I don't know, but 3 weeks before 403 boats race, and this

was completely separate where it was just two boats, wasn't national, unlike the

other one, even though it did have a lot of media resources and a lot of money put

into it. The race 3 weeks before is, is the premium rowing race in Britain.

Q. In terms of the impact of what you did on the 16 rowers, two coxes, the people

directly organising it, do you accept responsibility for that?

A. I do(?).

Q. Do you accept that you have harmed the general public in any way?

A. No.

MR NEWTON: Thank you very much, Mr Oldfield, if you could wait there.

Cross-examined by MR MABLY

MR MABLY: Mr Oldfield, from what you've just said, you're obviously a

dedicated man. Do you accept that?

A. That would be for others to say but that I think that might be the case.

Q. Responsible man?

A. I believe so, yes.

Q. And you have a social conscience.

A. That's correct.

15

Q. You have told us about your work in this country since you arrived here. We're going to fast forward to the 7th April, yes?

A. Hmm-mm.

Q. And we see, we've seen the footage, you're in the middle of the River Thames, yes?

A. Yes.

Q. Grinning away. Yeah?

A. Correct.

Q. Having upset an awful lot of people.

A. I mean, I don't accept that.

Q. You don't accept that. Looking back now, having seen the footage, having heard what you have said in this court room, are you proud of the achievements of the 7th April, or do you regret them in any way?

A. Pride is a word I would never use in my life.

Q. Well, content with what you did, or do you regret it in any way?

A. Er, I don't - I'm content.

Q. You're content.

A. Yes.

Q. Any regrets.

A. I'm content with what I did.

Q. Any regrets at all?

A. I'm content with what I did.

16

Q. I know, you've told us that, but going back to my question, do you have any regrets at all about what you did?

A. I don't have any regrets, I'm content with what I did.

Q. Okay. Now, when you jumped into the Thames, as you've said, you intended to interrupt the race. That's right, isn't it?

A. Correct.

Q. And it was obvious before you did that that interrupting the race was going to have a number of consequences.

A. Correct.

Q. That's correct, isn't it? And those consequences included, it was more than likely that the race was going to have to be stopped.

A. Correct.

Q. You were going to distort the progress of the race.

A. That, that was an unknown.

Q. Well, if the race is stopped, its progress is going to be distorted, isn't it?

A. Well, it was restarted so the race wasn't but...

Q. Yes, but it was stopped, wasn't it?

A. Temporarily.

Q. Yes. And it didn't run it's natural course.

A. What's interesting about that course is that it's a very difficult course where the, you know, there's often been boat - well, not often - but that boats have sunk, et cetera. So--

17

Q. Shall we stop beating about the bush--

A. It's not a particularly straight course like the other ones. One of the things about racing on that course is that it's, it's a tidal Thames, it's got bends and corners, and--

Q. We know it's got bends and corners, and we know it's got a tide, everyone knows that, but the point is that the course of the race was sabotaged. It's what you did, wasn't it?

A. I did protest in the river, yes.

Q. And it sabotaged the race.

A. That's for others to interpret.

Q. Well, how do you interpret it? You're giving evidence.

A. I interpret it that I did a protest, based on a very clear conscience, political conscience.

Q. Yes, and again, dealing with my question, one of the consequences which you envisaged before you did that was you were going to sabotage the race.

A. May I have some more water please?

JUDGE MOLYNEUX: Yes, of course. Madam usher, you might like to leave the jug there.

A. Thank you.

MR MABLY: Have your drink of water, Mr Oldfield. Now, doing your best to refocus, one of the consequences that your protest was going to have, as you envisaged, was that it was going to sabotage the race.

18

A. I don't - my protest was very clear. If you want to use the word sabotage, I understand.

Q. Well, shall we use a different word, see if you agree with that: it was going to distort the race.

A. It was, it was possibly going to temporarily delay the race.

Q. Possibly going to temporarily delay the race.

A. Yes.

Q. Okay. It must also have been apparent to you that you were going to disappoint a large number of people.

A. That wasn't, I mean, I imagine that some people would be upset, as you can see from some of the footage, most of the, some of the people were upset, a great number of people weren't. Some people were going to be, because it was a race between two organisations, or two clubs, or what have you, and that, some people would be upset, yes.

Q. Yes, because there were tens of thousands of people watching the race on the tow path, weren't there?

A. I've always been interested in the number - because I've worked in that area for a long time, I'm not sure if you notice on the video, there's vast areas and what's interesting is that nobody saw me go into the river because there's vast areas that are empty. It's only in certain pockets where there are people, so I, the tens of thousands I think would be possibly an, having worked in the area for those 4-5 years, I saw all of those boat races may exist in four small pockets, the people, if you look at the river, it's, it's almost empty for the vast majority of it.

Q. Well, Mr Oldfield, we can all see the footage, we can see the kinds of crowds that were there.

A. Yeah, there are crowds in pockets where the Local Authority puts on jumping castles and things for people, yes.

Q. So what are we to understand from your evidence, just so there's no misunderstanding? Are you saying that the course of this race, in terms of people watching it, was sparsely attended?

A. I think if you look at the footage, there are - most of the river is, especially on the side that I was on, which was probably why I was able to get in the river. If I was, if it was hugely populated I don't think I would have been able to get into the river.

Q. Is this an attempt, Mr Oldfield, actually to try and minimise the impact that you know that you caused, by trying to dispute the obvious fact that there were tens of thousands of people watching the race?

A. No, sir, not at all, I'm just saying exactly what there is, I'm not trying to reduce or anything, just saying exactly the facts, which I hope you can see on the film as well.

Q. Okay. Now, you don't like the phrase, tens of thousands, let's just say a large number of people, shall we, a large number of members of the general public? Are you happy with that phrase?

20

A. Correct.

Q. And you knew that you were going to disappoint a large number of them, didn't you?

A. I think I mentioned earlier that it was a - I made the decision within that few days to do something that would, that wouldn't be a major interruption, like stopping a road or an airport, or - that it was a very limited group of people who would be affected.

Q. And you knew that they would be affected, didn't you?

A. I knew that some people would be upset, yes.

Q. Because they hadn't actually come to see you, had they?

A. No, they hadn't come to see me.

Q. They'd come to see a boat race.

A. Yes, correct.

Q. And you would agree that they had the right to see that boat race.

A. Yes, and they did.

Q. Would you also agree that you obstructed that right? I mean, physically obstructed it.

A. Oh yeah, I mean, it's clear.

Q. And you did that deliberately.

A. Deliberately.

Q. And the result was it had the consequences that you had or that were entirely predictable.

21

A. I don't think anybody could know how predictable it was going to be. I was in the water for 5-and-a-half minutes. I could've been taken out long before the race had come close to me. Five-and-a-half minutes is a very long time to be in the water.

Q. Yes, but your objective wasn't to get taken out, your object was to actually interrupt the race.

A. Yes, but it may or may not have been successful.

Q. Yes, of course, anything's possible but you actually were successful.

A. I was successful in temporarily halting the race, yes.

Q. Yes. And when you did that, when you were in the Thames and you were swimming out towards the competing boats, did you have any consideration for your own safety?

A. I did, yes, I, what's very interesting about that part of the river, having worked there for quite a number of years, is there's a, there's a, actually a swimming race there, called the Great River Swim, which happens between Chiswick Eyot(?) and Chiswick Pier. So I know that area very well, and that's an annual race where people swim in that particular thing, between Chiswick Eyot and Chiswick Pier, which is the two areas where I was, so I knew of the kind of safety courses and the conditions of the river there. As people know, I grew up in Australia as well, and I grew up surfing, which I think I mention too earlier, and I also grew up rowing, and I know that rowing boats erm, are only that deep, they go very low in the water and those boats that are coming behind which have been mentioned, if you look at them

22

are all, they're old boats which have the propeller in the boat. They're not like the ones where you see now where there's those massive propellers that go at the back of the boat, so they're actually contained in the boat.

So in terms of my own safety, I, I felt very, very confident that nothing was going to happen. I thought perhaps that having been in the water for 5-and-a-half minutes it would never have even got to the situation where the boats were even close to me, that I would've, I would've been pulled out in the river much before the, the boats even came close. I'm sorry that Matthew Pinsent wasn't sort of looking up at the, at the river, it says in his statement he was looking down at the boats--

Q. Sorry, what do you mean by that? Are we to attach blame to Matthew Pinsent?

A. No, no, no, I'm just saying I was in the water for 5-and-a-half minutes. Let me move on. But I was very confident that there was no danger because also when an oar is only as, the most important thing when, when you row is that you don't stick the oar in too deep, otherwise you catch a crab and you throw yourself out of the boat, so an oar only goes as deep as the oar itself. That's one of the most important elements is that you don't do it very deep, so as we saw, I ducked very easily and I felt very confident that if the situation came, which I didn't expect, but if the situation came, there would be no danger to myself. And I'm a very strong swimmer, as it was pointed out from having grown up in Australia.

I mean, I was - a normal day for me would be surf boards come at you, those massive rowing boats that you see in the surf, having to dodge them,

23

enormous ones, erm, people on all sorts of craft in the water, rocks, coral, you know, I mean you grow up with this in Australia, this is very normal. I believe it's called wild swimming here, going in natural water. Most people swim in swimming pools but in Australia that's not the case, you swim everywhere. I mean, it's just the way, it's not called wild swimming, it's called swimming. So I had no erm, I was completely clear there, there would be almost no danger. To myself. And I know that part of the river very well, and there was the Great River Swim that happens there every year.

Q. Is there anything else you want to say about that?

A. About my danger?

Q. Or about the Great River Swim?

A. It happens annually, erm, I was a big supporter of it, I was very aware of it, erm, it gets bigger every year.

Q. Getting back to the events of the 7th April, when the boats were coming towards you, rather than anyone pulling you out, you actually swam towards them.

A. I swam into the middle of the stream, yes.

Q. Yes, into the path of the boats.

A. I was using the tide, yeah.

Q. And do you accept that there was a very severe risk to your welfare?

A. No, no.

Q. So you disagree with John Garrett and Matthew Pinsent in that regard.

24

A. Well, there's, there's never been a case where somebody has died from an oar. Or a boat.

Q. Well, it's not very often that people actually swim out in front of boats, is it?

A. I think it's very often--

Q. It's probably not surprising.

A. --I mean, rowing happens on, I mean, where I grew up (and rode?) in Australia, people were swimming all the time, there was - I mean, that particular course in Hammersmith & Fulham, I mean, I was once an industrial place, there was massive, you know, container ships going, well, not container ships but at the time, you know, big ships going up and down.

Q. Just focusing on the 7th April, Mr Oldfield, do you accept there was a serious risk to your welfare?

A. I don't, no.

Q. Well, what do you think would have happened if one of those competing boats had hit you in the head?

A. I hope I had explained carefully before that because of my fitness, because of my experience growing up in Australia and because my awareness of the types of boats that were out on the river on the day, that I was very aware, I wouldn't be in danger because I could duck, as I did and was shown, and that would've been the same with any of the other boats.

Q. What do you think would have happened if one of those oars had hit you on the head or slashed you across the face?

25

A. Erm, it wouldn't have happened because I would've ducked and gone under, which is a very normal thing to do in Australia, because if the waves are coming to you, you practice a lot to kind of diving under them.

Q. Or if one of the following launchers had hit you.

A. It's same thing, as I mentioned, most of those launchers are the old boats where the propeller is included in the, in the, I believe it's called the, I can't remember, the bottom of the boat that's in the water, so the propellers are, they're actually protected in those older boats, so people can't actually get hit.

Q. Yeah, never mind the propeller, what about if the boat itself had hit you.

A. It would be the same as the, the, the rowing vessel, I would've ducked, so there was no chance of - because you wouldn't have had to have ducked very low because you can see that they're very small boats, they go very low in the water.

Q. And how far would you have needed to duck?

A. Not very far, as you could see on the film.

Q. How far to get underneath one of those launchers?

A. A couple of feet.

Q. And no problem for you.

A. Absolutely no problem.

Q. And so what do we attribute then, the decision of the umpire and Matthew Pinsent, to, was it some kind of overreaction on their part?

26

A. I mean, I can't answer that other than perhaps that the different culture that people grow up with, that people don't swim and well, it's called wild swimming here.

Q. Is there any kind of gratitude on your part towards them for trying to do what they could to stop you being injured?

A. If they believed that that, I mean John Garrett seems like a very nice man.

Q. Yes, and the Oxford rowing crew, who stopped rowing? Made sure their oars didn't hit you. Any gratitude towards them?

A. I, I--

Q. Or did you have it all under control?

A. I think I ducked but yes, I mean, it's great that it all worked out.

Q. Or the Oxford cox, any gratitude towards her for ordering her crew to stop rowing?

A. It's brilliant that it all worked out, that nobody it was injured, yeah.

Q. Do you actually think it was fair to put those people in that position?

A. Erm, well, I think they'd mentioned earlier that it's quite a normal part of rowing to look out for things in the river and it's the role of the coxes, et cetera, to do that, to, you know, it can be a fridge or a, you know, piece of a tree--

Q. Sorry, a fridge? We're not talking about fridge, fridges don't swim out into the path of competing boats. You decided to do this deliberately--

A. I think in the statement there's a mention to the fridge--

Q. --and the question is do you think it was fair to put them in that position?

27

A.   Erm, I think protests aren't always fair.

Q.   Well, you have described this country as having a long history of protest. To what exactly were you alluding?

A.   I mean, right from the beginning - when do you want to go back to?

Q.   Well, you alluded to it.

A.   It's also not just this country but it's also--

Q.   What are you talking about, Mr Oldfield, what kind of category of protest are you placing yourself within?

A.   I mean, I think that's a bit unfair to suggest that I'm putting myself in that - I'm suggesting that there's a long history from which one can draw experience and inspiration from. I'm not suggesting that I'm one of those people. I'm suggesting that there's a long history of that which one can look at and say, this, you know, this part of British culture. I mean, and not only in Britain but within the colonial, you know, the British empire, of people that have, you know, really fought for independence, be it for civil rights, be it for women's rights, be it for land rights.

Q.   Mr Oldfield, people are still building statues to suffragettes. Are you thinking that in 100 years' time, people might be building statues to Trenton Oldfield?

A.   I've never thought that.

Q.   Well, what was it exactly that you were protesting about?

A.   I was protesting about the level of inequality in Britain, and that, the situation where it was only going to get worse in Britain because of these level of cuts that

28

were being brought in by the government, and that inequality is very unnecessary and very unfair.

Q. And that's what this was about.

A. Yes.

Q. And what did swimming in front of the Boat Race have to do with that?

A. The Oxford and Cambridge Boat Race is symbolic of a lot of issues in Britain around class. Around erm, 70 per cent for example of the government that were pushing through these, these very significant cuts, are Oxbridge graduates. It was a symbolic gesture to those kind of issues, all the way through of kind of inequalities - I mean, you will have seen in the paper in the last 2 days the extra funding that Oxford and Cambridge get in comparison to the other Universities, which is you know, increasing the inequalities, and I mean, the current Cabinet, five of them even did the same course at the same college, I think at the same time. So it very much represented, is symbolic of the situation that I've spent a decade here working on, and time back in Australia working on as well.

Q. So let's just understand this: are we talking about the Boat Race being symbolic of this? The Boat Race is symbolic of government cuts? Or is it Oxford and Cambridge Universities in their entirety?

A. You see, I mean--

Q. What exactly are we talking about?

A. I'm sorry, I've lost my train of thought, I think what's--

Q. It's your protest, Mr Oldfield--

29

A. Yes, thank you.

Q. --you tell us.

A. What I mean, perhaps it can be kind of articulated in that the race that happens

3 weeks before where there's 403 boats this year, which Oxford and Cambridge

chose not to participate in, when they - and all the resources 3 weeks later go to the

Oxford and Cambridge Boat Race, where all the media, all the funding, everything

goes to it, it's two boats that race, in comparison to 403, national event, brings

people from all around the country together. I think that's symbolic just in that,

within a 3-week moment, of the level of kind of inequality, the advantage, the two-

tier society that's existing in Britain, and was going to increase and is increasing.

Q. Now, obviously, Mr Oldfield, this is an issue you feel very strongly about, but

obviously, you understand that people do have the right to disagree with you.

A. Absolutely.

Q. And the right not to feel as strongly as you do about it.

A. Absolutely.

Q. And actually sometimes the right not to care.

A. That's a shame, that people don't care.

Q. But everyone has to get along together, don't they?

A. We're all in it together?

Q. Well, society has to work, doesn't it, Mr Oldfield?

A. Society, and that's everything I've been working towards.

30

Q. Now, those people who had turned up not to see you protesting but had turned up to watch the Boat Race, what consideration did you give to their rights?

A. I mean, I really considered where an appropriate - so it wouldn't be an airport or a road or something that could really disrupt, it was a very, very particular, very limited space. I believe protests unfortunately do cause inconvenience sometimes, brief delays, but that's very important in protest, that, for them to, that's part, unfortunately part of protests.

Q. Yes, unfortunately who decided, who was it who decided that they were going to be inconvenienced and delayed? All these people who had come to watch the Boat Race. Who decided?

A. Who decided?

Q. Yes.

A. I'm sorry I don't understand.

Q. Who decided they were going to be inconvenienced and delayed?

A. Who, I don't--

Q. It was you, wasn't it?

A. I don't understand the question.

Q. You alone, you on your own--

A. It was by myself, I didn't involve anybody else.

Q. No. You decided that your rights to protest, your views were going to take priority over the views and the enjoyment of everybody else.

31

A. I don't, I don't know if everybody, if it did take - I mean, lots of people thought it made it the most exciting Boat Race ever.

Q. What, these people that were booing you, and were shouting abuse at you?

A. There was a small handful of those people but that would be expected. That would be expected in any protest, I mean that happens all the time.

Q. And were the crowd coming up to you, slapping you on the backed and saying, oh, thank you very much, Mr Oldfield? Good job. Well done. No.

A. I don't, I don't know of many protests where that happens.

Q. No, no.

A. Do you? Could you (inaudible)--

Q. Just so there's no misunderstanding, it was you, wasn't it, you alone took upon the decision yourself that your rights, your views, took priority over those of everybody else? It's right, isn't it?

A. I don't really understand the question.

Q. Do you think there was any trace of selfishness in what you did?

A. No.

Q. Do you think there was any trace of arrogance in what you did?

A. No.

Q. Do you think there was any trace of egotism in what you did?

A. No, not at all. I completely not, I mean, do you think that you would go through this process if you thought it was about ego and, I mean, no. The incredible--

32

Q. It was about your views, wasn't it?

A. --the incredible pressure as a result of this? No.

Q. And on what basis in the future can these events take place?

A. Sorry?

Q. Well, on what basis in the future can the Boat Race take place?

A. I don't--

Q. Is it going to take place next year uninterrupted?

A. Every year's different--

Q. Or does that depend on what Mr Oldfield decides to do next year?

A. I don't think I will interrupt the Boat Race next year.

Q. Just something the public had to put up with this year.

A. Protests are very important in this, in how democracy works in this country.

Q. Yes. The rights of everyone are important, aren't they, Mr Oldfield?

A. They are, everybody should be involved in democracy.

MR MABLY: Thank you.

JUDGE MOLYNEUX: Any re-examination?

MR NEWTON: No, thank you. Does your Honour have any questions?

JUDGE MOLYNEUX: No, I don't. Mr Oldfield, thank you very much. You may resume your position now, thank you.

(The witness was released)

----ooOOoo----

Re-sources

Resources

Trenton Oldfield

Putting together this catalogue of resources has been one of the more difficult elements to this book. As you will know by now having read the preceding pages, I think the existence of prisons reflects more on our society than on 'prisoners'. In my mind prisons should be abolished. Charities and 'think tanks' could spend their time 'reforming' the political class and the legal-fraternity that has managed to significantly increase the number of prisons and prisoners rather than reduce them. It is these institutions and these people whose ignorance, prejudices and vested interests create and maintain the existence of a 'criminal class' and propagate the enduring idea of a 'vicious poor in need of reforming'.

Most organisations unfortunately are focused, often exclusively, on the endeavour of 'reforming' prisoners; making them 'useful parts of society again'. Some organisations won't even work with a prisoner if they don't profess a wish to be 'reformed'. These organisations rarely if ever propose the abolition of prisons. Neither do they acknowledge or put forward ending the mechanisms, culture, and economics that help to forge the idea of a 'criminal class'. I haven't included these organisations – they are easy enough to come across elsewhere.

There are some brilliant organisations doing amazing work to support those who are imprisoned and their families – I have listed them below. Check www.thisisnotagateway.net for a regularly updated list. I have arranged them under the following headings: In Jail, Families Left Behind, Women, Abolition of Prisons, Prison Reform, Miscarriages of Justice, and Books.

IN JAIL

Association of Prisoners

Advocate ending the use of imprisonment as a solution to social problems; work towards instituting restorative justice; campaign for the rights of those imprisoned (to education, employment and training). www.unlock.org.uk/xoffenders.aspx?sid=199

Inside Time: The National Newspaper for Prisoners

Voice for prisoners in British prisons, providing information and comments that are informative, interesting and entertaining. www.insidetime.org

Editorial Office
Botley Mills
Botley
Southampton SO30 2GB
Email Editorial: ns@insidetime.org
subs@insidetime.org

Mosquito Communications Ltd

Cheaper prepaid telephone solutions for prisoners. http://moscom.co.uk
2 Fagnall Farm Barns

Fagnall Lane
Winchmore Hill
Buckinghamshire HP7 0PG
Tel: 07007 MOSCOM
(07007 667266)
Email: info@moscom.co.uk

Prisoners Education Trust

Provides access to a wide range of vocational and academic learning opportunities for prisoners. www.prisonerseducation.org.uk

Wandle House
Riverside Drive
Mitcham, Surrey CR4 4BU
Tel: 020 8648 7760 Email: info@prisonerseducation.org.uk

Prisoners Pocket Directory

Directory of recommended law firms, rights in prison, details of all prison establishments, prison service orders, information on cell–sharing, recalls, segregation, adjudications, reception, induction, security categorisation, allocation, work and pay. www.prisons.org.uk/ppd.html

PO BOX 757
Stockport SK2 9AS
Tel: 08450 660011 Email: customer.services@prisons.org.uk

ConVerse: The Prisoners Newspaper

Highest circulation national newspaper for prisons. Highlights proven wrong-doings by public officials, be they corrupt prison staff, police, teachers, doctors or lawyers. www.spyholepress.com/converse.html

PO BOX 757
Stockport SK2 9AS
Tel: 08450 660011 Email:
customer.services@prisons.org.uk

Prison Radio Association

A 'by prisoner, for prisoner' radio service, with content presented and produced by serving prisoners in partnership with a team of professional producers.
www.prisonradioassociation.org/

HMP Brixton
London SW2 5XF

Prison Reading Groups

Supports the spread of prison reading groups, linking formal and informal education in prisons. www.roehampton.ac.uk/Prison–Reading–Groups
Sarah Turvey

Department of English and Creative Writing
University of Roehampton
Roehampton Lane
London SW15 5PU
s.turvey@roehampton.ac.uk

Citizens Advice Bureau

Each prison should have an office of the CAB who provide free, independent, confidential and impartial advice to everyone on their rights and responsibilities. http://www.citizensadvice.org.uk

Prison Phoenix Trust

Meditation and yoga workshops, correspondence, books and newsletters for prisoners and prison staff.
www.prisonphoenixtrust.org

PO Box 328
Oxford OX2 7HF
Tel: 01865 512 521 Email:
all@theppt.org.uk

Email A Prisoner

A quick, efficient, secure alternative method of communication for prisoners their families, friends, legal professionals and related

organisations.
http://emailaprisoner.com

PO Box 4335, Frome BA11 9AF
Tel: 0844 873 3111
Email: support@prison-
technology-services.com

English Pen

Distribute books and literary
magazines to those who have been
imprisoned.

www.englishpen.org/books-
to-prisoners
Free Word Centre
60 Farringdon Road
London EC1R 3GA
Tel: +44 (0) 20 7324 2535

Books to Prisoners

Provides educational literature
for prisoners who are attending
courses and dictionaries in English
and other languages to those
whose first language is not English.

www.havendistribution.org.uk

Haven Distribution
27 Old Gloucester St
London
WC1N 3XX
info2013@havendistribution.org.uk

Music In Prison

Deliver week-long creative
music projects in prisons, with
professional musicians.

http://musicinprisons.org.uk

The Irene Taylor Trust 'Music In
Prisons'
Unit 401, Bon Marche Centre
241 Ferndale Road
London SW9 8BJ
Tel: +44 (0) 207 733 3222
sara@musicinprisons.org.uk /
luke@musicinprisons.org.uk

No Bars To Reading

Training, resources and
support to enable one-to-one
peer mentoring and reading
lessons.
www.shannontrust.org.uk

89 Albert Embankment
Vauxhall
London SE1 7TP
Tel: +44 (0) 20 7582 4835
Email: communications@
shannontrust.org.uk

FAMILIES LEFT BEHIND

Families Outside
www.familiesoutside.org.uk

Prison Chat UK
www.prisonchatuk.com

Prisoner Families Voices
http://prisonersfamiliesvoices.
blogspot.co.uk

**Partner of Prisoners & Families
Support Group**
http://www.partnersofprisoners.
co.uk

Families Waiting Forum
http://familieswaiting.
createaforum.com

Jail Mate Cards
http://jailmatecards.co.uk

Mothers With Sons In Prison
http://motherswithsonsinprison.com

WOMEN

Women In Prison
http://www.womeninprison.org.uk

Rights of Women
http://www.rightsofwomen.org.uk

PRISON REFORM

Prison Reform Trust
www.prisonreformtrust.org.uk

**The Howard League for Prison
Reform**
http://www.howardleague.org

Legal Action Group
http://www.lag.org.uk

Penal Reform International
http://www.penalreform.org

Zahid Mubarek Trust
http://www.thezmt.org

Prison Movement
http://prisonmovement.
wordpress.com

Reclaim Justice Network
http://downsizingcriminaljustice.
wordpress.com

ABOLITION

**End The Prison Industrial
Complex**
http://endthepic.wordpress.com

Critical Resistance
http://criticalresistance.org

Prison Justice
www.prisonjustice.ca

Prisoners With Children
www.prisonerswithchildren.org/
our-projects/allofus-or-none

Alternatives to Prison
https://network23.org/londonabc/
alternatives–to–prison

**The Queer, Feminist and Trans
Politics of Prison Abolition**
http://
prisonercorrespondenceproject.
com/QFT_prison_abolition_full.pdf

Prison Activist
www.prisonactivist.org

Instead of Prisons
www.prisonpolicy.org/scans/
instead_of_prisons

Anarchist Black Cross Federation
www.abcf.net

Abolish All Prisons
http://abolishallprisons.webs.com

Visions of Abolition
http://www.visionsofabolition.org/
trailer.html

Campaign Against Prison Slavery
www.againstprisonslavery.org

MISCARRIAGES OF JUSTICE

**Joint Enterprise: Not Guilty By
Association**
www.jointenterprise.co

**Inside Doubt: Campaign
Against Miscarriages of Justice**
www.insidedoubt.co.uk

**Inquest: Working for Truth,
Justice and Accountability**
www.inquest.org.uk

United Against Injustice
www.unitedagainstinjustice.org.uk

**Innocent: Fighting Injustice
Since 1993**
http://www.innocent.org.uk

Wrongly Accused Person
www.wronglyaccusedperson.org.uk

The Innocent Network
www.innocencenetwork.org.uk

BOOKS

*A Little Book of Prison: A
Beginner's Guide*, Frankie Owens
(Waterside Press, 2012)

Victorian & Edwardian Prisons,
Trevor May (Shire Publications,
2006)

Victorian Workhouses, Trevor May
(Shire Publications, 2008)

*Discipline and Punish: The Birth of
the Prison*, Michel Foucault (Knopf

Doubleday Publishing Group, 1977)

Prison Rules: A Working Guide, Nancy Loucks (The Prison Reform Trust, 2000)

Are Prisons Obsolete?, Angela Davis (Seven Stories Press, 2003)

Perpetual Prisoner Machine: How America Profits from Crime, Joel Dyer (Basic Books, 2000)

Global Lockdown: Race, Gender, and the Prison–Industrial Complex, Julia Sudbury (Routledge, 2004)

Abolition Now! Ten Years of Strategy and Struggle Against the Prison Industrial Complex (AK Press, 2008)

Instead of Prisons: A Handbook for Abolitionists, Ed. Mark Morris (Prison Research Education Action Project, 1976)

Plague of Prisons: The Epidemiology of Mass Incarceration in America, Ernest Drucker (The New Press, 2011)

Abolition Democracy: Beyond Prisons, Torture, and Empire,

Angela Y. Davis (Seven Stories Press, 2005)

About
Myrdle Court
Press

Myrdle Court Press (MCP) advances critical, independent and rigorous inter-disciplinary work that interrogates contemporary notions and experience of 'cities'. It was established in 2009 to redress the incongruous situation that as the population, size and problems of cities are expanding, and despite the existence of many new cells of knowledge and urgent thinking, the spaces for critical public discourse are narrowing and the credibility of democracy rapidly declining.

An independent, not-for-profit organisation that straddles the spaces between the street and the academy, Myrdle Court Press commissions, collects and publishes work that tackles pressing and political concerns without restraint. It shares the experiences, astute insights and agitation of contributors from around the world including Beirut, Zagreb, Bogota, London, Hong Kong, Athens, Nicosia, Jerusalem, New York, Porto and Warsaw. Contributors come from the fields of visual arts, activism, education, property, architecture and planning, law, governmental policy, political economy, military strategy, filmmaking, philosophy and lived knowledge.

On Myrdle Court Press books:

"There is a dearth of critical commentaries examining the changes wrought by neo-liberalism. At last a multi-disciplinary collection of writing that brings together some of the best." Anna Minton, author of *Ground Control*

"This collection explicitly and honestly wears its politics on its sleeve. The exhilaration in the book lies in the stories told and in their transformative potential." Professor Jeremy Till, author of *Architecture Depends*

In Memory of Athiraman Kannan: Migration and Labour in the Early 21st Century (2013)

The Queen vs Trenton Oldfield: A Prison Diary (2013)

Estate: Arts, Politics and Social Housing in Britain (2010)

Critical Cities: Ideas, Knowledge and Agitation from Emerging Urbanists, Vol 4 (2013)

Critical Cities: Ideas, Knowledge and Agitation from Emerging Urbanists, Vol 3 (2012)

Critical Cities: Ideas, Knowledge and Agitation from Emerging Urbanists, Vol 2 (2010)

Critical Cities: Ideas, Knowledge and Agitation from Emerging Urbanists, Vol 1 (2009)

Myrdle Court Press is based in London, UK and is the publishing arm of This Is Not A Gateway. It takes a back-to-fundamentals approach to book production using design for readability, high quality ethically sourced materials, local printers and independent distribution.

www.myrdlecourtpress.net

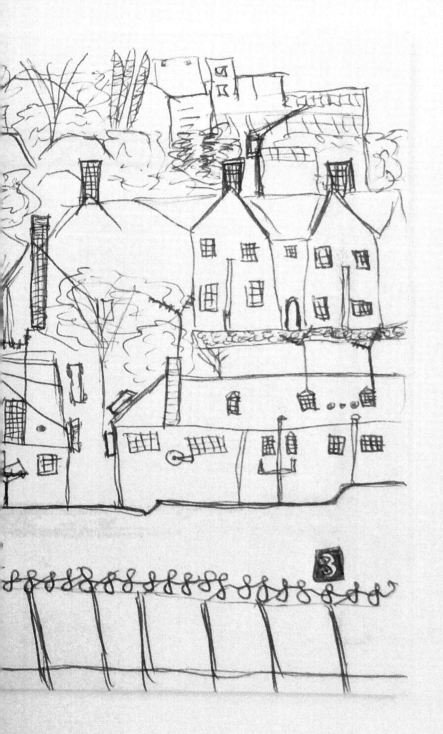